# BEASTS OF THE WORLD (VOLUME 1)

## HAIRY HUMANOIDS

### ANDY MCGRATH

# CONTENTS

# HOW MANY TYPES OF HAIRY HUMANOIDS ARE THERE?

To the uninitiated, and even to many hardcore fans of the *Bigfoot* phenomenon, there is a curious ignorance of the other numerous *Hairy Humanoid* reports from around the world. This Amerocentric focus on Bigfoot is, of course, unsurprising; when viewed through the lens of the media dominance of what was until recently the world's only superpower; combined with the pervasive effect that the hegemony of the English language has had upon international dissemination of fringe subjects, like cryptozoology.

Indeed, many *bigfooters* might be surprised to find that an even greater assortment of *Hairy Humanoids* is to be found in abundance outside of North America, in all of the world's continents, except Antarctica!

These *Hairy Humanoids* somewhat vary in size, description, and appearance, and in numerous instances, two or more '*types*' or '*species*' appear to be sharing a similar geographic area. Interestingly, these kissing cousins could represent unknown varieties of mystery hominids and primates, living within their niche' habitats and often alongside one another, in a type of non-symbiotic mutualism.

The ongoing effort to systematically classify these *Hairy Humanoids*, is at best, fraught with technical jargon and implied knowledge of fringe anthropological theorems; and, as such, is far too diffuse for we laymen to 'get a handle on' in a treatise as brief and diverse as this book. Consequently, as a replacement for the many categories and sub-categories that have been devised to differentiate between the minutiae of the many classes of *Hairy Humanoids* around the globe; we will instead utilise here a broad assemblage for these numerous '*Mansters*' as a coverall classification for 'similar types' in which the overall physiological appearance is comparable, even if some physical variation may be observable in size, colouration, and markings, etc.

Indeed, a model based upon bear speciation and specialisation around the world would make a fitting template on which to base these various – *Hairy Humanoids*. For example - a polar bear, brown bear, black bear, panda bear, sloth bear, and so on... all noticeably differ in appearance, behaviour, diet, and preferred habitat; yet, any observer who was at least familiar with one of these species would easily recognise the other members of this order with which he was unfamiliar, as belonging to the same family.

Thus, to uphold some veneer of differentiation between the primary types, we will, henceforth and in the spirit of simplicity, refer to several '*catch-all categories*' when describing the various kinds. These broad classifications will be sufficiently wide-ranging; enough at least in an exposition as encyclopaedic as is this book, to give an overview of what appear to be general *'classes'* of *Hairy Humanoids* and will absorb the following categories:

- **Man Apes:** *A massively built, hair-covered, upright, bipedal hominoid. Standing from 7 – 9 ft. tall, with large, wide, flat feet, similar to humans, that appear to have no arch; but instead exhibit a type of midfoot flexibility, commonly known as the midtarsal ridge.*

- **Wildmen:** *Caveman-like, or Neanderthal-like, the Wildman is bipedal, largely hair covered, well-built, and muscular, standing between 5 – 7 ft. in height and often appearing to have distinct head hair, which is separate to that of its body. Its feet are human-like in appearance but broad and arched and closely match fossilised tracks that have been attributed to H.Neanderthalensis.*

- **Relicts:** *Standing from 5ft. 6in. to 7ft. 6in. in height, these stocky apes, as opposed to the Man Apes and Wildmen, appear to occupy a position that is closer to that of true apes. And although they, too, like other Wildmen, are bipedal, they are also reported to walk quadrupedally and leave tracks that show a suspiciously ape-like, divergent medial toe. Something that may suggest an arboreal nature, suitable for climbing trees and rocky slopes.*

- **Littlefoot:** *The less common, smaller form, is a type of small upright ape or proto-pygmy, standing between 2ft 6in - 5ft 6in tall; some of which, in the former, bear some resemblance to the ape-like Orang pendek of Sumatra and in the latter, the pygmy-like Ebu Gogo of Flores. Its feet are small and exhibit an ape-like divergent medial toe, with a rounded, tapered heel.*

- **Monkey Monsters:** *Similar in appearance to known species of platyrrhines and catarrhines, in some respects, though massively outsized. Standing from 5 – 6 ft. in height. These monstrous primates are usually highly aggressive and are just as comfortable* *on two legs as they are on all fours. Most types possess a tail. They have long, narrow, clawed feet.*

- **Dogmen:** *A large, muscular, wolf-like, or dog-like humanoid, standing from 5 – 8 ft. tall, that was once widespread throughout the ancient world but is now rare. Perhaps related to the monkey monsters still seen in Asia, Africa, and South America in the present day. Its feet are dog-like or wolf-like and leave large clawed tracks.*

- **Amphibious Anthropoids:** *These semi-aquatic, anthropoidal forms are always described with both arms and legs and with ape-like or, sometimes reptilian characteristics. Unlike the Merbeings of old, they do not have tails and prefer rivers, lakes, ponds, and swamps to the open sea. Their tracks are 3 toed and webbed.*

It will not escape the attention of the reader that although the creature features contained within this volume are but a selection of a far wider phenomenon (of which there are many diverse and far-flung members around the world) that one particularly important character, the giant, 'Man Ape' known as – *Bigfoot*, has been omitted. There is a good reason for this exclusion, which I hope that the reader will understand.

The history of *Bigfoot*, or how *Bigfoot* came to be, demands a separate book of its own, and in an exposition as fleeting as this, wherein each creature is generally allotted a 3 – 5 page inventory, there is little room for even the most cursory account of the history of this animal. A history that is not fixed mind you, but ever-growing and adding to itself with every passing year. To that end, it could be said that in the world of Cryptozoology, the North American *Bigfoot* (or *Sasquatch*) has become a genre in itself and one that needs a detailed analysis, which the author feels cannot be delivered here.

If a comprehensive study was undertaken to list all of the alleged Bigfoot sightings in North America, there is no doubt that the results would fill several thick volumes of what would constitute nothing less than a 'stock take' of *Bigfoot* reports. And, even though the utility of such an endeavour as a data resource would be invaluable to researchers worldwide, it would surely make for dreary reading to those of us seeking a more accessible overview of this fascinating phenomenon. It is certainly my intention to fully investigate this cryptid character within a later work, in which I hope to bring some new perspectives to the field of *Bigfoot* enquiry.

# MAN APES

*"A massively built, hair-covered, upright, bipedal hominoid. Standing from 7 – 9 ft. tall. With large, wide, flat feet, similar to humans, that appear to have no arch; and instead exhibit a type of midfoot flexibility, commonly known as the midtarsal ridge."*

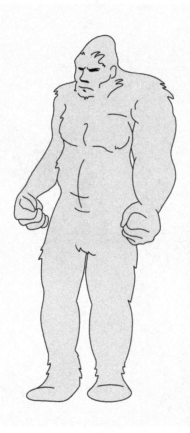

In 1957, the Brazilian newspaper 'Ultima Hora de Rio de Janeiro' reported that the villagers of Tolar Grande were terrorised by eerie calls emanating from the mountains!

## UCUMAR

This Bigfoot-like beast is a semi-mythical giant man-bear, which is believed to terrorise rural communities who live in the foothills of the Andes in Argentina and Chile. Local legend has it that the Ucumar is the bastard child of a field maid and the ranch pattern that was rejected by his father and left to die in the mountains by his mother, only to survive thanks to the help of Lucifer. In revenge, he now haunts the area of his exile, taking cattle and sometimes humans in payment for his abandonment. Although this legend is concentrated in the Andes of Argentina and Chile, stories of the Ucumar also exist in Peru, Bolivia, Ecuador, Venezuela, and Colombia.

**What's in a name?** Named after its mournful or ululating call, it's also colloquially known as *Sachayoj, Ucu, Ukumar-zupai, jukumari, ukumari,* and *ukuku. Ucumar* also means *bear* and most of the interpretations of this legendary beast seem to be centred around its bear-like characteristics.

**Monstrous Measurements:** According to local folklore, it is a hair-covered, bipedal, half-man/half-bear. A wild and ugly humanoid form, standing 5-7ft tall, with immense sharp teeth, small eyes, a long beard, and a narrow forehead. It has large hands and legs and feet with opposed toes.

**Terrifying Tracks:** Human-like tracks, 17 inches in length, said in some cases to show an opposable toe!

**Beastly Behaviours:** Bipedal. Makes Eerie, mournful calls at night that sound like: *"Uhu, Uhu."* Incredibly strong and agile and able to climb trees with ease. Attacks and kills, using the element of surprise. Abducts women for breeding. Sometimes abducts children and forces them to live with him.

**Deadly Diet:** Appears to be vegetarian, feeding on fruit and wild honey. It is reputed to be very fond of the Payo plant that has an inside similar to cabbage. Although some folktales surrounding the legend of the creature state that it occasionally feeds on corn and farm animals, whose meat it eats raw. A facet that may be indicative of a large omnivore, like a bear, being responsible for the legend!

*The Ucumar is said to be fond of the cabbage-like insides of the Payo plant (Aechmea distichantha)*

**Hairy Habitat:** The Ucumar inhabits mountains, caves, and rocky areas and is distributed throughout the Tolar Grande, Umahuaca, El Chorro, and Baritu national Park in Salta Province, as well as Caliliegua province and Chaco Province in Argentina. According to legend, he lives in caves at the bottom of the ravines and likes to walk along the rivers, especially to bathe in them.

**Scary Sightings:**

*1958:* In 1958, a group was camping in Rengo, in the Cordilleras, Province of Santiago, Chile, when they encountered a large *"ape-man."* The group was so terrified by the strange beast that they called the police, who later arrived and took statements from the witnesses, who swore that they had seen *"an enormous man covered with hair!"*

*1957:* Newspapers reported that the residents of Tolar Grande were being woken nightly by a chorus of eerie calls coming from the Curu-

Curu Mountains. The cries, which the locals believed to come from an Ucumar, terrified them for some time. The semi-folkloric reality of the Ucumar, like many creatures ingrained into the tradition and superstition of other nations, holds the duel position of ghoul and beasts, which is enough for local peoples to believe it at once to be a supernatural being that cannot be captured and a beast-like animal that can inflict physical harm upon the unwary. Indeed! In Argentina, tales of these giant ape-men continue to this very day! Argentina.

**Beastly Evidence:**

Tracks:

*In 1956,* Geologist Audio L. Pich was travelling in the Andes Mountains (Argentina) at a height of over sixteen thousand feet when he came upon unusual human-like footprints, seventeen inches long.

*In 1957,* tracks similar to those discovered by Audio L. Pich were also found in the province of La Salta, Argentina.

**Beastly Theories:**

*Spectacled Bear:* Theories about the identity of the Ucumar vary from its being a South American Sasquatch to an extinct Ground Sloth like the Mapinguari, and although it is described as a half bear-half Apeman; the most likely known monster impostor that would fit its purported dimensions is the spectacled bear; which, although primarily found in the Andes, does occasionally venture as far south as northern Argentina. The bear is rare, nay almost extinct, and aside from around 3000 specimens which are currently located in Peru and thankfully protected by law; it would likely be an unexpected animal and if encountered, physically or audibly, by unprepared witnesses, after dark; this rare bear could surely transform into a Bigfoot-like being, like the Ucumar. But this animal can't emit a sound like that attributed to the Ucumar. Interestingly, in Peru and Bolivia, the spectacled bear is known as Ucumari or Jucamari. There is certainly universal agreement that the Ucumar materialised from the spectacled bear or ukumari of the jungles of the Chaco yungas, in the Baritú National Park, in Salta province, Argentina, Indeed, in Quechua and Aymara languages, Ucumar, means 'bear' and most interpretations of the legendary being are based on this meaning. And yet, one wonders whether this etymological plagiarism of the Ucumar is due to its bear-like appearance or simply because, as is the case in many countries, the name itself is a catch-all term for large animals of a similar description?

Could the endangered and rarely seen account for some sightings of the Ucumar?

*Surviving Gigantopithecus*: A surviving, *'evolved'*, Gigantopithecus Blacki, a huge Pleistocene ape, known only from jaw fragments found in southern China and Vietnam. As much as this fossil ape would seem to be to most Bigfoot believers, the golden ticket to the main event: i.e., a paleontological promissory of an evolutionary forefather to our modern-day bigfoot phenomena, there are some understandable difficulties with this theory; the most obvious of which is the subjective speculation upon which the physiological dimensions of this animal has been reconstructed. In fact, were it still in existence today, it might be more gorilla-like in appearance and very likely, though not categorically, quadrupedal.

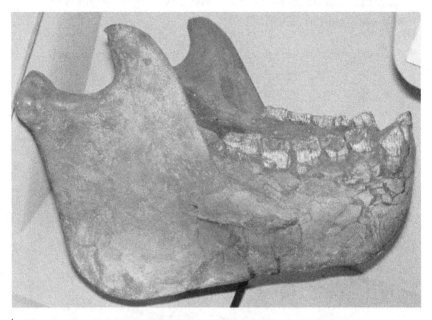

*Gigantopithecus lower jaw (cast) from the Cenozoic of eastern Asia. Public display, Cleveland Museum of Natural History, Cleveland, Ohio, USA.*

Could a type of giant Man-Ape, or "Big Yeti," exist here on the Tibetan Plateau?

## JEZ-TYRMAK

There is some overlap between the *Jez Tyrmak*, the *Dzu-Teh,* and *Rimi*, and although mildly differing in some respects, their overall description as giant Man-Apes as well as their distribution throughout the Himalayas and the Tibetan Plateau is sufficient, I believe in this case, to amalgamate all three creatures into one. Viewing their distinct names simply as indigenous appellations, colloquially conferred upon them by the diverse cultures that pepper the vast expanse of the Tibetan Plateau.

**What's in a name?** The name Jez-Tyrmak is derived from the Mongolian *Jelmoguz-Jez-Tyrmak* (pronounced, *dzhel-moghul-dzh-tura-muk*), meaning: *"Great big living things not found in all but in most hilly places."* But it is also rendered, confusingly as: *'copper fingernails'*. As is often the case in culturally diverse yet symbiotic regions, it is also known by the etymologically plagiarised appellations of *'Dzehez-*

Tyrmak' & 'Zes Tyrmak', which have similar meanings. Correspondingly: *Dzu-Teh*, ("*big, or hulking thing*") and *Rimi* ("*A Man-Creature of the Mountains.*") are similar in their implied iterations.

**Monstrous Measurements:** 6 – 9 ft. tall, human-like, with a pronounced brow ridge. Covered with long shaggy hair that is dark grey to black, in colour, that gets lighter as it ages, or according to altitude. It has long, powerfully built arms and huge hands. As indicated by its unique name, at least one variety of this giant *Man-Ape* has 'copper-coloured fingernails'.

**Terrifying Tracks:** similar in appearance to the tracks of the Sasquatch, but exceptionally large, ranging between 18 to 20 inches in length.

**Beastly Behaviours:** The giant Man-Apes of the Himalayas live primarily on calves or older, sick and dying yaks, but they also seem to have undertaken a vocation out of seeking out animal victims of bad winters and storing the carcasses away in their high altitude larders (caves). They are thought to covet bones, which they crack open for the marrow.

**Deadly Diet:** The Giant Man Apes (like the interchangeable Jez-Tyrmak, Dzu-Teh and Rimi,) who inhabit these high altitudes have become specialised beef-eaters and live almost exclusively on yaks, which they kill by catching them by their horns and twisting their necks. In the case of the *standout-ish* copper coloured nails of the Jez-Tyrmak, these could be from Staphylococcus aureus, caused by the tearing up of animal carcasses.

**Hairy Habitat:** Infrequently encountered throughout the Tibetan Plateau, Tibet, at higher altitudes from 13,000 to 15,000 ft. The Jez-Tyrmak is likely the same animal as the '*Dzu-Teh*' reported in the Himalayas, in and around Sikkim State, India; Bhutan and Tibet, and the '*apparently*' vegetarian '*Rimi*' of Tibet and Eastern Nepal. All three of which are colloquially referred to as '*Big Yeti*' throughout the

Himalayas. Local old-timers in this region often tell stories about seeing *Jez-tyrmak* and his footprints and say. *"...There are two types of them. One is big and does not come down to the river, he often appears in the snowy mountains, and the smaller one walks in the water..."*

**Beastly Evidence:**

*Gates' Track:* Television explorer – Josh Gates discovered the tracks of a large hominoid in the foothills of the Himalayas in 2007. The tracks were remarkably similar to those of Sasquatch tracks found throughout North America, indicating that a similar giant, *'Man Ape'*, distinct from the *Yeti* (*Meh-Teh*), may inhabit the Himalayas.

**Beastly Theories:**

*Blue Bear:* These giant man-apes could not be ordinary bears, as they generally live at a higher altitude than the usual (blue) bears do and the ranges for other species of bear are also entirely different. The other main reason is that it has taken up a life as a specialist yak-raider which is not ordinary bear behaviour in Tibet. So it would seem that they go up the mountains which these bears do not. This detail, combined with the fact that their tracks are entirely different from those of a bear, indicates that misidentified bears are not a good fit for these mysterious creatures. Even in the case of the *Dzu-The*, whose name does mean *Yak-bear*, it is still identified as one of the *Big Yeti*; because, in this case, the word *'bear'* is generic for a large predator.

*Surviving Gigantopithecus:* A surviving, *'evolved'* Gigantopithecus Blacki, a huge Pleistocene ape, known only from jaw fragments found in southern China and Vietnam. As much as this fossil ape would seem to be to most Bigfoot believers, the golden ticket to the main event: i.e., a paleontological promissory of an evolutionary forefather to our modern-day bigfoot phenomena, there are some understandable difficulties with this theory; the most obvious of which is the subjective speculation upon which the physiological dimensions of this animal has been reconstructed. In fact, were it still in existence today, it might be more gorilla-like in appearance and very likely, although not categorically, quadrupedal.

*A trifling 1.9% of Scotland's landmass is covered by urban sprawl; if a giant, 'Man Ape' could survive undetected anywhere in Britain, then surely it would be here! (Carn a' Mhaim from Ben MacDhui.)*

## AM FEAR LIATH MÒR

It has long been thought that the Big Grey Man of the Cairngorm Mountains, and in especial, the summit of Ben MacDhui, is a folkloric throwback to when this misty land, now colloquially known as Great Britain, was populated by cruel giants who ruled a land that was then known as Albion; (or to their Irish neighbours in the east - *The Land of the Mighty*). Ben MacDhui is the biggest mountain in the Cairngorms and the second highest in the UK. It is a sterile environment not conducive to supporting a large omnivore and on its harsh, barren slopes, nothing really grows - save the most resilient alpine plants. In the winter, the northern sun barely penetrates the thick cloud cover and mist, which rolls in unexpectedly and can cover the land for days; creating an eerie landscape shrouded in mist, from which the uninitiated can begin to feel assailed and that they are being secretly watched by mysterious beings that could emerge from the mists at any time. Strange sounds, like cracks, whines, and even the sound of heavy footfalls, are often heard by lonely climbers trapped in the mountain's mists. Whether these are the environmental and meteorological groans of this enigmatic area, steeped in shadowy antiquity, no one knows. Yet, some believe that the mountain hides a hairy hominid of giant proportions, known in Scots Gaelic as *Am Fear Liath Mor – The Big Grey Man of Ben MacDhui.*

**What's in a name?** *The Big Grey Man of Ben MacDhui* is also known in Scot Gaelic as *Am Fear Liath Mor, Ferlas Mhor, Ferlie More,* and *Fomor.*

**Monstrous Measurements:** Standing stands erect at 10 – 20 ft. tall and covered with thick but short grey, olive, or brown hair. It has pointed ears and broad shoulders. Long, waving arms, long legs, and finger-like talons on its hands and feet.

**Terrifying Tracks:** - On December, 2nd 1952, James Alan Rennie photographed a series of tracks in the snow - 19 inches long and 14 inches wide, with a stride of 7ft. The tracks were travelling in a perfectly straight line on the mountain and at one point, they even appeared to have entirely jumped a distance of 30 feet over a road that must have been perceived as an obstacle, impeding the creature's onward journey.

**Beastly Behaviours:** The Big Grey Man is said to be more aggressive than its Asian and American counterparts, often appearing in thick fog or mist and frightening lonely travellers on the mountain. It makes odd crunching noises that sound like heavy footsteps and a high-pitched droning hum, echoing across the mountain. Its presence is preceded by an icy feeling in the air that induces distress and dread, or depression and apathy. There is a strong belief among climbers that it has the power to affect one's emotional state with strong and irrational impulses, with some witnesses even claiming that they felt irresistibly compelled to hurl themselves from the summit. Its presence is also sometimes accompanied by ghostly music, voices, and laughter.

**Hairy Habitat:** The Summit of Ben MacDhui and throughout the Cairngorm Mountains, Grampian, Scotland.

**Scary Sightings:**

*1891*: One of the earliest modern witnesses of the Big Grey man was Norman Collie, a professor of chemistry at the University College London. He was also a passionate hill-walker. During the annual general meeting of the Cairngorm Club in Aberdeen on a dark, winter's night in December 1925, he told a story to its members of a most strange experience he had on the mountain in 1891. An experienced climber, he had been returning from the summit when he heard the crunch of footsteps behind him. For every step he took, he heard another crunch nearby as if someone were following him but with a stride three or four times the size of his own. Collie stated, *"For every few steps I took, I heard a crunch. It was as if someone was walking after me, but taking steps three to four lengths of mine."* Although he never saw anyone, he was certain something was there. Terrified at the prospect of meeting this giant stalker, He ran downhill for the last few miles.

*Professor Norman Collie. Image Credit: UCL Chemistry Collections. CC BY 3.0*

*1904:* Hugh Welsh and his brother were studying plants and arachnids near the summit of Ben MacDhui and were conscious of soft-sounding footsteps around them whenever they were moving. Curiously the footsteps did not match their own footfalls, which would be expected if they were the result of an unexplained echo effect produced by the obtuse topography in the area. They noted that these curious sounds were more distinct during the daylight hours and throughout their excursion, the brothers were *"very conscious of 'something' near them"*.

*1920s:* Tom Crowley, an experienced climber and former president of the Moray Mountaineering Club, also heard the footsteps as he was descending Braeriach (a peak to the west of Ben MacDhui, across the Lairig Ghru pass) into Glen Eanaich. He paused and turned his head to cast a glance over his shoulder and was alarmed to see a tall, grey figure, with *"pointed ears, long legs and finger-like talons on its feet"* approaching him from behind.

*1920s:* Alexander Mitchell Kellas, a very experienced climber and scientist (Chemist). Together with his brother Henry, Kellas was ascending to the mountain's summit when they spotted a *"giant figure"* 10 feet tall and moving towards them from the direction of the Lairig Ghru pass. The Scottish chemist watched the shape *'walk'* to the summit, circle the cairn there (with which it was equal in height), and then disappear back into the pass.

*1940:* In his book, *'The Big Grey Man of Ben MacDhui'*, Richard Frere detailed an encounter related to him by a friend, who had been camping at the very top of the mountain in 1940. His friend had settled down in his tent for the evening and fallen asleep when Frere awoke suddenly and noticed movement outside his tent's opening. And as he peered out of his tent into the night, he observed a large, broad-shouldered, brownish, humanoid creature that must have been twenty feet in height. The terrifying creature seemed to swagger as it moved around the camp, emitting an air of insolent strength before eventually moving off. (Richard Frerer too had claimed to have experienced similar strange sensations and fears as other climbers in the cairngorms, on a trip upon the mountain in 1948)

*1942:* Legendary climber William Sydney Scroggie was camping out at the shelter stone by the Garbh Uisge on Ben MacDhui when he saw a tall, imperial figure taking large deliberate steps towards the burns flowing onto Loch Avon.

*1943:* Naturalist and mountaineer Alexander Tewnion had a harrowing confrontation with the Big Grey Man. His account appeared in 'The Scots Magazine' in June 1958:

*"I am not unduly imaginative, but my thought flew instantly to the well-known story of professor Collie and the Fear Liath Mhor [Big Grey Man]. Then I felt the reassuring weight of the loaded revolver in my pocket. Grasping the butt, I peered about in the mist here rent and tattered by the eddies of wind. A strange shape loomed up, receded, came charging at me! Without hesitation, I whipped out the revolver and fired three times at the figure. When it still came on, I turned and hared down the path, reaching Glen Derry in a time that I have never bettered. You may ask, was it really the Fear Liath Mhor? Frankly, I think it was. Many times since then, I have traversed MacDhui in the mist, bivouacked out in the open, and camped on its summit for days on end on different occasions — often alone and always with an easy mind. For, on that day, I am convinced I shot the only Fear Liath Mhor my imagination will ever see."*

**Beastly Evidence:**

Tracks:

On December, 2nd 1952, James Alan Rennie photographed a series of tracks in the snow in a straight line on the mountain. Each print was about 19 inches long and 14 inches wide, with a stride of 7ft. At one point, the tracks even jumped a road over a distance of 30 feet.

**Beastly Theories:**

*Brocken Spectre Effect*: Are sightings of the Big Grey Man, nothing more than meteorological hallucinations! According to some sceptics, a common atmospheric anomaly called a *Brocken Spectre Effect* is responsible for eyewitness accounts and not a flesh and blood monster. This rare alien atmospheric anomaly is produced when the sun hits the mist and magnifies a person's elongated shadow on clouds, mist, and fog. This, the sceptics say, gives the illusion of a giant humanoid form looming out of the mists towards the justifiably terrified witness, who is blissfully unaware of this literal trick of the light that is being played upon him. This effect, which is also sometimes accompanied by a *'Glorie'* (a rainbow-like halo), adds to the otherworldly experience which the witness believes that he is undergoing.

A Brocken Spectre occurs when the sun casts an enormous shadow in front of an observer.

*High Altitude Hallucinations:* Other researchers have suggested that people are experiencing high altitude hallucinations brought about by oxygen starvation and that the legendary Big Grey Man is commonly imagined by people suffering from these hallucinations because of its commonly disseminated imagery and legendary place in Highland legends. Indeed, high altitude and the disorientation created by the featureless peaks of the Cairngorms could also add an element of panic and irrational behaviour to sufferers of this common condition, in which all manner of sounds and shapes might migrate from the subconscious into the delirium of a waking dream. Such as one might experience when falling asleep, at the end of a long and strenuous day! However, it should be noted that many of the witnesses were rational men of science and experienced climbers, neither inexperienced in the strange effects of the terrain nor subject to the atmospheric burdens of the climb. And yet they are seeing something.

In the words of Peter Densham, leader of the Cairngorms RAF Rescue Team 1939-45.

*"...tell me that the whine was but the result of relaxed eardrums, and the Presence was only the creation of a mind that was accustomed to take too great an interest in such things. I shall not be convinced. Come, rather, with me at the mysterious dusk time when day and night struggle upon the mountains. Feel the night wind on your faces, and hear it crying amid rocks. See the desert uplands consumed before the racing storms. Though your nerves be of steel, and your mind says it cannot be, you will be acquainted with that fear without name, that intense dread of the unknown that has pursued mankind from the very dawn of time."*

*A Paranormal Portal:* Grey Man theories range from the sensible to the surreal. Among the favourites is that the beast is some type of giant *Man-Ape*, a *True Giant*, if you will - long thought extinct! This may sound implausible, yet, there are many more risible esoteric theories from which to choose, such as that he is a transcendental holy man or a hairy hermit; or even an extra-terrestrial, engaged in some sort of alien excursion on the mountain! More recently, it has even been suggested that the mountain itself is a *portal*; a porous border between two realms, and of which the Grey Man is an ancient guardian.

*Surviving Gigantopithecus:* A surviving, 'evolved' Gigantopithecus Blacki, a huge Pleistocene ape, known only from jaw fragments found in southern China and Vietnam. As much as this fossil ape would seem to be to most Bigfoot believers, the golden ticket to the main event: i.e., a paleontological promissory of an evolutionary forefather to our modern-day bigfoot phenomena, there are some understandable difficulties with this theory; the most obvious of which is the subjective speculation upon which the physiological dimensions of this animal have been reconstructed. In fact, were it still in existence today, it might be more gorilla-like than bigfoot-like in appearance and very likely, although not categorically, quadrupedal.

In 1960, two prospectors observed a group of huge gorillas ranging in height from 7 – 10ft. tall as they destroyed their hut at Lake Ballard, Western Australia.

## JOGUNG

All cultures feature cautionary tales that utilise bogeyman-like monsters that lurk on the edge of civilisation, waiting to devour disobedient and inattentive children and in this respect, aboriginal Dreamtime narratives are no different. These tales often reflect our deepest anxieties as parents about the vulnerability that our little ones have to external forces and our attempts to lighten the burden of the cruel reality of life from their tiny minds, with elaborate tales of the ogres and goblins, which can be found lurking on the borders of our towns and villages. Coincidentally, along with all of the real-life dangers that we know so well. Indeed, in aboriginal cultures, a veritable pantheon of monstrous manifestations abound, including that of the hairy *Pangkarlangu* (Pankalanka), a large, lumbering, hairy hominoid, with razor-sharp claws, that feeds on the flesh of wandering babies and toddlers, whose heads it dashes open upon the hard earth, before carrying their lifeless bodies back into the sparsely populated desert. This mythical giant, which is also known as the *Jogung*, by all accounts, is something quite separate from the *Yowie*. A type of giant, hairy, club carrying '*Man-Ape*', 13ft. tall and greedy for human flesh.

**What's in a name?** The meaning of the name *Jogung* is unknown. Although the etymologically similar terms, *Jingy* and *Chingah*, meaning "*devils*" or "*evil spirits*", were in common usage in Western Australia by the nineteenth century. As is common in countries as tribally diverse as Australia, this creature is known by a myriad of wonderfully dissimilar names, such as *Barmi birgoo*, *Illankanpanka* (In central Queensland), *Jimbra*, *Jingra* and *Jinka* (in Western Australia), *Kraitbull* (in South Australia), *Lo-an* (in Yarra Flats, Victoria), *Pankalanka* (in Northern Territory), *Tjangara* (in South Australia), and *Wolumbin* (in Victoria).

**Monstrous Measurements:** Gorilla-like in appearance. Bipedal. 7 – 13 ft. tall. Covered in dark brown or black hair. The males are said to have large genitals and females, large breasts.

**Terrifying Tracks:** 24 inches in length with splayed toes (large tracks with opposable toes or sometimes even three-toes, are sometimes reportedly made by giant Man-Ape-like creatures in other parts of Australia!)

**Beastly Behaviours:** Nocturnal. Makes guttural sounds. Has a rotten smell. Carries a club or tree limb with which to kill people. Raids aboriginal camps.

**Deadly Diet:** Kangaroos and other animals (including humans!)

**Hairy Habitat:** reported throughout the Great Sandy Desert, Western Australia; Arnhem Land, Northern Territory; Mount Kosciusko area, New South Wales; central Queensland; Murray region, South Australia; Yarra Flats, Victoria. Lives in rock crevices and caves underground.

**Scary Sightings:**

*1861:* During July of 1861, three European explorers, Dempster, Clarkson, and Harper, were warned by Aborigines at Lake Grace, Western Australia, about a fierce, monkey-like animal called the Jimbra or Jingra that killed solitary travellers.

*1960:* Two prospectors, Andy Hoad and Brett Taylor, observed a group of huge, gorilla-like creatures emerge from the scrub in the Lake Ballard area, Western Australia. They saw that one of the creatures was noticeably female, with long breasts and dark brown hair, standing approx. 7ft. tall, and the other somewhat larger creature, which was male, stood 9 ft. tall. Running back to their hut, they were horrified to find a 10 ft. gorilla tearing it down. Both men hid until the coast was clear, then raced to their truck and drove away. Later, Aborigines in Kalgoolrie-Boulder told them that the gorillas they had encountered were called Jimbra.

*1970:* In June 1970, mountaineers Ron Bartlett and Frank Sinclair noticed huge, human-like tracks in the snow near their camp, northwest of Mount Kosciusko, New South Wales. As they were leaving, they felt that they were being watched and noticed a strange odour. After breaking their camp, they were moving through the scrub when they saw a dark, hairy, 8ft. tall figure staring at them. It moved away into the thick bush.

*1977:* Vince and Trevor Collins encountered an enormous black gorilla while driving north of Jimberingga Well in the Great Sandy Desert, Western Australia. The giant creature emerged from the bush and strode into the road, wielding a tree limb.

*1989:* Two carloads of four-wheel drive enthusiasts were shocked to see a 13ft. tall, hairy giant wielding a club along Cooper Creek, between Maree and Birdsville, South Australia.

**Beastly Evidence:**

*Homo Giganticus:* Australian Cryptozoologist Rex Gilroy believed these giant beings could reach heights of between 9 – 13ft in height and alleged that a mineralised skull fragment, that he unearthed at Coolah, central western NSW on August 5th, 2000, showed the left projecting eyebrow ridge and low, receding forehead, from an approximately 9ft. 8 in. tall hominid. And, thus, concluded that this was evidence that a giant form of *Homo erectus* may have lived in Australia until comparatively recent times.

*Gigantopithecine relics:* Over many years, Rex Gilroy, along with his wife, Heather, have netted a large collection of photographs and casts of huge tracks that they believe are *"something else entirely..."* and a species quite distinct from the Yowie. Noting that, many of the large tracks they have catalogued have an opposable big toe, not unlike the Himalayan yeti, which, they hypothesise together with the large, mineralised skull of an ape-like creature discovered in Queensland, supports their theory that a population of Gigantopithecus, once roamed Australia.

**Beastly Theories:**

*Demons from the Dreamtime:* When examining legends and reports of amazing animals around the world, I must confess to experiencing difficulty in drawing out the real from the religious, especially in cultures that have a thin barrier between the world of the material and the spiritual. In this respect, the beings of the *Aboriginal Dreamtime* are no exception in their belief that all of Australia's animals once existed in human form. This often leaves one wondering if the aboriginal stories of the hairy men are allegorical in nature or an extended form of a real-time creation mythos that has increased in stature and spread, along with the slow march of assimilation and European incorporation of the beliefs and ideas of

Australia's former landlords. In these Dreamtime beliefs, as well as the depiction of known animals as amalgamations of man and beast (Kangaroo-men, Koala-Men, etc.), there are also tales of monstrous-humanoids that haunt the landscape and occasionally assail its human inhabitants. Could modern-day hairy man reports be nothing more than the societal imbibing of these demons from the Dreamtime?

<u>*Manifestations of Immorality:*</u> The largest and most famous of all hairy giants are the Quinkin, from Queensland's Cape York Peninsula. Although these creatures had unusually three clawed fingers and toes and were generally used in aboriginal lore as a moral manifestation of the evil embodiment of human lust (as depicted in the prehistoric cave paintings in Cape York's Laura rock galleries). There is some small possibility that this region's (possibly inbred - three toes/fingered) giants are/were regional versions of a giant *Man-Ape*, like the Jogung, that were simply woven into the fabric of aboriginal morality myths.

'Quinkin' Rock Art, some of the world's most extensive and ancient rock painting galleries surround the tiny town of Laura, Queensland

*Giant man Apes:* Most researchers believe that there are two types of *Yowie* species in Australia. The larger stands at around 6-10ft tall and a smaller species which stands about 4-5ft tall. However, this would seem to be a simplification of the many types that are reported throughout this enigmatic island. And, in keeping with the theoretical outline of this chapter, there would seem to be evidence, in part at least, that Australia harbours at least three types or discernible forms of *Hairy Humanoids*.

1: *Man-Ape*: The rare giant *Man-Ape* type, like the *Jogung*, *Quinkin/Turramulli*, *Jingra*, *Jimbra* and *Jinka*, *Kraitbull*, *Lo-an*, *Pankalanka*, *Tjangara,* and *Wolumbin*, that are Bigfoot-like, but also reported huge, *'true giant'* proportions, above 10 ft. in height.

2: *Wildman:* The more common *Yowie* is a Neanderthaloid or wildman type, like the Almas of the Caucuses Mountains or the Yeren of China (although such a creature in Australia would more likely be related to a robust australopithecine, like the highly contested Paranthropus than to Homo Neanderthalensis). The general appearance of these primitive beings recalls Homo erectus (Java man).

3: *Littlefoot:* The less common, smaller form of *"hairy man"* – colloquially referred to as the *Junjadee, Jingarra, Jingera, Jongari, Net-net, Nimbinjee, Nyol, Waaki,* and many other names besides; which is a type of a small upright ape and/or, an undiscovered tribe of pygmy aborigines; standing between 2 – 2.6 metres tall; some of which, in the former, bear some resemblance to the Ape-like *Orang Pendek* of Sumatra and in the latter, the pygmy-like *Ebu Gogo* of Flores, Indonesia.

*Surviving Gigantopithecus*: A surviving, *'evolved'* Gigantopithecus Blacki, a huge Pleistocene ape, known only from jaw fragments found in southern China and Vietnam. As much as this fossil ape would seem to be to most Bigfoot believers, the golden ticket to the main event: i.e., a paleontological promissory of an evolutionary forefather to our modern-day bigfoot phenomena, there are some understandable difficulties with this theory; the most obvious of which is the subjective speculation upon which the physiological dimensions of this animal have been reconstructed. In fact, were it still in existence today, it might be more gorilla-like in appearance and very likely, although not categorically, quadrupedal.

*Are the stories of Malaysia's 'Man Ape' simply the folktales of yesteryear repackaged for a modern audience, or could this ape-like giant have a basis in biology?*

## ORANG DALAM

Peninsular Malaysia occupies the southern half of the Malay Peninsula in Southeast Asia. Its rich Montane Rain Forests support several large species like tigers, elephants, rhinoceros, tapirs, and a smorgasbord of other rare animals. Could this ecoregion be a refuge, not only for several of Asia's large fauna but a hitherto unknown species of giant *'Man-Ape,'* universally known throughout the region as the *Orang Dalam*?

**What's in a name?** Orang Dalam is a Malay word, meaning – *"man of the interior"*. As in many culturally diverse regions, these creatures have several variant names, and the *Orang Dalam* being no exception, is also known as *Ensut, Hantu Jarang Gigi* (thin tooth demon), and *Kaki Besar* (Bigfoot).

**Monstrous Measurements:** 6 – 10 ft. tall. Bipedal humanoid. Covered with dark brown hair. It has red eyes.

**Terrifying Tracks:** Tracks are 4 toed (a characteristic of the *True Giants*, according to some researchers), averaging 16-19 inches in length and 8- 10 inches in width.

**Beastly Behaviours:** Bipedal. Powerful smell like urine. Fish eater. Approaches humans' initially in a friendly manner before suddenly becoming frightened and running away.

**Deadly Diet:** Eats Fish.

**Hairy Habitat:** Pahang Jahor, Melaka and Perak states, Malaysia.

**Scary Sightings:**

*1959:* a mining engineer named Arthur Potter was sleeping in his boat by the side of Lake Tasek Chini, Pahang State, Malaysia, when something lifted part of the roof of the boat. He switched on a flashlight and saw a huge, red eye. The next day he found 18-inch tracks in the mud.

*1979:* Students at a vocational institute near Lumut, Perak State, reported seeing 10 ft. tall hairy creatures at night in August 1979.

*2007:* Malaysian Bigfoot researcher and journalist Harold Stephens shared curious tracks that were discovered shortly after three individual *Orang Dalam* sightings in Felda Semenchu, Johor, Malaysia. Stephens received the reports from Prince Mahmood of Johor, Malaysia, who of the three eyewitness who had seen the "Bigfoot", managed to interview two of them; a guard named, Shahrul and another man named Raslan, who saw the creature with a friend. Shahrul described the creature as being very hairy and large, standing in a stooping posture at approximately 9.8 ft. in height. The creature was breathing loudly. He was unable to see its face properly. The second witness, Raslan, who, along with a friend, had observed the creature crouching under a palm tree, described the creature as very large and having an ape-like face with fiery red eyes.

**Beastly Evidence:**

<u>Tracks:</u>

*1961:* Large, four-toed tracks were reportedly discovered in the Johor State.

*1966:* Ape-like footprints 18 inches long, 6 inches wide, and 5 inches deep were found near Segamat, Johor State, in early August 1966.

*1970:* Harold Stephens and Kurt Rolfes launched an expedition to find the Orang Dalam. Although the expedition failed to reach the plateau, these giants are reputed to inhabit. They did manage to photograph some giant hominid tracks, 19 inches long and 10 inches wide, on a sandbar in the upper reaches of the Sungai Endau River, Pahang State.

*1995:* Huge four-toed footprints were found near Cape Tanjung Piai, Johor State, on January 12th, 1995

*2007:* Alleged tracks of an *Orang Dalam* were found and photographed, around the same time as three eyewitnesses reported seeing the creature in Felda Semenchu, Johor, Malaysia.

*Rubber Estate Tracks:* On 15th June 2013, Adnan Pungut discovered 200 Bigfoot-like footprints while clearing rubbish and wood at his rubber estate near Kampung Kepis Baru, Kuala Pilah.

**Beastly Theories:**

*Malayan Sun Bear:* the critically endangered Malayan Sun Bear *(Helarctos malayanus),* once endemic to this region and now only numbering between 300 – 500 individuals, is the smallest member of the bear family at 1.5 metres in length. It is also easily distinguishable by a bib-shaped golden (or white) patch on its chest. Colloquially known in Malay as *Beruang Badu* - *"honey bear"*, due to its pooh-like love of honey, it is certainly rare enough to meet the conditions of an *'unexpected encounter'*. It is also known to inhabit the same remote, dense tropical forests of South East Asia as the Orang Dalam, but sadly, this most endearing and least understood of all bear species is a poor stand-in for the giant *Man-Ape* of Malaysian Peninsular.

*Life Apes...?* Could the *Orang Dalam* be an outsized Lar Gibbon? Gibbons will naturally appear to *ape,* human-like locomotive characteristics, like walking bipedally, which they will do on occasion, albeit with their arms outstretched, for balance. Their faces, too, are somewhat flatter than other apes with a faintly protruding muzzle, which may initially give the impression of a *humanesque* appearance. However, even an outsize gibbon species would be hard-pressed to upscale from what is usually a maximum height of 1.64 ft. to the towering 10 ft. tall Orang Dalam.

*Undiscovered Tribes?* Throughout Malaysia and Indonesia, the title – *Orang Dalam ("man of the interior")* is in common use to describe a person belonging to one of the tribes that live in the jungle or hills, and in peninsular Malaysia, it specifically refers to the *Senoi People.* However, the title is far more intriguing when used by the Senoi themselves to denote other hominids or rudimentary tribes. When looking objectively at the lifestyle of the Senoi, which is almost wholly symbiotic with the natural environment, one wonders how far removed from civilisation the *Orang Dalam* would need to be (if human) to be considered *'rudimentary'.*

*Could the indigenous Senoi people of Peninsular Malaysia, who are also sometimes referred to as Orang Dalam ("man of the interior"), have inspired the legends of this mysterious 'Man-Ape?'*

<u>*Surviving Gigantopithecus*</u>: A surviving, *'evolved'* Gigantopithecus Blacki, a huge Pleistocene ape, known only from jaw fragments found in southern China and Vietnam. As much as this fossil ape would seem to be to most Bigfoot believers, the golden ticket to the main event: i.e., a paleontological promissory of an evolutionary forefather to our modern-day bigfoot phenomena, there are some understandable difficulties with this theory; the most obvious of which is the subjective speculation upon which the physiological dimensions of this animal has been reconstructed. In fact, were it still in existence today, it might be more gorilla-like in appearance and very likely, although not categorically, quadrupedal.

An aerial photo of the Tana River, which is in the Rift Valley, Kenya.

## NGOLOKO

Largely owing to its diverse topographical landscapes and habitats, Kenya plays home to many large African animals, like the lion, leopard, rhino (black and white), elephant, cape buffalo, wildebeest, waterbuck, warthog, hippo, crocodile, spotted hyena, cheetah, African wild dog and many, many more. Yet, none of these intimidating beasts can compare to a hairy humanoid called the *Ngoloko*, believed by some to stalk the inhabitants of this fruitful region.

**What's in a name?** The name *Ngoloko* is of unknown origin. However, there may be a clue as to its meaning in this creature's local appellations: *Loldaika*, or *Milhoi*, meaning: *"evil spirit"*.

**Monstrous Measurements:** 8ft. Tall. Covered in thick grey hair. Dark skin. Receding forehead. Hairless face. Huge ears. Prominent nose. Small mouth, with big teeth. Long head hair. Very long hair on the upper torso (about 3 feet long.) Only a thumb and finger on each hand, with the thumb having a 2.5-inch claw.

**Terrifying Tracks:** One prehensile big toe and three small toes. (Although, similar tracks, found on Mt. Kilimanjaro, appeared three-toed) It has a stride of 18 inches while walking and 9 feet while running.

**Beastly Behaviours:** Walks on 2 legs. Has a bad odour. Stalks humans?

**Deadly Diet:** Eats wild honey and drinks blood and buffalo milk.

**Hairy Habitat:** Occupies forests and mangrove swamps. Found throughout Kenya, near the coast, from Mombasa to the Tana River. Mount Kilimanjaro, Kenya; Lake Baringo, Kenya and the Yaida Valley in Tanzania.

**Scary Sightings:**

_1800s:_ Hweri Wa Mabruko and some friends were out tapping rubber trees, along with some Mboni Bushmen in the Witu District, Kenya, when they observed an Ngoloko stalking them. The Mboni Bushmen promptly fired off an arrow at the creature, which found its mark. The injured creature fled its prey, now turned predators, who followed in hot pursuit, only to find it lying prostrate and dying, about 500 yards from where it had been hit. The men described the creature as being 8 feet tall, male, and covered in thick grey hair, the strands of which measured 3 feet in length. Its chin and forehead were reticent and its skin, which was observable on its hairless face, was dark. Its face bore large eyes, a prominent nose, large elephantine ears, and a small mouth with large teeth. The men also noticed that its hands were peculiarly formed, having only a large finger and a thumb. Its feet were equally odd, possessing one prehensile thumb and three toes, one of which featured a large claw.

**Beastly Evidence:**

*Audio Encounter and Tracks:*

J.A.G. Elliott, who recorded this account in his 1934 book, *Tales of Africa*, also heard the creature's distinctive cry, which he described as being: *"more frightening than a gorilla's"* and was also able to study several tracks alleged to belong to the creature, while travelling through the Wa-Sanje, a lagoon filled area of mangrove swamps and bush that borders the Kenyan coast. One particular set of footprints he discovered definitely belonged to a bipedal animal, with a stride ranging between 1.5 feet (walking) to 9 feet (running).

**Beastly Theories:**

*Nineteenth-Century Sensationalism:* Far from being the scientifically saturated age of exploration that we all attribute to this period in human history, the nineteenth century was full to the brim with tall tales told by travellers eager to entertain their audiences with terrifying trials and unassailable obstacles; or, more often it seems, by mercantile monster hunters eager to beguile their would-be investors with the promissory of indisputable evidence, that would bring infamy and commercial interest to the bankroller of their beastly expeditions! One need only be reminded of P.T Barnum's *"Feejee mermaid"* (a composite chimaera, with the body of a monkey and the tail of a fish) to appreciate that the paying public, during this period, were ever hungry for hairy humanoids and slippery serpents, to titillate their voracious voyeurism!

An advert for P.T. Barnum's "Feejee Mermaid" around 1842. By P. T.
Barnum or an employee.

_Inbred infirmity:_ Is it possible that the _Ngoloko_ represents an example
of an undiscovered, inbred tribe? One has only to think of its claw-
like hand (featuring only a finger and thumb) to be reminded of the
Ectrodactyly (V-shaped feet) of the nomadic vaDoma Tribe (also
known as the _"two-toed"_ or _"ostrich-footed"_ tribe.) This condition,
resulting from a single mutation, has persisted within the tribe due to
their small gene pool and their tribal law, which forbids them from
marrying outside the tribe. Could there be other similarly insular
communities in Kenya which have, over time, developed several
genetic deformities like Ectrodactyly, hypertrichosis, and
acromegaly?

Could isolated tribes like the Vadoma (or Ostrich people) have been viewed through the eyes of 19th century Europeans as a form of ancient man?

*Surviving Gigantopithecus*: A surviving, 'evolved' Gigantopithecus Blacki, a huge Pleistocene ape, known only from jaw fragments found in southern China and Vietnam. As much as this fossil ape would seem to be to most Bigfoot believers, the golden ticket to the main event: i.e., a paleontological promissory of an evolutionary forefather to our modern-day bigfoot phenomena, there are some understandable difficulties with this theory; the most obvious of which is the subjective speculation upon which the physiological dimensions of this animal has been reconstructed. In fact, were it still in existence today, it might be more gorilla-like in appearance and very likely, although not categorically, quadrupedal.

# WILDMEN

*"Caveman-like, or Neanderthal-like, the Wildman is bipedal, largely hair covered, well-built, and muscular; standing between 5 – 7 ft. in height and often appearing to have distinct head hair, which is separate to that of its body. Its feet are human-like in appearance but broad and arched, and closely match fossilised tracks that have been attributed to H.Neanderthalensis."*

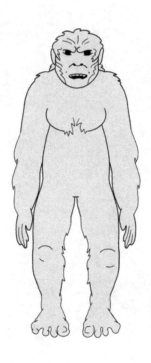

| Caucasian mountains. Kabardino-Balkaria. Russia:

## ALMASTI

The Caucasus sits astride both Europe and Asia, sandwiched between the Black and Caspian seas, like a haughty no man's land of dense forests, steep-sloped hills, and lofty mountains, which, at least historically, been constituted a natural barrier between Europe and Asia. The area, which comprises the countries of Russia, Armenia, Georgia, and Azerbaijan, and the contested nations of Artsakh and South Ossetia, is also littered with a myriad of Autonomous republics and federal regions, which comprise a veritable smorgasbord of peoples, languages, and dialects... yet, within the diverse peoples of this region, there is agreement that a hairy, humanoid people, commonly referred to as the Almasty, have lived alongside them from time immemorial.

**What's in a name?** *Almasti* is a Kabardian word meaning *"forest man"*, which is almost certainly derived from the Mongolian word *Almas*, meaning *"wild man"*; this name, possibly having been socially transmitted through the region by Mongolian speaking Kalmyk's. However, the Mongolian moniker, *Almas*, and its possible derivative, *Almasti*, are not all that these two geographically disparate creatures have in common. Could the *Almas* and *Almasti* represent two regional variations of one distinct species of Wildman, or is their presumed relationship nothing more than an etymological artefact of Genghis Khan's lost Asian empire?

**Monstrous Measurements:** The Almasti is bipedal, standing between 5ft – 6ft tall (although individuals of 7ft or more are occasionally observed), the toes are spread out in a fan and it can weigh up to 500 pounds. It is covered in reddish-brown or dark brown, shaggy hair, with the hair on its head, which is noticeably different to that of its body appearing, long and tangled; the hair of the male reaching down to the shoulder blades, and the female, down to the waist. Its eyes are slanted and reddish in colour and almost seem to emit a luminous red glow at night, with eyewitnesses describing them, 'lighting up with a bright red colour and sparkling, like lit cigarettes!' Its face has a prominent eyebrow ridge (almost overhanging its eyes), high cheekbones, a wide, flattened nose with flared nostrils, and a receding rounded lower jaw. Its ears are high and elongated. The lips are thin and monkey-like and although it does appear to possess a muzzle of sorts, this is described as being less prominent than that of a monkey, producing the impression of a being, halfway between man and monkey. In another universal similarity with other Wildmen, its head is placed directly on the shoulders, giving the animal the appearance of having a very short neck or no neck. Its teeth are larger than that of a man's and regularly sized, except for two pairs of pronounced and intersecting canines that mesh together, like a dog's teeth. Its hands superficially resemble those of a human', except that they have flat palms that lack a thenar eminence and also exhibit a curiously short thumb, which sits in alignment with the other four longer fingers. Its fingernails are long but not pointed. Its legs are short and bowed and its feet splayed.

Sexual dimorphism is visible in this species, with females sporting pendulous breasts; (although large adult females are just as tall and as strong as males.) The skin of the face is black and the skin of the palms of the hands is a dark reddish-brown, as is the skin on the buttocks, where fur/hair is absent. Curiously, its young are reputed to be born pink and hairless and remain so until they reach age one. Like many Wildmen around the world, it has a strong odour, which has been described as being akin to that of *"a dead dog"*, *"a cesspool,"* etc. With some witnesses observing that in the area where one animal had been sitting, *"its odour remained for almost a week"*. Recently deceased (at 101 years of age, no less!) Wildman researcher Marie Jeanne Koffmann, to whom, among a precious few trailblazing researchers, we owe most of what we know about the Almasty; noted that the odour left by these animals was primarily attributed to the male of the species.

**Terrifying Tracks:** Like a human footprint, but larger, especially at the base of the toes, with a wide heel and spread out (splayed) toes. There appears to be evidence that its feet are turned in, with tracks showing a characteristic inflexion of its distal part.

**Beastly Behaviours:** Primarily nocturnal, but also active at dusk. It sleeps during the day on a nest made of leaves. Has no discernible language but mumbles and bellows. Has an immensely loud call or cry. Its odour is particularly pungent and unpleasant and can be detected long after it has left an area. Will occasionally wear discarded pieces of cloth or clothing, but do not fashion anything themselves. It shows no fear of humans but has a great fear of dogs, which in turn feel a great animosity towards the Almasty. Capable of running at great speeds. In times past, local people often took pity on the *Almastis'* and gave them food and clothing in the cold winter months. It was also common in those times for Almasty to steal food and clothing left unattended while in the forest. This led to the belief that Almastys would follow humans in the forest in the hope of obtaining any provisions left unguarded. Indeed! Local lore is replete with tales of bathers emerging from a leisurely dip to discover that all of their clothes and provisions have been stolen. The *Almasti* is observed alone and in family groups, with many abandoned cabins in the caucuses historically reputed to have been tenanted (albeit temporarily) by families of *Almasti*. They do not appear to fashion or utilise any tools, apart from stones (which they throw) or a simple club, the like of which has been found at suspected nesting sites. Although they do appear to understand the process of keeping a fire going, as attested to by some eyewitnesses accounts, they do not appear to possess the knowledge to make their own.

**Deadly Diet:** Omnivorous, but primarily vegetarian, preferring to eat, grasses, hemp, corn, melons, and cherries (the fields of which they can be happily heard raiding, at night, through their loud chewing, nose-blowing, and odd mumbles, which sound like: *"Boom, boom, boom!".)* Also known to eat frogs, lizards, rodents, and occasionally, the placenta of domestic animals and horse dung. They also seek out pieces of rock salt, which they lick.

**Hairy Habitat:** Prefers remote mountains and woodlands, where it makes temporary nests of specially chosen leaves and grasses in summer and occupies empty cabins, barns, and caverns in winter. It is reported throughout the Russian Caucuses Mountains, Abkhazia, Georgia, Armenia, the Dagestan Republic, and Azerbaijan.

**Scary Sightings:**

*10<sup>th</sup> Century AD:* Arab traveller and Historian Abdul Hassan Ali Masudi (known as the Herodotus of the Arabs) wrote of the Caucuses, that they were inhabited by: *"...a sort of monkey, having an erect stature and round face..."* and said that: *"...sometimes they are brought to the kings of those nations, and they are taught to stand by them and to taste what is on the table; for the monkeys have the peculiar quality of knowing if poison is present in food or drink."* Ali Masudi goes on to mention that: *"The same is the practice of most Chinese and Hindu sovereigns..." "...of the use which their kings make of monkeys for testing their food."* It is interesting here that while these other kings could simply be using known species of monkeys to test their food, Ali Masudi makes no differentiation between them and the *'erect monkeys'* of the Caucuses.

*Early 1930s:* In the early 1930s, late in May, early June, shepherd Zagoureev Chaghir was tending sheep high up on the slopes of alpine pastures of Elbruz, in the Republic of Kabardino-Balkaria. When he was forced by heavy rain to take refuge under a rocky overhang. When he approached it, he saw that three *Almastis'* were also sheltering under it. Although a little frightened, he decided to stay there anyway, as the rain was now falling very heavily. Both Chaghir and the Almastys kept their distance from one another and, asides from observing each other, had no further interaction. When the rain stopped, Chaghir came down from the mountain but kept quiet about his sighting for fear of a local superstition he had heard that maintained that anyone who saw an *Almasti* for the first time and spoke about it would get a bad headache. The following morning he was awoken by the cries of his fellow shepherds, who were frantically trying to take their herds down the valley because three Almasty had been spotted under a rock. Chaghir, being forced then to confess his sighting to the elders and his fellow shepherds, confirmed that he had seen the very same Almasty the previous day. Up to 15 shepherds curious to see the creatures ascended the slope, made a half-circle around the rock and watched the creatures until dinnertime. Of the three creatures they witnessed, two were of medium size and had the breasts of women but extremely long and covered with hair, and the third, which was bigger and seated between the two females, had the chest of a man. They were sitting on rocks, facing the shepherds, and were hunched over, with their heads down, only raising their heads slightly, now and then to look at their spectators from beneath their brows. One of the witnesses to these animals, an elder, and leader of the group, Koumychev Talib, described the creatures thusly:

*"Their heads were very ugly, not nice at all. They resembled a human face a little, but the nose is shorter and flattened. The eyes are slanted and reddish. The cheeks are very prominent, like those of a Mongol or a Korean,*

*but more so. The lips are thin. The lower jaw is receding, as though cut on a bias. The hair is long, like that of a woman, and tangled...The entire body is covered with shaggy hair, resembling that of the buffalo. In some places, this is long (torso, chest) and in other places, it is shorter (arms, legs). The hair was very dirty. The stink was so strong that we could not stand it. The odour resembled that of wild flax when it grows thickly. Once, the one seated on the right mumbled something. I did not see their hands clearly, as they were held between their legs. The legs are rather short and bowed. The foot is like that of a man but more spread out. All were wearing, wrapped around their waists, an old piece of a shepherd's cape. A young shepherd proposed to throw a lasso around one of them and bring it into the village. But, all the others cried out that it is forbidden, that they must not be harmed, and that they must not be disturbed. I watched them from a distance of 3-4 metres, and I even approached to within about 1 metre..."*

<u>1930s:</u> Koumykov Feitsa claimed to have seen many Almastys every summer, over a period of 5 years, in a rocky area where there were caverns, in the mountain pastures near Elbruz, Republic of Kabardino-Balkaria. Of his many experiences with the *Almastis'* in this region, one was particularly close. He said of his encounter:

*"One day, I was coming back from the village. It was very far. I had a small bag with food – cheese, bread, a piece of mutton. Toward evening, it began to rain very hard. I went into a cavern, made a wood fire, and spread out my woollen cape. At night, the rain fell even harder. All at once, something entered the cavern. It was very big, covered with reddish fur, and walking on two legs. For a moment, I thought it was a bear, and then, no, I saw it was an Almasty. I was very frightened. I was not armed and had only my dagger. I was seated sideways to it and pretended not to see anything. But, I was more dead than alive. I had my dagger in my right hand, hidden on my chest so that it could not see it, in order not to make it angry. Then, I calmed down a bit, remembering that the old people always say that, if one does not do it any harm, it never touches man. Nevertheless, the Almasty sat down near the fire, at one side, and began to squeeze water out of its fur, for it was soaked... Then, it sat down close to the fire, turning first one side and then the other to the fire. Finally, it was leaning almost against my feet. I*

*moved aside a little, very carefully, but it leaned against my feet again. In this way, little by little, it pushed me away from the fire. I was completely reassured because I could see that it was not dangerous. Moreover, it was a woman. She had very long breasts, which hung down across her abdomen. I said several words to it, and then I tried to talk to it, in Kabardian, in Balkar, and then in Russian. But it only mumbled incomprehensible sounds. I began to be sleepy, as it was already very late. But, I did not dare to sleep. Finally, I finished by dozing, lying on my left side. During the night, I very clearly heard it biting and chewing. I thought, "Good God, my food!" But, I didn't say anything. I heard it sucking on the bones. In the morning, I awoke very early and saw that it was no longer there. My bag had been opened and was empty. It had eaten everything, the wretched creature, and had left me nothing. The bones from the mutton were carefully lined up beside the bag."*

*1939/40:* Pchoukov Mohamed, a Kabardian stonemason, had an unexpected visitor to his vegetable garden in the summer of 1939 or 1940. His encounter which, lasted well over a week, shows a human-like emotional intelligence and conversely compounds the animal-like behaviours of this species. Pchoukov said of his long observation of the creature:

*"It was in 1939 or 1940, in summer...Where she came from, I do not know, but one day a female Almasty appeared in our vegetable garden and settled in the corn section. She made a nest there with old rags and grass. She passed a week with us without ever leaving the vegetable garden. She ate green corn. She was entirely covered with fur. Her hair was very long. The breasts were elongated, and hung like on a woman, but very low down. The nails were long. The eyes were slanted and red. The teeth were larger than in man, and the lips were the lips of a monkey. During the day, she always remained lying down. In general, she lay on her side, but she turned all of the time, and never stayed in the same position for long. Many people came to us to see her. If several people approached at the same time, she became nervous, sat up, cried, stood up and pulled on her hair. She cried in a very loud voice, like a woman. When she was calm, if there was someone near her, she would come up slowly and begin to lick the person, like a dog.*

*When you left her, your shirt sleeve was all wet; she would lick your entire shoulder."*

1940s: Khakonov Danial claimed to have seen many *Almasti* while working as a shepherd in the Akbecheyouko Valley in the 1940s. Even claiming that he and the other shepherds were aware of an old cabin nearby, where a family of six or seven Almasty lived. Khakonov said that toward evening the creatures would stir and become agitated, squealing, shouting, crying, and speaking sounds that sounded like *"Boom–boom–boom."* And that one time, he and the other shepherds were even kept awake all night by the sounds of them 'playing' on a drainpipe they had dragged into the house. Of one particular experience with the Almasty, Khakonov says:

*"One evening, at the end of October, we were cooking meat. At this moment, the sheep scattered. We went running around to get them back together. When we came back, an hour later – no more cooking pot. It was a pot of some fifteen litres! What did we think? We didn't think anything. We didn't have to think: We knew without thinking that it had been done by Almastis..."*

He goes on to say: *"I worked for three years in that place. They were there all of the time, especially in summer. Our dogs became accustomed to them. They growled but didn't touch them. However, if the dogs surrounded one, the Almasty began to cry out very loudly. I often saw their tracks: Five toes, no plantar arch, round heel, wide sole. Their prints resemble somewhat those of a bear. I have not returned there since 1947. "*

1944: In October 1944, several policemen attempted to trap a female Almasti in a hemp field in the Caucuses Mountains south of Nal'chi. Erjib Koshokoyev, one of the men present, said of their unusual encounter:

*"Our detachment (of police) was on horseback, crossing a field of hemp, on the steppe... Suddenly, the horse of the first man stopped so abruptly that I almost ran into it. I was riding second in line... He said to me: "Look! An Almasty!" Just in front of us, a few meters away, an Almasty was stuffing*

*into its mouth the ends of stalks of hemp, with the grains on them. Behind us, the detachment was gathering around and making some noise. It saw us and ran away very rapidly – it ran extraordinarily fast – toward a shepherd's cabin, which was not far away. While it was running, several men of our detachment took their rifles from their shoulders and prepared to fire, but our chief, a Russian officer from Nalchik, cried out: "Don't shoot, don't shoot. Let's capture it alive and take it to Nalchik." We dismounted and surrounded the shepherd's cabin. We were quite numerous and were able to form a solid circle around the cabin. I was just opposite the door and saw everything very well. When we approached, the Almasti came out of the cabin two or three times, in one bound. It appeared very agitated; it came out, moved around, jumped to one side, but then saw the men. It went back in one jump, leaped out again right away, jumped to another side, but there also it saw the men. In doing this, it grimaced, with its lips moving very, very fast, and it mumbled something. Meanwhile, our cordon was approaching. We had closed ranks and were advancing elbow to elbow. At this moment the Almasty appeared again, jumped in all directions and, suddenly, gave a terrible cry and ran straight at the men. It ran faster than a horse. To tell the truth, the men were taken by surprise. It easily broke through our cordon, jumped into the ravine and disappeared in the brush surrounding the river. It was about 1m80 in height, and very robust. One could not see its face well because of the hair. Its breasts hung down to its middle. It was covered with long shaggy red hair, like that of the buffalo. The hair could be seen clearly through the pieces of the old handmade Kabardian caftan which it was wearing, and which was completely in tatters. "*

Interestingly, Erjib, in relating the background of his encounter to Marie Jeanne Koffmann, mentioned casually that: *"...before the war, there were many Almastis around our area, even masses of them, one can say. Today very few are encountered...* This same sentiment is echoed by many of the older witnesses that Koffmann meticulously interviewed during her long sojourn in this region. Could the 2nd World War have had a detrimental effect on the Almasty population, or even upon, what was at that time, an extended range of habitation, which has since shrunken with the encroachment of man and the memory of his noisy warlike machines?

*1950:* In the summer of 1950, Didanov Dina, an electrician from Baksan, had been engaged to make an inventory of the collective farms in the mountain pastures of Elbruz when he made a startling nigh time observation of a female Almasty in the shelter in which the workers slept. He said of his encounter:

*"Toward midnight, we went to lie down. The shelter had three walls of stone. There was no fourth wall; it was open on that side. Everyone lay down on the ground, on hay, under our woollen capes, heads toward the interior wall, and feet toward the exterior. I was lying at the edge. Between the sidewall and me there was a space where the soup pot and a frying-pan full of grilled meat had been stored. Everyone fell asleep quickly. Me, I was young, a little excited by the conversation, the meal, the unusual surroundings – it was the first time that I was sleeping in the mountains – and I did not go to sleep. My neighbour, an old man, was not sleeping either. From time to time he would doze off, then wake up, smoke, and fall asleep again. All of a sudden, a sort of woman entered the shelter, rapidly and silently. She was hideous, with long hair down to the waist. She looked at the wall where a bridle was hanging, a Caucasian bridle decorated with metallic pendants. She took down the bridle, turned it over and over again, examined it from all sides, and then hung it up on the wall again and went out quietly. I was petrified with fear. At that moment the old man was not sleeping. I asked him, "What was that?" He answered me calmly, "It's nothing, don't pay any attention. If you stay here, you will see a lot of things like that." And he went back to sleep. All at once, she reappeared, stopped, stood motionless, examined very carefully the sleeping men, rapidly approached the saucepans and found herself one or two meters from me. The pot was covered with its lid and, as is our custom, the frying pan was covered with another frying pan. She stooped down, took the cover off the frying pan quickly and quietly, and began to eat. She ate at random, at times the meat from the frying pan, at times the soup. She dipped into the soup with the big wooden ladle which she had taken from the cover. She did not hold it as people would, but with all five fingers on one side. Her fingers*

*were very long, except for the thumb, which was shorter than a man's. Her appearance was hideous; not attractive at all. She was completely hairy, with dark reddish-brown fur covering her entire body. Long breasts extended down to the abdomen. The hair was loose, long and tangled. The nose was small, not turned up... but flat. The mouth stretched very wide, much more so than ours, and the lips were thin, as in monkeys. The skin was black. The cheeks were prominent, as in Chinese or Koreans. However, there are Chinese and Chinese. Some have more prominent cheeks, and others less so. As for her, she had very prominent ones, like a true, authentic Chinese. The eyes slanted sharply and their colour was like this: If, in place of the eyes, one put little bulbs from a pocket lamp and then placed a red glass in front of them, well, that would be exactly like her eyes. She was wearing a sort of dress, all torn and disgusting. She ate very quickly, seated on her heels, grabbing now the meat, now the soup, with very rapid movements. She chewed very quickly. In fact, I don't even know if she chewed or swallowed directly. But she devoted close attention to eating, without stopping for a second to look to the right or to the left. What struck me was the speed, the precision and the silence of her movements. On my word of honour, if I had begun to eat I would certainly have made some noise. I would have knocked against something. As for her, she did everything in complete silence. Just like in a silent film at the cinema. For example, when she took the bridle: The bridle had national ornaments in metal, and they should necessarily have jingled together. Well, she took it down, turned it around, and hung it back up again without the slightest sound. When she had finished eating, she put the lid back on the pot, quickly and silently, she closed the frying pan with the other frying pan, she put the wooden ladle back on the cover, at exactly the place where she had found it, and went out. If I had been alone I would probably have died of fright. But, although I was afraid, I felt calm, because there were a lot of people around. I said to myself if something happens I shall start to shout, and they will all get up. I was not able to go to sleep for a long time. In the morning, everyone began to eat the meat and the soup and to offer it to me. I declined: Me, I had seen what had been eating it during the night! I said that I was not accustomed to eat in the morning. "*

_1950:_ Khadji Mourat, an Azerbaijani chauffer, got the shock of his life one night, in the Autumn of 1950, when returning home in secret with a stolen sack of rice that he had _'commandeered'_ from a local mill. Believing to have spotted his neighbour's wife bathing in the river, what happened next would turn this would-be-peeper's midnight treat into a horrifying hairy assault upon the eyes. This is what he saw:

_"I was walking at night along the edge of the Belokane-chai River. I was carrying a sack of rice which I had "pinched" down there at the old mill. It weighed some twenty kilos. Plainly, I did not want to meet anyone. As if intentionally, the moon was shining as brightly as possible. Also, I had not taken the main street but, rather, the back alleys of the village, along the river. All at once, I heard a noisy splashing. I thought at first that the wind was carrying the sound of the rapids. But, there was no wind and, also, the rapids are quite small. The splashing was repeated regularly, as if someone were emptying a bucket all at once. I said to myself, "That must be the neighbour across the way, who is taking a bath – the devil take him. What am I going to do to get by?" I came up to the river bank carefully, and looked around from behind a rock. In the moonlight, I saw a person, very tall, standing in the water. He was standing up straight, and throwing enormous handfuls of water over himself. "That's curious, I thought, the neighbour isn't that big." At that moment I saw the long hair on the head. "Bah, that's better! I said to myself, it's not the neighbour, it's his wife! Well, I said to myself, I'm going to watch her take a bath." I was a young fellow, a bachelor. Not yet married. So, in any case, it was interesting to see a good-looking woman! I put down my sack and crept up carefully. I arrived at the water's edge, but just at that point, there were bushes which got in the way, so that one could only see very poorly. I had to retreat. She was just behind a rocky outcropping. I went down on my chest, crawled toward the rock, and raised my head slowly, exactly at the level of the water, right beside her. I almost gave up the ghost right there. In the water was standing a dreadful-looking woman, abominable. It wasn't a face that she had, but a frightful muzzle. And enormous hands, long ones. She was filling them with water and throwing it on her shoulders. On my word of honour, it was a_ *half-bucketful that she scooped up each time. Then, she took her breasts and began to throw them on the water. Now, her breasts were enormous, very long, and made a loud slapping sound on the water. Then, she started to throw water over herself again. My hair was standing up on my head. I crawled slowly backward, then I jumped to my feet and ran across the road to the neighbour, the same one of whom I thought it was himself or his wife who was bathing. I knocked at his door for quite a long time. Finally, he came out. I said to him: "Get your rifle and come quickly, there is a Kaptar (a horrible mythological creature) which is taking a bath, come see." At first, he hesitated, and then we left. When we arrived, there was no one in sight. The neighbour helped me to carry the rice and so, clearly, I had to share it with him."*

<u>1956 – Angry Almasty:</u> N.Ya. Serikova was staying at a collective farm in the Zolsk area of the Kabardin-Balkar Republic, Russia. She was listening to the sounds of a wedding party next door when an Almasti came into the room, screeched twice and left the hut, slamming the door behind it. It frequented a nearby house, where an old woman had befriended it.

<u>1959:</u> Omarov Ramazane, director of the veterinarian and zoological station of the district of Tliarata, in the Republic of Dagestan, was returning home across the Mountains of Antzoug at 6 o'clock on the 20th August 1959, when he spotted what he thought was a bear moving in the valley below. He would go on to witness a creature he had only known from the folktales of his childhood. The importance of his testimony, which certainly adds a level of scientific credibility and confirmation of the physiological appearance and behaviour of the Almasty, cannot be overstated. This is what he saw:

*"...I was coming back across the mountain to Antzoug. It was about 6 o'clock in the evening. The visibility was very good. I was coming down a small valley where the trees were quite sparse. When I reached the big white rock...I noticed an animal that was moving at the base of it. I thought that it was a bear and I hid behind a bush. I had no arms of any sort on me. I had only my bridle and the bag in which I carry the supplies needed for*

*vaccinations. While hiding behind my bush, I began to observe. The animal which, so far as I could see, had been seated, got up suddenly and started in my direction on its two legs. It was a creature which resembled both a man and a monkey at the same time. Since I was a child I had heard stories of Kaptar, but I did not believe in them. Well, this was one, which I now saw with my own eyes. Its fur was long and black, like that of a goat. The neck was virtually non-existent, the head resting directly on the shoulders. Long hair hung down from it. The Kaptar approached. It was going not toward me, but to one side. It was a man. The head was long and tapered to a point toward the top. In other words, it was conical or ovoid in form. Its long arms hung almost to the knees. It swung them while walking, and they jerked, as though they were articulated on bolts. They gave the impression of having been assembled in joints, like a child's plaything. At about 200 m from where I was, this strange creature crossed the path and sat down again. It remained seated two or three minutes, with its hands touching the ground. It reminded me of an athlete doing warming-up exercises. Then, it got up again and went toward a bush on the other side of the crest and disappeared. I did not see it anymore. I abandoned my bush and came calmly back to the house. What struck me the most? It went up the slope very quickly, taking steps of a meter and even more. A man would not be able to go up such a steep slope in such great strides. I thought of the chimpanzee which I had seen in the zoo of Tbilisi. The fur of the chimpanzee is shorter, and its head more round. Its arms and legs are also shorter. It must be said, it is true, that its size is much smaller. The Kaptar did not measure less than 1m80, and it resembled more a man than a monkey. It walked erect, with just the head inclined a little forward from the shoulders. There was no tail. Another typical thing: With wolves and bears, one always sees the ears, even if they have short ones, whereas here the hair covered the ears, and they were not visible. Clearly, I was afraid. But, my curiosity was even stronger than my fear. I have lived 37 years, and I had always thought that the Kaptar was the invention of superstitious people. Now, I know that to be false; I saw it myself. "*

<u>1964</u>: On the 10th August 1064, Kabardian farmer Akhaminov Khouzer Bekanlouk was busy scything in a field of sunflowers near the village

of Planovskoye. What he would bear witness to is almost unheard of in the field of wildman research and provides valuable information about the productive cycle of the Almasty. This is his encounter:

*"...I was scything in a field of sunflowers where there remained some open places where seeds had not been sown. Suddenly I heard a strong noise, as if someone were blowing noisily - like a dog, when a fly gets into his nose... When the sound occurred a third time, I put down my scythe and went to look. Suddenly, two arms, like human ones but long, black and hairy, extended out of the foliage in my direction. I ran immediately to my cart and climbed up on it. It had been unhitched about ten meters away. Standing on the cart, I saw a silhouette, resembling a human one, which was bent over, and was pushing into the sunflowers. I only saw clearly the back, which was covered with long reddish fur, like that of the buffalo, and the long hair of the head. I did not see its face. When the Almasty had left (I recognized it at once, because formerly I had seen others), I came down from my cart and returned to my scythe. At that moment I heard a squealing at the same place. I advanced carefully, and pushed the stalks apart. On the packed-down grass, as in a nest, were lying two newborns. It was clear that she had just given birth. They were exactly like human babies, except that they were smaller. They must have weighed around two kilos, not more. Apart from that, you would not have been able to distinguish them from our little ones. They had rosy skin, like human infants, exactly the same head, the same arms and legs. They were not hairy. No, I stress this: They were not hairy. They looked like newborn humans or newborn rats – bare, and with rosy skin. They were waving their little arms and legs, just like our newborns, and squalling. I got away from there in a hurry. I quickly hitched up my donkey and returned to the village. Two or three days later I came back, but there was no one around."*

What is so very interesting about this encounter is its description of the newborns as being – *"bare, and with rosy skin"* and *"exactly like human babies"*. Is there more than just a passing resemblance between Almasty and humans? Could an extant form of undeveloped Neanderthals exist in the wild places of the world, or does this species, like several other mammals, simply give birth to hairless young? This sighting reminds me of another uncovered by Marie Jeanne Koffmann in her research of the Almasty, in which the witness says: *"In the corner of the cabin, an Almasty was sitting on some hay; it had in its arms a tiny little one... the baby had a black skin, entirely covered with black hair, but these were short and not thick" "With one hand she was holding her little one, all covered with fur, two or three years of age."* How the witness knew the age of the animal, we do not find out, although it is probable that the estimate was based upon proportions of a human child of similar age. What is interesting, however, is that in this sighting, the child is now hair-covered and not bare.

*1991:* On August 25th, 1991, RSC Board member and biologist Gregory Panchenko observed was on a field expedition in Kuruko Ravine (add photo) in the Kabardin-Balkar Republic, Russia, when he had an encounter with an Almasti. The Almasti entered through a window of a barn that he was sleeping in and as Panchenko was partially hidden and not noticed by the Almasti, he was able to observe the animal closely as it made high pitched, twittering sounds while plaiting a horse's mane. The horse did not offer any resistance and after a short time, the Almasti departed through an open window above the barn door. Panchenko verified that the Horse's mane had new clumsily plaited braids that were not there the day before. Some Kazakhstan herders believe that the wildman uses these plaits to hang, back to front, beneath mares and drink their milk. However, wildman researcher Igor Bourtsev claimed to have solved this puzzle of the plaits by watching many night expeditions to watching horses through night vision device, concluding that the horses hair plaited itself through their habit of perpetually shaking their heads and necks.

*(Note: There are many more Almasty sightings that could be included here and even though this story is far broader than a book of this nature could investigate holistically, I feel it impingent upon me to give a reason for omitting the case of Zana, the Wild woman of the Caucuses. The subject of her capture, domestication and 'breeding'; not to mention her descendants and their remains, are fraught with scientific disparity and warrant a*

*meticulous and forensically focused investigation – which I mean to conduct on the matter, in one of my forthcoming titles – 'Tales of the Wodewose: The Wildman Goes Global.')*

**Beastly Evidence:**

*Koffmann Tracks*: French researcher Marie-Jeanne Koffmann found a set of tracks in the Dolina Narzanov Valley in the North Caucuses in March 1978.

*Koffmann/Kozlov Tracks:* In 1992, Marie Jeanne Koffmann and Andrei Kozlov cast several alleged Almasti tracks in the Kabardin-Balkar Republic where eyewitness Doucha Aspikova had seen an Almasti only a few days previous.

*Bourtsev Tracks:* 14-inch tracks discovered and cast by Wildman researcher Igor Bourtsev, in the Pamir Mountains, in 1979.

*Art and Archaeology:* Could two hairy humanoids, engraved upon a funerary mirror of gold and silver, which was discovered in a Scythian tomb from the 7th to 5th century BC in a village of Kelermes in the North Caucuses, possibly be representations of the Almasty? Among the hirsute couple, both male and female, many other known local species are engraved upon the mirror. Could this rare treasure simply represent an ancient animalium of revered species that were known to the Scythian tribes in this region?

**Beastly Theories:**

*Inbred Ancestors:* Could the Almasti be nothing more than a close-knit tribe, that through interbreeding, have passed recessive genetic abnormalities down through successive generations until these conditions have become endemic amongst its members? It certainly seems unlikely that a community of humans, so interbred that their physiological traits have begun to resemble a hybrid of human and simian characteristics, could have managed to evade scientific discovery, although as seen in other parts of the world, some uncharacteristic human societies, have at least successfully avoided assimilation and detection in other parts of the world (one is reminded of the pygmies of the Congo and the Ostrich people of Kenya not to mention the recent aerial photos of the *"isolated Indians of the upper Humaitá,"* an amazon tribe whose discovery was made without human intervention and of whose physiological uniquity, such as it might be, being genetically cut off from the wide population, we know nothing about.

| *Uncontacted indigenous tribe in the Brazilian state of Acre.*

*Relict Neanderthal:* Are the Almasti a form of a prehistoric human, like the tall Neanderthals found in Shanidar in Kurdistan, Iraq, or the descendants of a human-like race of apes, altogether unknown in the fossil record? Certainly, the caucuses have produced fossil remains of Homo erectus, Archaic Human, and Neanderthal fossils, which may seem enough to justify this assertion; correspondingly, homo erects fossils have been found (not particularly close by) in Beijing, as well as possible Neanderthal-like tools in Mongolia. Sadly there is little in these scant fossil finds that would indicate how these assumed anthropological antecedents of man might have looked were they alive today and we are left, as always, with these uncertain remnants as paltry restitution for our inability to categorise these man-like beings.

Model of Homo Neanderthalensis elder man in The Natural History Museum, Vienna.

*The Waning Wildman:* Are we present at the end of this unique and ethno-known species, of which the occasional member, whom we spy, is himself a lonely wanderer in a land he once filled with energetic family groups, both tolerated by the local human population and even, on occasion, aided by them, with food and clothing? Could its former geographic dominance have been hampered by the growing industrialisation of the nations in which it once lived, or perhaps, were the horrors and carnage of the second world war enough to drive it ever further away from man; up onto the unassailable heights and deep within the impenetrable forests, where few humans dare to tread!?_Perhaps, in the regions adjoining the caucuses, the population of these magnificent Wildmen is still what it once was, but in the caucuses themselves, even in at the time when Koffmann recorded many of these eyewitness reports, there was a general consensus among the people in this region, that the Almasty were in terminal decline.

| *Virgin forest in Shennongjia Forestry District, Hubei, China.*

## YEREN

The *Yeren*, although reported in many remote regions of China, is most closely associated with the tall, hairy, man-like creatures that are believed to be endemic to Western Hubei Province's Shennongjia Forestry District. This district was created on May 28th, 1970, through the amalgamation of the neighbouring areas of Badong County, Baokang County, Fang County and Xingshan County into an area covering 1,256 square miles. Due to its rare flora and fauna, it has World Heritage Status and boasts a diminutive population of approximately 80,000 residents, giving it an average density of 61 persons per square mile and making this mountainous morass a genuine sanctuary for the Chinese Wildman.

**What's in a name?** The name *Yeren* means '*Wild man*' in Mandarin Chinese (some archaic spellings render it: *Ye-Ren*, *Yeh Ren*, and *Yiren*.) It is also known as, *Mao-Ren*; *Suet-juen* and *Xuren*, all of which mean "*Snowman*". It has three proposed scientific names, the first of which,

*Predatopithecus Sinensis*, which was proposed by G.N. Mao in 1964, and the second and third, *Pongo Erectus* and *Yeren Sinensis*, which were proposed by Grover S. Krantz in 1998.

**Monstrous Measurements:** There seem to be two basic types of hairy humanoid that carry the name – *Yeren*.

*The larger*: is bipedal, muscular, and stands from 6 - 10 ft tall, with an average height of 6ft, 6 inches. Its head is human-sized with differentiated long head hair that is 12 – 21 inches long and that stands up at the front of the head but hangs down at the back. It has a high, sloping forehead that rises above the eyes, a narrow face that is covered in short hair, including the nose, and eyes that are deep-set, black, and human-like. Its ears are also superficially man-like but large, and its nose is upturned or flared at the end like an orangutan's or a human's nose that is missing the root. It has high cheekbones, protruding teeth, and jaws with everted lips. It ranges in colour, from black in Yunnan Province to white in Tibet, and reddish-brown in Hubei Province and long red hair can often be seen on its arms, which are long and hang beneath its knees. The palms of its hands and soles of its feet are hairless. It has long hands and fingers (about 6 inches in length) with long fingernails. Its thumb is only slightly separated from the fingers. Its calves are thickset and longer than the thighs. Its feet are more than 12 inches long and 6 – 7 inches wide. Its broad shoulders are 3 – 4 ft wide, and its waist, 18 inches across. Some sexual dimorphism is visible in the large breasts and buttocks possessed by the females (males are also reported with large buttocks!) It does not appear to have a tail.

*The Smaller:* is quadrupedal, standing from 4-5ft tall, appears (long) thin, and has smaller feet than its larger namesake, and may be comparable to the *Ren-Xiong*.

**Terrifying Tracks:** there are also 2 types of tracks attributed to this animal which may correspond to both the larger (bipedal) and smaller (quadrupedal) types that have been categorised under this name.

*The larger:* are 12-19 inches long and 6 – 7 inches wide. The toes are oval and webbed. The length of the toes is one-fourth that of the entire foot. With a stride 3 – 5 ft in length.

*The Smaller:* are 8 inches long with big toe separated from smaller four, and pointing outward.

**Beastly Behaviours:**

*The larger:* Bipedal. Walks with a loping gait. Reclusive and Solitary (rarely seen in groups of two or three). Migrates through remote mountains and forests. Employs various vocalisations and calls that might sound like: *"jia-jia-jia-jia" "ah-ah!" "Wa-wa-ahaha"*, and *"go-ro, go-ro."* Makes temporary nests out of leaves. Not afraid of humans and sometimes, as is the case with other *Wildmen* around the world, is suspected of abducting women for sex. In the case of the *Yeren*, however, local superstition maintains that the females will also abduct men for this very same purpose. A stele that was erected in a grotto in Ping Feng hill, Zhuxi County, (Hubei Province) in 1790, commemorates the site as the former haunt of a Yeren, who would kidnap passers-by.

*The Smaller:* Both quadrupedal and bipedal. Reclusive and solitary, yet curious. Afraid of humans, but also supposedly laughs when coming across them. Migratory and builds temporary nests of leaves upon which to sleep.

**Deadly Diet:** Both types are omnivorous and have been observed eating wild chestnuts, fruits.

**Hairy Habitat:** Both types are migratory. Residing in the cool high mountains during summer and migrating to deciduous woodlands and gorges in the winter and spring. Both are also reported in Sichuan and Hubei provinces (especially the Shennogjia Forest Reserve, which has the greatest number of significant reports); Guizhou, Yunnan, Shaanxi, Zhejiang, Gansu, Fujian and Anhui Provinces.

Inscription in cliff face next to the entrance of the "Yeren Cave" in Western Hubei Province, China. The inscription reads "Ye Ren Dong" ("Wild Man Cave").

**Scary Sightings:** Some scholars have dated the *Yeren* phenomenon as far back as the Shang Dynasty (1600 – 1046 BC), asserting that the pictographs of hairy *Wildmen* from this era closely match modern wildman descriptions. Indeed! Even the *Shan-hai Ching* (4th Century BC), an encyclopaedic collection of Chinese geography, flora and fauna, speaks of a people called the *Mao-min*, or *"Hairy People."* In more modern times, Yeren-lore appears to have re-emerged in the 1920s and since this period, officials in Shennogjia have recorded more than four hundred sightings, many of which include reports from government officials. Since then, many notable researchers have undertaken the challenge of *discovering the Yeren*, and although reports were somewhat stifled during the Mao era, the veracity and continuity of reports has more or less remained stable.

Below I have included several well-known sightings that constitute the core of the *Yeren* phenomenon:

*4th Century A.D.* The Soushen Ji (In Search of the Supernatural), a compilation of 'mysterious phenomena', recounted the tale of a man named Tai Jing, who encountered a hair-covered man, over 6ft 6in tall, in the mountains of Wuchang (Wuhan).

*454 -456 AD:* County official, Chen Cangqi, wrote that two reddish-haired humanoids, both male and female, were captured in Anchang County (Hepu County) and were sent as tribute to the imperial court of the Emperor Xiaojian, whereupon the emperor ordered that their images be recorded.

*539 – 552 A.D.* According to the Nanshi (History of the Southern Dynasties), hundreds of hairy men jumped over the village walls of Ying (Jiangling County, Hubei Province) with loud cries (539 A.D.) Some years later (552 A.D.), groups of Yeren destroyed buildings in the Huainan area (Anhui Province). It was in this incident that the term, *Yeren,* was allegedly first recorded.

*1915:* Wang Laozhong, a hunter from Fang County, claimed to have been kidnapped by a reddish-haired female *Yeren* and forced to live with it in its grotto.

*1922:* A crowd of onlookers watched the 22nd prefectural militia drive away a large *Yeren* that had been captured in Fang County. 3 of the witnesses, 6-year-old Huang Xinhe, 17-year-old Huang Xinkui, and Xinming, attested to having witnessed the release of the creature, which was neither an orangutan or a bear, but a large, muscular hairy humanoid, with a large face, a prominent mouth, and big feet.

*1926:* Du Jinhai was walking through a bamboo grove in Shanshuwan when he spotted a large, reddish-haired *Yeren* walking nearby.

*1929:* Hunter, Qin Shaoqun, shot a *Yeren* in Liuchi.

*1930:* A woman named Xiao Zongrun was walking on Suluoshu Mountain when she observed the incredible spectacle of a *'wild man'* trying to ride a wild boar while bleating out laughter-like cries.

*1934:* A family was sheltering from the elements somewhere in Shennongjia Forestry District when they were alerted to a strange creature after hearing some 'unusual noises'. These were followed by a visitation from a 6.6 ft tall humanoid, covered in yellowish hair that hung down from its shoulders; that walked around their camp, before leaving.

*Late 1930s:* A famous amusement arcade and entertainment complex in shanghai exhibited a male *Yeren*. According to one eyewitness, a man named Wang Helin, the creature resembled a man, totally covered in brownish-black hair and 6.6 ft tall, with a large mouth, hands and feet.

*1937:* A man named Wu Yunqing was travelling on Wu Mountain in Chongqing City when he spotted something climbing the slope. The animal, which was 160 – 200 feet away from him, was 6.6 ft tall and covered in reddish-brown hair, and though bipedal, climbed the steeper slopes on all fours.

*1938:* Cai Shixiang and five or six companions were taking a trip in Shennongjia Forestry District. When they discovered strange human-like tracks in the snowfield at Tielugou. The group described the tracks as manlike, although the big toes were significantly larger. Later, the group travelled on to Yanziling, where they encountered two *Yeren*, one large (6.6 ft tall) and one slightly smaller, who were *"stroking each other's hair."*

*1940s:* A man named Cao Liangkun claimed to have witnessed a whole tribe of red-haired Yeren' of various sizes (and presumably ages and gender) roaring at the sun and waving their hands in unison.

*1940:* Biologist Wang Zelin examined a *Wildman* that was killed by hunters near Niangniangba, Gansu Province. It was a female, covered with greyish-brown hair that stood about 6ft. tall. Its face was overgrown with hair. Its teats were reddish, suggesting that it had been breastfeeding a young one recently. Wang Zelin stated that: that it: *"...appeared to be a cross between ape and human."*

*1945:* According to an eyewitness, Zha Chengxian, two dead *Yeren*, an Adult female and a juvenile, were displayed in the Changfang Township.

*1947:* A large adult female *Yeren* and a younger juvenile were encountered by Zhai Ruisheng, leader of the 359ᵗʰ brigade of the Eighth Route Army. Zhai described the larger creature as being unmistakably female due to its having large breasts. The smaller creature did not have any distinguishing sexual characteristics and was only slightly shorter than the large female. Both creatures had human-like faces with large eyes, large hands and feet and were covered in hair (the larger, in reddish-black and the smaller in light-brownish hair). Curiously, the large female was wearing a covering of leaves over her genitals.

*1948:* An 8-Year-old boy named Zhao Benxiu witnessed an entire *Yeren* family, consisting of adults and juveniles and even a mother with large breasts that was actively breastfeeding a baby while walking in the Shennongjia Forestry District.

*1950s:* On two separate days, geologist Fan Jingquan watched two Wildmen, a female and a young male, as they were picking wild chestnuts near Baoji, Shaanxi Province. The smaller one was about 5 ft tall and even bold enough to approach the awestruck geologist closely.

*1952:* A Doctor named Lei Yucheng was travelling from Jiudaoliang to Hong Hua Township in the Shennongjia Forestry District when he noticed a *Yeren* moving along a slope. Lei described the creature as being 6.5 ft tall and covered in long reddish-brown hair.

*1953:* A man named Dong Xingda was stalked by a *Yeren*, not unexpectedly, at a place named Yerenkong ("Wildman Ravine") in the

Shennongjia Forestry District. The creature followed him for 500 metres until he threw a rock at it, after which it went away.

*1953:* A man named Yang Shipan was walking in the Shennongjia Forestry District in the summertime when he thought that he had spotted a fellow villager. Twice calling out to his neighbour but receiving no reply, he approached a little closer only to realise that he was looking at a *"wild man"*.

*1955:* A factory worker named Hu Yuanren was on his way to Bandengenya in Shennongjia forestry District when he encountered a 'man-like' creature. The creature, which was covered in reddish-yellow hair, slapped its hands together and made a magpie-like call that sounded like *"jia-jia-jjia-jia"*, at which Hu became afraid and ran away. Later, recounting his encounter with the locals there, he was informed that they had seen this animal before and that it was never aggressive to people.

*1956:* June 10th, 1956: The We Wei Po, a major Chinese daily newspaper, reported in 1961 that Giant Bipedal Chimpanzees, that were 6.6 ft Tall and covered in dark hair, had been chasing people on the border between Western Hubei Province and Eastern Chongqing City.

*1961:* A 4 ft tall female *Yeren* was reportedly killed by road workers in the Xishuangbanna Nature Preserve area, Yunnan Province. Later, the Chinese Academy of Sciences attempted to investigate this story but was hindered by the alleged body of the creature having disappeared by the time they arrived on the scene. Failing to obtain any direct evidence, they concluded that the creature was likely a large gibbon. Curiously, more than twenty years later, a journalist, who claimed to have been involved in the original investigation, alleged that the animal that he saw was no gibbon, but a large unknown creature, shaped like a human.

*1965:* A cadre named He Xiantong claimed to have observed a strange primate in Wenjia Mountain in Shennongjia Forestry District. The creature, which was apparently sleeping in a tree, had a monkey-like face with a flat mouth, human-like five-toed feet, and was completely covered in greyish-black hair.

*1968/69*: A worker in a wood processing plant in Shennongjia Forestry District witnessed Yeren, two years running, in 1968 and 1969.

*1970:* A farmer in Panshui, Shennongjia Forestry District, killed a *Yeren* and sold its legs to the local Yangriwan Mess Hall. Seventeen witnesses in all claimed to have seen the creature's legs, which were covered in brownish-black hair, weighed 33lbs, and sported man-like feet that were 1.3 ft in length.

*1971:* Zeng Xiangzhong, a teacher at the Mugua School in Shennongjia Forestry District and six other people, witnessed a bipedal creature that was covered in long greyish-white hair. The creature emitted a call that sounded like *"ah-ah!"* as it quickly made its way across the mountainside adjacent to the school.

1973: A man named Liu Guangming claimed to have fought with a large red-haired *Yeren* while on his way to Youluya, in Shennongjia Forestry District.

*1973:* Two cadres, Zeng Guanghou and Zhang Zhiyong, attempted to shoot at a pair of *Yeren* in Zhushan County. The animals, which the men described as monkeys larger than humans and covered in yellowish-grey hair, ran away unharmed.

*1974:* On May 1st, 1974, Yin Hongfa, a cadre of the Qingxigou Production Brigade of Qiaoshang Commune in Fang County, was gathering herbs on Qinglongzhai Mountain, when he encountered a female *Yeren*; which he described as being covered in long greyish-white hair, with prominent brow ridges, oval, reddish coloured eyes and a monkey-like mouth that was wider than a human's. It stretched out its long arms, which had large hands and long fingers, to grab Yin, who reflexively grabbed it by its head hair and hacked its left arm with a machete, causing it to run off into the forest, making a sound that sounded like *"wa-wa-ahaha"*. After which, Yin was left holding 20 or 30 strands of its hair in his hand.

*1975:* The commissar of Zhushan, Meng Qingbao, observed an animal that resembled a long-legged, tailless monkey as it slowly moved off into the forest.

*1975:* In April 1975, two workers, Wang Chenggen and Zhang Yingze, encountered a large reddish-brown haired animal from a distance of 330 ft in the Shennongjia Forestry District.

*1975:* In May 1975, a Yeren tried to steal the walking stick of 30-year-old Gan Mingzhi while he was collecting firewood in the mountains of Xingshan County, Shennongjia Forestry District. The creature, which Gan described as a 'hairy man', 6.6 ft tall with large teeth and thick fingers and toes, grabbed the man's stick while at the same time emitting laughter-like cries. After a brief struggle, Gan managed to free his stick from the creature and made his escape.

*1976:* On Jan 29<sup>th,</sup> 1976, Zeng Xianguo, a 19-year-old farmer from Yusai Village in Qiaoshang Commune, was scratched during a confrontation with a *Yeren* in the local mountains. Zeng described the creature as resembling a large Orangutan, approximately 6.2 ft Tall, covered in reddish-black-long hair, and with a prominent mouth that was larger than a human's.

*1976:* On February 20<sup>th,</sup> 1976, a farmer in the Shennongjia Forestry District claimed that a *Yeren* had stolen his pig.

*1976:* On May 14th, 1976, six officials travelling by jeep encountered a Wildman near Chunshuya village in the Shennogjia Forest, Hubei Province, at 1:00 AM on May 14<sup>th,</sup> 1976. They got out and started to surround it but did not dare advance on it. One of the men eventually threw a rock at it and it slipped away into the woods. They described the creature, which they had initially spotted in the illumination of their headlights, as man-shaped and covered in long bright red hair, tailless, with a long face, prominent brow ridge, human-like eyes, a slightly pointed mouth, thick legs and large buttocks. This incident, reported by official sources, became the impetus for several wildman expeditions, including one joint venture between scientists and the army, 110 members strong, drawn from 32 research institutions, museums, zoos, universities, and colleges throughout the country as well as photographers, and a special army infiltration unit of 56 soldiers, equipped with tranquillizer guns, audio recorders, and sniffer dogs. This expedition was not without success, with several large manlike tracks being cast and several hair samples being collected as well as one of the search party's involved allegedly ambushing one of the creatures. Alas, the nerves of one of the soldiers present got the better of him, causing him to accidentally discharge his weapon, shooting himself in the leg and warning the fortunate *Yeren* of their approach.

*1977:* On June 6th, 1977, Pang Gensheng was approached by a hairy man 7 ft 6 inches tall in the Qinling-Taibaishan Reserve, Shaanxi Province. They confronted each other for an hour until Pang hit it in the chest with a stone, whereupon it went down a gully muttering *"go-ro, go-ro."*

*1978:* In August 1978: Three local farmers were seated around a fire in a shed in Fang County when a *Yeren* walked in through the door. A stare-off ensued between the men and the creature until the creature finally turned and left the shed, walking off in the opposite direction.

*1979:* Liu Minzhuang, affectionately nicknamed the *"Professor Wildman"*, turned up the skeleton of a *'monkey-boy'* who was reputed to be the child of a local woman who was once kidnapped by a *Yeren*. *(See a more detailed dialogue on this in the Beastly Evidence section at the end of this chapter.)*

*1980:* On February 28th, 1980, Li Guohua, who often worked alongside Liu Minzhang, was investigating a series of tracks at Fanwanliang in Shennongjia Forestry District when he observed a brownish haired *Yeren*, a 6.9 ft tall *Yeren* traversing the snowfield 230 ft away from him. Li immediately gave chase, at which the creature fled and climbed a steep escarpment, prompting Li to draw his rifle and to try to shoot the creature. Fortunately, on this occasion, the damp had adversely affected the gunpowder and the *Yeren* vanished from view.

*1980:* From May to December 1980, The Chinese Academy of Sciences conducted expeditions into the Shennongjia Forestry District and the Daba Mountain in Sichuan Province, in which nests made of bamboo, hair samples, tracks and faeces were recovered. During the expedition, two members who had made their way to the Xiangshui River in Shennongjia Forestry District, Li Guohua and Li Renrong, witnessed a long-haired humanoid-like primate sitting on a rock approximately 1000 ft away from them.

*1981:* On September 15th 1981: Three explorers were travelling through the mountains near the Xiangshui River when they witnessed a tall, reddish-haired *Yeren* running on two legs.

*1984:* On October 23rd, 1984, a small, hairy *"wild-man"* threw sand and stones at two young women of Shuitou village, near Rulin in western Hunan Province. The next day, thirty-two peasants and eleven hunting dogs tracked down and netted the creature in a neighbouring county, but not before it clawed the ear off of one of its captors. The animal was exhibited in several cities before it was turned over to the Chinese Wildman Research Institute and identified as a Rhesus monkey.

*1985:* On May 10th, 1985: Two local cadres, Pei Yunquan and Zhi Guanghua of Yangjiawa in the Shennongjia Forestry District, saw a small *Yeren*, approximately 4.3 ft. tall.

*1993:* On September 3rd, 1993, ten staff members of the Chinese Ministry of Railways spotted three *Yeren* not more than 66 ft away from them while travelling by motor vehicle through Yanziya in the Shennongjia Forestry District.

*1995:* In April 1995, Chen Anju, a farmer from Tangjiapo, Shennongjia Forestry District, observed a tall, bipedal animal eating wild fruits.

*1997:* In September 1997, retired Teacher Zhao Tan witnessed a black haired *Yeren* near the borders of Fang and Baokang County.

*1999:* On August 18<sup>th</sup>, 1999, several passengers of a tourist bus travelling through Shennongjia Forestry District witnessed a *Yeren*, approximately 6.6 ft tall, with greyish-black shaggy hair, crossing a road in the mountains. Later, local authorities searched the area and found footprints, 1 ft. in length, with a stride ranging between 3 – 3.9 ft.

*2000:* On September 6<sup>th</sup>, 2000, eight employees of Shiyan City's telecommunications Office were travelling in a motor vehicle through Liangfengya in Shenningjia Forestry District when they observed two blackish brown-haired *Yeren* about 160 ft. away from them. Upon their approach, the creatures disappeared into the forest.

*2001:* On October 3<sup>rd</sup>, 2001, tourists visiting Houzishi in Shenningjia Forestry District attempted to take photos of a large hairy bipedal animal situated several hundred feet away from them. Unfortunately, and not unexpectedly, their pictures were inconclusive.

*2002:* On January 28<sup>th</sup>, 2002, two officials, Qui Hu, deputy town chief of Hongping and Fu Chuan Jin, deputy head of the Hongping Forestry Depot, encountered a 'wild man' crossing the road, 66ft. in front of them, while driving near Yanqiaodonggou in Shennongjia Forestry District. They described the strange creature as resembling a human and a monkey that was covered in greyish-yellow hair and which had a loping gait. They estimated its stride as being from 6.6 to 7.2 ft.

*2003:* On June 29<sup>th,</sup> 2003, four people witnessed a 'hairy man' while travelling in a motor vehicle on No. 209 national Road, near Tianmenya in Shennongjia Forestry District. The creature they observed was bipedal, 5.2 ft tall and covered in grayish-white hair, and darted into nearby woods when it saw their vehicle approach.

<u>2004</u>: A 14-year-old student, Zhou Jiang, encountered an old-looking biped, covered in grayish-white hair, as it hastily made its way somewhere in Shennongjia Forestry District.

<u>2007</u>: On November 18<sup>th</sup>, 2007, four tourists visiting a remote area called Chalihe on the northern slope of Laojujn Peak, in the eastern Shennongjia Mountains, observed two animals that they described as looking like a cross between a bear and a monkey.

**Beastly Evidence:** In 1981, the China Wildman Research Society, formed with the help of the famous Chinese paleoanthropologist Jiǎ Lánpō, offered a cash reward for a *Yeren* body, dead or alive. Later in October 1994, the Chinese government set up a scientific committee to study *Yeren* evidence. Again in 1995, another reward was offered to anyone who could obtain a *Yeren* specimen, Dead or Alive, with lesser prizes for photographs, hair or faeces! This time, the offer came from the China Travel Service in Hubei Province, but like those before it and despite its financial incentive, it failed to yield any tangible evidence! The arena of *Yeren* research is not without its purported evidence, however, and many intriguing discoveries have been made in the period since its resurgence in the modern era.

Tracks:

*Songbai Tracks:* A large scale expedition near Songbai in the Shennongjia Forest documented more than two hundred footprints on Mount Quiangdao. The tracks were approx. 18 inches long with a stride of 6 feet.

*Luchizi Tracks:* A doctor named Guo Deixang found human-like tracks in a cave in Luchizi, Shennongjia Forestry Park, that were 1.3ft in length. Additional tracks were also found in the same location at a later date.

*Ranger Tracks:* In 1995, ranger Yuan Yuhao sighted a *Yeren* walking into the forest in the Shennongjia Reserve. He tracked the animal and cast several of its tracks at a place where it had squatted down to drink from a spring. The 15-inch tracks appeared to show signs of a midtarsal pressure ridge, a morphological feature that is frequently observed in North American Sasquatch tracks.

*Shennongjia Giant:* On August 1999, Chinese officials investigating *Yeren* sightings found giant footprints in the Shennogjia Reserve.

*Tourist Trap Tracks:* On November 18th, 2003, four tourists claimed to have seen two *Yeren* near the Licha River. Upon noticing their car approaching, the two creatures fled into the dense forest. Later that day, the tourists returned to the site of their encounter accompanied by two forest rangers who, along with the tourists, found several footprints, as well as broken branches and wild fruits scattered around the area. This prompted the China Association for Scientific Expedition (CASE) to visit the area 4 days later, whereupon they conducted a thorough investigation of the location and discovered two visible footprints, one 11.8 inches long and one smaller and four strands of soft white hair, 0.7 inches long on one of the broken branches nearby.

Hair: Suspected *Yeren* hair samples that have been subjected to modern testing methods of Microscopic keratin Content and Particle Induced X-ray Emission (PIXE) have often yielded intriguing results, with some hair samples even showing chemical and structural distinctions that differ from known animals, including humans and primates.

*Sanchatou Hairs:* In 1955, a man named Yuan Congzhen claimed to have collected *Yeren* hair samples in Sanchatou, Shennongjia Forestry District.

*Maota Hairs:* In 1965, a farmer named Zhang Fanke witnessed two *Yeren* while gathering herbs at Maota in Shennongjia Forestry Park. The Yeren, one of which had reddish hair and the other grey, appeared to be passing through the area and did not stop. After the creatures had left, Zhang found a 0.8 ft long hair belonging to one of the creatures.

*Wichigou Hairs*: In April 1986, a piece of hair measuring 1.1 ft and attached to the skin of an unknown animal was found at Wichigou, Shennongjia Forestry District.

*Hair Analysis*: In 1988, several hairs attributed to the *Yeren* were examined by Liu Minzhuang at Shanghai's Huadong Normal University and were found to contain higher levels of calcium, iron and copper than samples from nine other known species.

*Hair and Tracks*: Another scientific expedition to Shennogjia Forest from April to July 1995, headed by Wang Fangchen, recovered more hair samples, while a further search in June 1997 turned up hundreds of large footprints.

Nests:

*Dajiuhu Nests*: After receiving several *Yeren* reports from villagers in Dajiuhu, Shennongjia Forestry District, the militia made a search of the local mountains and discovered strange nest-like structures made from grass.

*Daba Mountain Nests*: From May to December 1980, The Chinese Academy of Sciences conducted expeditions into the Shennongjia Forestry District and the Daba Mountain in Sichuan Province, in which nests made of bamboo, hair samples, tracks and faeces were recovered. During the expedition, two members who had made their way to the Xiangshui River in Shennongjia Forestry District, Li Guohua and Li Renrong, witnessed a long-haired humanoid-like primate sitting on a rock approximately 1000 ft away from them.

Body of Evidence:

*Macaque Monster:* In 1957, villagers reportedly killed a *Yeren* in Zhejiang province. A biology teacher, who at the time believed that the creature might be of some scientific importance, preserved the hands and feet of the animal and presented them - some years later in 1980 - for scientific analysis. Anthropologist Zhou Guoxing of the Beijing Natural History Museum concluded, after examining the preserved extremities of the alleged *Yeren*, that they likely belonged to a large macaque monkey.

*Monkey Child:* In 1977, the Chinese Academy of Sciences surveyed Fang County and the Shennogjia Forest Reserve and turned up a few footprints, head hair, and faeces. A revived investigation in 1979 and 1980 turned up the skeleton of a 'monkey child' in neighbouring Sichuan Province, though it most likely was a deformed human. Sadly, persons with certain birth defects are commonly referred to as Monkey babies in China and are often believed to be the product of a union between a Wildman and a human female. Could some of these Monkey babies, driven into the forests and cut off from society, have given birth to the *Yeren* legend? Purported "monkey boy" skulls, supposed evidence of *Yeren*-human hybrids, could have belonged to fully human children who suffered spinocerebellar ataxia.

Art and History:

*Pictograms:* Dating from as early as 1600 – 1046 B.C. – The Shang Dynasty Pictograms appear to show humanoids with long shaggy hair.

*Bronze Lamp:* A Han Dynasty Lamp, dating from 206 B.C. – 221 A.D. unearthed in Fang County, Shennongjia in 1976, is decoratively painted with what appears to be a long-haired ape-man.

Literature:

*The Shan-hai Ching (4th Century BC):* an encyclopaedic collection of Chinese geography, flora and fauna, that speaks of a people called the *Mao-min*, or "Hairy People."

*Shangui:* In the ancient poem *Shangui* ("The Mountain Spirit") by Qu Yuan (340 – 278 B.C.), this statesman and poet describe a hairy bipedal man-like creature that inhabits the mountains of Kui (present-day Zigui) in Hubei Province.

*Hong Mai Treatise:* Official and writer Hong Mai collected reports of *Yeren* encounters and wrote a treatise about the wildman in the 12th century.

_Yeren Classification System:_ Official and scholar Luo Yuan catalogued and classified different types of _Yeren_ in the 1260s.

_Pen-Tsao Kang-mu_: Li Shizhen, mathematician, doctor, herbalist, and acupuncturist, wrote a Materia Medica, known as the Pen-Tsao Kang-mu in the sixteenth century, in which he listed the properties of plants, animals, and minerals and noted that the _Yeren_ was a transitional species between ape and man.

_China Illustrata:_ In his book, China Illustrata (1667), Athanasius Kirchner, a Jesuit and natural historian, recorded the accounts of bipedal hairy humanoids from other Jesuits who had travelled in China. He noted that black hair-covered, human-like animals, with long arms that ran swiftly and laughed like men, were to be found in Fukien (Fujian Province) and the provinces of Junnam and Gannan (Yunnan & Jiangxi Province).

_Frontispiece depicting Adam Schall von Bell and Matteo Ricci, China Illustrata by Athanasius Kircher._

*Zibuyu:* In the eighteenth century, Yuan Mei wrote in his work, *Zibuyu*, that Fang County was haunted by tall 'men' that were completely covered in long hair.

**Beastly Theories:**

*Chinese Orangutan:* A surviving population of Orangutan. Orangs were present in China during the Pleistocene and are thought to have even persisted into comparatively recent times. A surviving population might at least account for the quadrupedal attributes of the smaller - red-haired *Yeren* that is sometimes reported but is somewhat lacking in physiological equivalence to the larger bipedal *Yeren*. Indeed it is hard to imagine that any species of *Orang* could have become so outsized, or, moreover, how it may have adapted to an upright existence.

*Asiatic Black Bear*: Although this species has a distinctive white V on its chest and would be difficult to mistake for a large unknown primate.

*Homosapiens Escapicus!* Throughout history, for one reason or another, many peoples have chosen to live isolated lives, far away from civilisation. Could the *Yeren* (Large and small) represent human communities that, through stealth and nocturnal secrecy, have managed to remain undiscovered by living in small family groups and resisting the urge to settle in any single location through continual migration? Choosing instead to live off the bounty of the forest and are forced to propagate through a limited gene pool, physically altering their appearance through the predominance of recessive gene traits. Some researchers have proposed that the Yeren are the descendants of convicts who were used to build the Great Wall of China (which began in the $7^{th}$ century BC). Escaping from their penal labour, they went into hiding in China's vast wilderness, eeking out a living, as best they could, in secrecy. Such a tale, if true, would certainly explain away the propensity that Yeren is believed to have for kidnapping and breeding with human females and would most certainly better explain children being brought forth from such unions, far better than the miracle of interspecies propagation would.

The Great Wall of China.

*History Repeating*: Could the *Yeren* be an extant form of ancient ape, like Paranthropus robustus, an extinct australopithecine? The fossils of which have been found in South Africa, although there is no evidence in the fossil record that Paranthropus migrated as far as Asia. Dryopithecus is another extinct genus of ape known from east Africa and Eurasia, from the late Miocene. They had large brains, gracile jaws and suspensory forelimbs that more closely resembled monkeys than modern apes, which might account for some monkey-like reports. Sivapithecus, too, was an extinct genus of Miocene ape, although this creature more closely resembled the orangutan and would therefore be less likely to be mistaken for the Yeren.

*Irati Forest, Navarre, Spain.*

## BASAJAUN

The long tradition of orderly historical record-keeping, inherent in the cultures of the former vassals of the Roman and Greek empires, has left a detailed and largely intact smorgasbord of wildman representations throughout Europe, that is found, not only upon the ancient edifices of our holy houses but also woven into the clannish standards of our noble families and inculcated into the illustrations of our ancient animaliums. This, in combination with the large literary and oral history of human encounters with the wodewose, or wildman; means that the average researcher, spoiled for choice, can choose instead to focus on individual cases or regional wildman varieties, finding sufficient fodder in the single as one would in the whole. Within this bygone pantheon, the Basajaun of the Basque nation (Euskadi) that straddles southwest France and northeast Spain, is a minor player, but nevertheless important, due to its honorific title: *"Lord of the forest"* or *"Forest man"*, in which its contiguous affiliation with its semi-mythical continental cousins is confirmed.

**What's in a name?** The name, *Basa-Juan* is a composite title, combining the Basque words - Baso (forest) and Jaun (man); which, when united, render the all too familiar habitational title present throughout crypto-hominology of: *"Man of the Woods", "Lord of the Woods", or "Forest Man"*, etc. It is, in concurrence with other wildman legends, likewise branded with other appellations throughout the region, such as *Anxo, Basandere* (woods-woman), *Bebrices, Iretges, Mono careto* (ugly ape), *Nonell de la neu* (Catalan – Nonell of the snows), *Peladits* (finger peeler), *Tartalo* (Cyclops), *Torto*, and *Yan Del Gel*; attesting to its ethno-known, or at the very least, long folkloric tenure in Basque culture.

**Monstrous Measurements:** In the Basque folk tradition, the Basajaun is a mostly peaceful giant that possesses great strength and agility. It is bipedal, standing 5 – 10 ft tall, with a large, man-like body that is covered in long, reddish, or dark brown hair that hangs down to its knees, sometimes even reaching its feet. The male (*Basajaun*) has a beard, the female (*Basandere*) does not.

**Terrifying Tracks:** Leaves 'mysterious tracks' that do not match any known local species or; circular tracks shaped like the hooves of a cow.

**Beastly Behaviours:** Legend has it that the Basajaun protects flocks and warns shepherds of incoming storms or roaming packs of wolves through loud yells, whistles, and hollers, in return for bread, which it collects while the shepherds are asleep. It is generally benevolent but also carries a large stick or a club and occasionally abducts shepherdesses. Screeches like a cat when angered or distressed. Reputed in Basque folklore to have taught blacksmithing and agriculture to men. Wears animal skins.

**Deadly Diet:** Grasses, roots, and game animals.

**Hairy Habitat:** Lives in caves, deep in the woods. Believed to inhabit the forests of Ataun and Gorea in the Basque region; the Irati jungle in Navarre; Maladeta Massif, Aragon; and especially the Pyrenees Mountains of France and Spain.

**Scary Sightings:**

<u>1774</u>: Engineer, Julien David Leroy wrote in his work on logging in the mountains of the Pyrenees that the pastors of the Iraty Forest region of Saint-Jean-Pied-de-Port and its neighbouring areas along the border with Spain, claimed that a shaggy-haired *Wildman*, superficially resembling a bear, was known to inhabit the region.

*Unknown Date:* Local folklore holds that long ago, 2 hairy brothers named Iretges lived in the woods near Bedeilhac-et-Aynat, Ariege Dept. France. The brothers wore animal skins and were notorious for abducting shepherdesses; until one day, the villagers, tired of their depredations, lured them into a trap and killed them.

<u>1979</u>: In May 1979, six woodsmen encountered a 6ft. tall ape-man in a sparsely-populated area in the Pyrenees Mountains of Huesca Province, Spain. After hearing a scream and squealing nearby, one of the men, Manuel Cazcarra, went off to investigate, only to discover a hairy man-beast, 6 ft. tall, standing before him. The creature, perhaps alarmed by Cazcarra's sudden appearance, climbed up a pine tree, where it stayed, clutching a branch with its arms and legs and seemingly berating the man with its loud screams. Cazcarra called the other men, who came running up, one of them, Ramiro López, who was just in time to see the ape-man climb down from the tree and hide behind a dense bush, before suddenly launching a hefty tree branch in their direction. The men decided not to pursue the creature further. The two men who had witnessed the creature were experienced woodsmen and were familiar with the bears that inhabited this region and swore categorically that the animal they had seen was not a bear. One week later, The Guardia Civil (Spanish Police), accompanied by one of the woodsmen, returned to the area and found 'mysterious footprints'. Shortly afterwards, a family

driving towards Prats de Molló witnessed an ape-like animal crossing a road close to the French border.

*1993:* In June 1993, a group of cave researchers (Speleologists) decided to spend the night at a ruined church near Collada de Vallagrasa in the Catalan Pyrenees Mountains of Spain when they heard strange noises that sounded something like those of an enraged cat. Approaching the source of the clamour near the church door, they were astonished to see a bulky, man-like creature, 5ft. tall and covered in shaggy hair that appeared to be frightened and agitated. Upon seeing the group, it fled into the woods. Later, the same wildman was seen again in the woods between Fargo De Bebie and Ripoll, Gerona.

*1994:* In the spring of 1994, a mountain climber named Juan Ramo Ferrer saw an apelike creature while hiking from Peña Montañesa to the village of Bielsa close by. The strange creature, which was shorter than a man and covered with reddish hair, with very long ape-like arms, jumped from tree to tree and squealed at the terrified hiker, who fled to a local campsite near Peña Montañesa. According to Ferrer, his hirsute harasser *"exuded a musky odour."*

*Unknown Date:* Two *Wildmen* pounced upon two palaeontologists and struggled with them briefly before running away.

**Beastly Evidence:**

Art and Archaeology:

*Isturitz Cave Art:* The Isturitz and Oxocelhaya caves in the Arberoue Valley in the foothills of Pyrenees, in Lower Navarre, southwestern France, are sites of Palaeolithic significance and contain the physical, material, and artistic remnants of both Neanderthal and Homo sapiens societies that have been deposited within their insides, between 60,000 and 600 BC. In the cave of Isturitz, one can even see a rupestrian engraving of what appears to be hairy, of a wildman, in profile.

*Isturitz carved bone:* Another possible representation of the wildman was found in the same cave and features two hairy hominoids that are not Homo sapiens. One of the hominoids has an arrow in its leg and links around its neck and leg, possibly indicating that these creatures were killed by hunters.

*Holy History:* Wildmen grew in popularity during the medieval period, where they are depicted as wild, hair-covered men, upon the architectural adornments of cathedrals, tapestries, and in the heraldic coats of arms of prominent European families.

A depiction of a Wildman alongside a person commonly assumed to be its *"Shower"* or *"Handler",* adorns a portal in an 11th-century church in Semur-en-Auxois. Does this depiction of the commercial exploitation of a wildman indicate that the wildman, albeit rare in those times, was ethno-known among the myriad cultures of Europe?

Literature:

*Basa-Jauna, The Wild Man:* A folk tale from the Basque region tells the story of a Basque farmer's wife with 3 sons and a daughter. Her sons leave home to seek their fortune and become enslaved by a *Basajaun* and *Basandere* (husband and wife) in exchange for not being eaten, after seeking shelter at their castle, one night. Years later, their sister, finding out that she had once had three brothers who disappeared, goes in search of them and, seeking shelter at the same castle, also becomes enslaved by the *Basajaunak*, who vampirically drains her life force by sucking on her finger. After several twists and turns, including her brothers becoming oxen for a while, she threatens to roast the *Basandere* who sends her away to find some hazel sticks, and in a characteristically predictable old-world tale of family misfortune turned unlikely happy ending, she and her brothers, end up living happily alongside the *Basajaun* in their castle... This somewhat mediocre tale is too long to include in full here and ends rather abruptly, yet nevertheless, it testifies to the folkloric antiquity of the *Basajaun* and, remarkably, is the only case where it is represented with vampiric qualities.

**Beastly Theories:**

*Relict Neanderthal:* It is now known that the Iberian Neanderthals persisted around the area of the Ebro River in the Pyrenees (which encompasses much of the modern Basque region) until relatively recent times. Do the hairy portrayals that both Neanderthals and Bajaunak share prove human and Neanderthal coexistence in the Basque region? Could modern-day reports be those of a surviving Neanderthal? Sadly, I think not. The average Neanderthal man stood at an unimpressive 5 ft 5 inches tall, which sits right at the lowest height range for the Basajaun. Furthermore, Neanderthal is now known to have been skilled in stone tool use, as well as weaving, fire, art, seafaring, music, and so on; which doesn't make it a particularly good fit for the modern wildman type, that eyewitnesses usually describe seeing; but does constitute a closer fit with the fabled megalithic builder and protector of flocks, that the folkloric Basajaun was reputed to be.

*Neolithic Migrants:* Some authors have suggested that the *Basajaun* myth is a folk memory of early human contact with migrating Neolithic settlers? These peoples, clad in furs and skins, and accompanied by flocks of domesticated animals, were megalith builders who would have brought agriculture, domesticated animals, and new tools to the region. Indeed, there is a Basque myth that speaks of Saint Martinico (Martin Txiki), who, through trickery and ingenuity, stole these technologies from the Basajaunak and imparted them to 'mankind'.

*Unknown Ape Species:* Could an extant form of ancient ape, like Paranthropus robustus an extinct australopithecine, from South Africa or Dryopithecus, an extinct Miocene ape from east Africa and Eurasia, be responsible for historical encounters with creatures like the *Basajaun* and other European Wildmen? Besides their hairy appearance and gracile nature, the *Basajaun* and other European Wildmen seem to be more man than 'monkey', as is evident from their multitudinous depictions, which adorn European cathedrals and noble heraldry throughout the medieval period.

*The god Pan (pictured here with Daphnis) an ancient embodiment of the Wildman?*

*Faunic Folklore:* The European Wildman's behaviour and appearance are closely related to and possibly inspired by other mythical entities of Europe, such as the Satyr, Faun, Ogre, and Leshy; which are similarly described as shy, forest-dwelling, hair covered beings; who are not beyond carrying off the occasional maiden, from time to time! One would also be remiss to overlook the similarity it bears to the pagan hero, Heracles. This enigmatic fellow is regularly depicted as a powerful, hair-covered, club-wielding man whose recycled origins and myriad names transverse most of pagan history. Therefore, it could be contended that the image of Heracles (or Hercules) is ingrained upon the cultural memory of the peoples of Europe and the near east and that the Wildman is but a watered-down amalgamation of this deified character and that of Pan (Silvanus) the ancient Greek god of the wilds, and protector of shepherds flocks, who is thus represented as a hairy bearded man with the legs of a goat and carrying a shepherd's staff.

Note: Some ancient representations of Balkan shepherds depict bearded men carrying staffs and wearing fleece trousers made from goat's hair.

Tirich Mir is the highest mountain of the Hindu Kush range located in
the Chitral District of Pakistan

## BARMANU

High in the inaccessible Chitral and Karakoram Ranges,
between the Pamirs and the Himalaya and especially in the
forested regions the Shishi Kuh Valley, near Chitral, North-West
Frontier Province, Pakistan, the Kalash people, and their Nuristani
neighbours, tell tales of a legendary creature that is reputed to be
half-man and half-ape. The traditional stories surrounding this
creature, which seem to be a cross between true life tales of yeti-like
encounters and a local version of the 'Beauty and the Beast' fable, are
ingrained into the belief systems of many cultures in the Northern
Areas of Pakistan, and, not unlike many such cryptids around the
world, occupy both the material and the immaterial realm of these
isolated communities. Of the few researchers that have braved this
wild frontier in search of its unsung cryptid, Spanish scientist Jordi
Magraner (an expert on European and Central Asian Neanderthals)
is probably the most significant. In 1987, He became convinced, after
interviewing several locals over a 19 month period, that an

undiscovered wild-man inhabited this area. So much so, in fact, that he spent the next fifteen years searching for it. And, although his untimely murder in 2002 is marred with rumours of an illicit lifestyle, the research he conducted in this area is probably still the best resource tool we have at present regarding this elusive *wildman*.

**What's in a name?** *Bar-Manu* is likely derived from the Sanskrit, *Ban-Manus*, which means *"Man of the Forest"*. The Kalash and Nuristani refer to it as *Barmanu* in their local dialect and it is also known as *Barmanu* in the Khowar, Shina, Hindko, and Kashmiri languages, in which it also means: *"Man of the Forest"*; *Barmanou* or *Baddmanus* in Khowar, Urdu, Shina, Pashto, and Kashmiri. The Chitral people use *Barmanu* to denote a large object, a big man or chubby child, as well as the creature itself but also use another word, *Jangali mosh* (man of the forest), to identify the wildman, an appellation that is likely related to the *Jangli Adami* (forest man) in the Urdu language.

**Monstrous Measurements:** Bipedal. Standing from 5 – 7 ft. tall. Muscular build (although it can also appear pudgy or plump). Covered with black, brown, red, grey, and beige hair, which is longer on the head and covers the entire body, except for the face, which is nearly hairless and sports a beard from the lower jaw down its neck. The head hair is differentiated from that of the body and is of varying length. The skin is dark and is visible through the hair. The head is large and longer in the back to front direction, with little to no forehead and a massive neck that is hunched into the shoulders. The lower jaw is massive, without a noticeable chin. The torso is relatively long, broad, and thick; the thorax is well developed. Ears are bigger than a man's. Eyebrows are large with a protruding ridge that almost forms a visor-like protuberance over the eyes. The eyes are wide-set and the cheekbones prominent. The nose is flattened and upturned with broad nostrils. The mouth is wide with no discernible lips and contains large, human-like teeth; no canines are present. Arms are long with large human-like hands and long fingers with a weak opposable thumb appears to be on the same plane as the other fingers. Legs are generally short compared to its body and to those of humans. Feet are turned inward, are short and very broad, especially in the front Toes are all about the same size, crooked and fanning out. The big toe is spread sideways; the small toe is curved inwards. Fingernails, both on their hands and feet, are curved downwards. The penis is large when erect but small when at rest. Body odour is foul, like a dead animal. Sexual dimorphism concerning stature is not apparent, although obvious genitalia has been observed on both male and female specimens. The females have long hairless breasts descending to their belly.

**Terrifying Tracks:** Human-like, but wide and turned inward. Feet are short and very broad, especially in the front Toes are all about the same size, crooked and fanning out. The big toe is spread sideways; the small toe is curved inwards. Feet are human-like but wide and turned inward. Fingernails. Both on hands and feet are curved downwards

**Beastly Behaviours:** Agile and strong. Can *"Run as fast as a dog"* and *"climb as fast as a goat"*. Possesses no articulate language but makes loud cries that are short, guttural, or high pitched, and that sound like *"aha"*. Has a foul body odour, which smells like carrion. Reputedly loves beautiful women and tries to abduct them for sex. Occasionally wears animal skins on its back and head. Most active in spring and autumn, rarely seen in winter, when it is believed to hibernate, emerging seldomly to feed. Primarily nocturnal but also seen during the day. Leads a nomadic existence, only staying in one location for a few days before moving on. Generally, not aggressive, choosing instead to leave an area if spotted by a human male, although its behaviour is different towards human females, whom it will approach and allegedly, even attempt to abduct.

**Deadly Diet:** Omnivorous, but mainly vegetarian. Observed eating ant larvae & nymphs, Juniper berries, roots, and carrion; likes the corpses of dead goats and sheep. Possibly predates on small animals, like pica and lizards. Likes honey.

**Hairy Habitat:** Nomadic in nature but temporarily inhabits caves, dense thickets, trees knells, and empty human buildings. Found between altitudes of 6,500 – 9,800ft, throughout the Hindukush, Chitral, and Karakoram ranges (situated between the Pamirs and the Himalayas) and especially in the coniferous forest regions of the Shishi Kuh Valley, near Chitral, North-West Frontier Province, Pakistan.

**Scary Sightings:** Much of what we currently know about the *Bar-Manu* is centred upon the work of zoologist Jordi Magraner and his colleagues, who mounted several field expeditions in the north of Pakistan between 1988 and 2002. Magraner documented over 50 eyewitness reports and several key pieces of evidence, as well as experiencing unidentifiable guttural sounds, himself, on two separate occasions, which he believed could have been made by the elusive Wildman. Most significantly, the witnesses interviewed by Magraner had never been contacted before by other researchers, making their virgin accounts all the more intriguing.

<u>1977:</u> In September 1977, Goatherd, Purdum Khan was grazing his herd in a prairie on the mountain in the Hindu Kush Range in Pakistan's North-West Frontier Province, at an altitude of 7,600 ft, when he became aware of a foul stench, like that of a dead. The shepherd, who had been sitting on a rock watching his sheep, noticed, approximately 3 to 9 – 13 ft below him, a 'young' hairy man, approximately 5ft 8 inches tall, that was sitting crossed-legged and eating ant larvae. The shepherd, who observed the creature in silence for 2 hours, noticed that the well-built creature, whose body was covered in dark reddish hair, was eating the ant larvae nymphs by picking them up between his thumb and forefinger and that its penis was large and erect. When a large dog approached, the hairy man walked upright, on two legs, downhill towards the forest. Pardum noticed that it had dark skin *"like that of a Gujar" (a local brown-skinned person),* which was visible through the hair. It did not wear any clothing. A few days after his encounter, in the early morning, the shepherd, who was coming down the mountain with a young woman,

and passing the same location, saw the hairy man again. The beast grabbed the woman but released her and fled when Purdum brandished his axe.

_1985, 1986 & 1987:_ Lal Khan, a Gujar shepherd, saw the same hairy man on three separate occasions. On the first two occasions, he saw the creature from a distance, which, upon seeing the shepherd, slowly left the area, leaning on a stick. However, on the third occasion, he had a particularly close encounter while herding his goats across a slope at 11,300ft. The hairy man, who must have been sleeping below the low hanging boughs of a large fir tree, was awoken by the coughing of Lal's goats, quickly emerged from the tree and threw a stone at Lal, before calmly walking away across the prairie, using his large stick for support. Now and then, the wild man stopped to gather plants and eat them, idly making his way uphill before eventually disappearing behind a ridge. The sighting lasted more than 10 minutes and caused the shepherd to become so frightened that he gathered his goats and went back down the hill. Lal Khan described the creature as being covered in dark, except for its chest, which was white, and its cheeks, palms, knees, and ears, which were hairless. It had a beard below its chin, differentiated, short head hair, broad shoulders, and massive man-like teeth.

_1987:_ One afternoon in April 1987, A Gujar shepherd, Nur Hamid, and his sister were gathering morels in a conifer forest in the mountains at about 9,480 ft. when they observed a hairy man crouching in a bush, about 20 meters downhill from them. Upon noticing the siblings, it began moving towards them. Nur and his sister, alarmed, began shouting and throwing rocks at the creature, prompting another man to come and help them drive the beast away. Finally, one of the rocks found its mark and hit it on the head, at which the hairy man _"ran as fast as a dog"_ and disappeared into the forest, further downhill. The witness described the beast as stocky and well-muscled, approximately 5.7 ft – 5.9 ft tall, with dark skin was entirely covered with reddish hair, with long head hair reaching to its shoulders. Its face was hairless, with a flattened, upturned nose and a wide mouth with human-like teeth but no fangs.

_1987:_ One evening at around 9:00 pm, in July 1987, a Pathan shepherd, Mohamed Nabi, was returning to his village with his goats. He suddenly found himself face-to-face with an adolescent hairy man who repeatedly tried to touch Mohamed with his long outstretched fingernails. The shepherd was not afraid of being scratched and hit the young hairy man with his stick every time it attempted to touch him. The two rivals, separated by a large bush around which they circled, attempted to outsmart the other for the next two hours, throughout which the young hairy man would try to grab Mohamed and Mohamed would hit it with his stick. The creature, in its frustration, uttering guttural noises that sounded like: _"ahan!"_ throughout the encounter, eventually fled uphill to the nearby forest. The shepherd added that during his encounter, the young hairy man stood erect on its hind legs. He described the creature as being: 3.5 – 3.9 ft. tall and entirely covered with greyish-brown hair with dark skin. It smelled like a rotting corpse.

_1990:_ On May 24th, 1990, at 10:30 am, three children, 2 boys and a girl, were playing by a canal close to their village. The girl, _Chitralis Ata Ul Llah,_ suddenly noticed a hairy woman; with a big scary face come down the mountain and hide behind a rock. The woman who was 5.4 – 5.6 ft tall, with dark skin and long hair, wearing a _"great coat and high boots of dark hair"_ and who had _" two enormous breasts that stuck out of the coat."_ walked over to the two boys, who had not noticed her approach and grabbed the smallest, 4-year-old, Gul Naz, before turning and running back up the mountain with him. The larger of the two boys, Abdul Hafiz (4 years old) and the (6-year-old) girl, Chitralis Ata Ul Llah, then fled in terror to the village. The village mounted a search party for the boy and a thousand people scoured the mountain in vain. After failing to find him, the villagers concluded that a _Pari_ (spirit) must have abducted him. Three days later, some blue clothing was spotted on the mountain and the missing child was found dead on a rock, his death occurring barely half an hour before. The body did not show any other wounds or signs of ill-treatment other than those consistent with a fall and remarkably, the villagers did not believe that the hairy woman had killed the child, but rather that the fatal wounds he sustained were caused by a fall. Wildman researcher Jordi Magraner, who documented the case, theorised that perhaps the hairy woman had 'adopted' the boy as a replacement for her own lost child; perhaps later abandoning him. Trying to find his way home through the rocks, the boy had fallen and died, sadly, just a short time before being discovered by the villagers. The villagers later found footprints at the location where the child had been abducted that were 9-10 inches long by 5-6 inches wide.

## Beastly Evidence:

### Tracks:

*Sar Tor Tracks:* One day, in September 1987, wildman eyewitness Sar Tor also found footprints in soft ground while walking in the conifer forest, at an elevation of 6500 to 8000 feet. He described the track as being human-like, but with a much wider forward section with a width of around 6 inches and length and an overall length of approximately 10 inches. The prints revealed at their boundary evidence of hair on top of the foot. The tracks were heading in the direction of the mountain top and here and there, traces of broad hands with short narrow fingers were also visible.

*Mohammed Nabi Tracks:* Mohammed Nabi, the shepherd who had fought a young hairy man for 2 hours in July of 1987, also saw the tracks of a larger hairy man on two occasions. The first set, which looked quite fresh, were discovered at 8,200 to 8,500 ft. elevation on April 3rd, 1988, and appeared to be crossing a ridge through the valley, heading up to the top of the mountain. The second set, which he discovered on April 8th, 1988, at around 11,500 ft elevation, were descending from the summit and crossing the valley. In both cases, the tracks were identical in shape and size, measuring approximately

11.8 inches and appearing man-like, albeit much wider at the front. The shape of the toes, too, was visible, with the big toe being particularly well represented. There was no sign of claws.

*Mohamad Khan Tracks:* On a sunny September afternoon in 1989, Mohamad Khan, a Chitrali farmer/breeder, was leading his goats to a pasture when he came across large man-like tracks in a conifer forest, at an elevation of about 11,500ft. The tracks, which were 10 inches long and 6.3 inches wide, had spread out or splayed toes, which appeared crooked. The heel was just like that of human tracks, but the stride was very long. The tracks which impressed deep into the moist ground appeared to come from the snowy mountain top and had been witnessed Mohamad in this same location, at exactly the same time of year, in 1987 and 1988, leading the shepherd to believe that they might have been made by the same individual.

*Magraner Tracks*: Tracks were also found during a 1994 expedition by French explorer Jordi Magraner.

Audio encounters:

*Maureen's Audio Encounter:* Maureen Lines, an Englishwoman who had lived among the Kalash people for more than thirty years, learning their language, and becoming a leading authority on their culture and folklore, claimed that locals often sighted the 'Barmanu' in the mountains of that region and claimed to have even heard its cry from across the river while taking a walk with her driver and a local friend.

She said: *"It was no ordinary cry. It was extremely loud... It came from across the river, it seemed and it was like a woman's scream, but it was definitely animal-like like somebody was in great agony...The hyenas, jackals, mountain lions, even the elusive snow leopard of the Kalash region all have distinctive calls. This was beastly & clearly different. And I still shudder every time I think about the experience."*

According to Maureen, the sound, which lasted for a few seconds, echoed and reverberated in the valleys for a while afterwards and as it was nearly night, she and her companions became frightened and left the area.

*Magraner Audio Encounters:* In 1988 and again in 1994, Jordi Magraner and his team heard what they believed to be the cry, or call, of the *Barmanu,* while on an expedition in the mountainous forest of Chitral and described the following:

*"The first time we heard it was at 600 or 700 metres... The voice is strong; the expression contains some cries and guttural sounds without identifiable articulate speech... These sounds were heard at nightfall. They were powerful and echoed through the mountains like plaintive human calls. The voices were high-pitched, recalling of a teenager or a woman. The emissions of sound lasted less than one minute. We had no time to record these cries. No animal in Chitral is able to produce such sounds. Even the jackal living in this country cannot produce such a powerful whine... The next day, shepherds who heard the cries maintained it was a 'Forest Man' (a Wild Man)".*

The second time Magraner claimed to have heard the cries was during a search with Anne Mallasse and another associate, at an elevation of 6560 ft. in the Shishi Kuh valley, Chitral. During the late evening, the team heard unusual guttural sounds which only a *'primitive'* voice-box could have produced

## Beastly Theories:

*Home Erectus:* Some scant fossil remains of Homo erectus were found in Selungur Cave, Kyrgystan, as well as some artefacts believed to belong to archaic humans in Darra-I-Kur Cave, in Afghanistan. However, if the *Bar-Manu* is a form of ancient man, it would seem likely that its presence in the region is not related to these much-lauded archaic antecedents!

*Homo Pongoides:* All the witnesses to whom Magraner showed reference imagery for the wildman (post-interview) almost categorically and immediately selected the morphological features of

Bernard Heuvelmans reconstruction of the apelike Homo Pongoides as their match for the *Barmanu*, from Magraner's ID kit drawings of apes, fossil men, aboriginals, monkeys, and the Minnesota Iceman. Does this then indicate that the Minnesota Iceman was indeed a genuine specimen, or if hoax, as it has long been suspected to be, did the rural residents of the isolated mountainous regions of North-West Pakistan and their Afghani neighbours simply strike it lucky? Or, could the dissemination of the western sensationalist news of yesteryear have penetrated even here, painting a subconscious portrait in the minds of these indigenous observers of what they might have encountered upon the pristine peaks of their pastoral paradise?

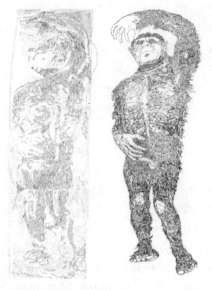

Almost all of Magraner's Barmanu eyewitnesses identified the Minnesota Iceman as a match for the animal they encountered. Could the sensational image of this Barnumesque hoax have reached even here, influencing the minds of these isolated shepherds?

*Kissing Cousins:* Tales of hairy Wildmen abound in this region and are bordered by other similar Wildmen legends of the *Almasty* of central Asia and the *Yeti* of the Himalayas and are variously described as man-like or ape-like. The author agrees that there are several different species, or types of Wildmen, that are morphologically distinct; and that the Neanderthaloid *Barmanu* has other relatives around the globe, with whom it is practically identical, such as the *Almas, Almasty, Yeren, Yowie,* and *Wodewose,* etc. However, as is common in these regions, The *Barmanu* might also be a general name for several different types of hominid and similar to that of the *Yeti* or *Bigfoot,* if the investigator is forensic in his examination of witness reports, he will frequently find several types; such as the giant *Man-Ape, Wildman,* and *Relict Ape,* umbrella'd and sheltering, beneath a common designee/appellation.

*Genie in a bottle:* The Kalash tribe and other shepherds who live in the high valleys and spend much of their time in the higher elevations particularly believed in the existence of *Barmanu* and considered them to be men, but not '*human*'. Whereas their neighbours who inhabit the valley bottom, rarely encountering these creatures, consider them to be (Pari) spirits, genies, ghosts, etc. These superstitious beliefs of these latter peoples, who coincidentally are also more likely to have contact with the outside world, are more likely to be brushed aside as fantasy or folklore due to their superstitious cultural container, and yet it would seem that between these two geographically adjacent peoples there is a lesson for the western mind, to exercise caution when dismissing folklore as, well, just folklore... I am reminded of the abduction of the young boy, Gul Naz, documented by Magraner, in which we are reminded of the villagers self-acquittal of responsibility for the boy, simply claiming that as "*a Pari*" (spirit) had abducted him, that there was nothing further that they could do.

Could a tribe of Wildmen live hidden within the impenetrable forests of the Amazon?

## MARI-COXI

Lieutenant Colonel Perceval "Percy" Harrison Fawcett DSO (18 August 1867 – during or after 1925) was an English geographer, artillery officer, cartographer, archaeologist, and explorer. He is regarded as a trailblazing adventurer, and although best known for his disappearance in the Amazon whilst searching for the "Lost City of Z", he is also considered as something of a *'storyteller'* on account of the many improbable animals that he claimed to have come across during his expeditions in South America. One of these fantastical beasts is the *Mari-Coxi*, with whom Fawcett and his party had an intense encounter while exploring the Serro dos Parecis plateau, in Mato Grosso State, of west-central Brazil.

**What's in a name?** *Maricoxi* comes from an Arikapu word; it is also known as *Morocco*

**Monstrous Measurements:** As hairy as a dog. Looks like a primitive man, with a sloping forehead and pronounced eye ridges that overhang its eyes, which are pig-like, in appearance. Has exceptionally long arms.

**Terrifying Tracks:** Unknown?

**Beastly Behaviours:** Makes grunting noises that sound like: *'Eugh! Eugh! Eugh!'* Lives in villages comprised of primitive shelters. Can make its weapons, like bows and arrows and spears, which it will aim at trespassers upon its territory, usually in bluff, unless the intruder refuses to leave. Dances from leg to leg in a gesture of intimidation or threat. Uses a horn when hunting.

**Deadly Diet:** Unknown?

**Hairy Habitat:** Lives to the northeast of the Maxubi tribe (to whom it is well known) in Serro dos Parecis, Mato Grosso State, Brazil.

**Scary Sightings:**

<u>1914:</u> During an expedition in Mato Grosso State, Brazil, Lieutenant-Colonel Percy H. Fawcett encountered two hairy men who threatened him with bows and arrows and then ran away. Later, he came across a village in a clearing where he encountered an entire village filled with the same mysterious *ape-men*, who, despite his overtures of friendship, drove Fawcett and his party away by force. In the book *Expedition Fawcett* (1953), compiled from his field notes, by his son Brian, we read of his encounter with these mysterious ape-men:

*"As we stood looking from right to left, trying to decide which direction was the more promising, two savages appeared about a hundred yards to the south, moving at a trot and talking rapidly. On catching sight of us, they stopped dead and hurriedly fixed arrows to their bows while I shouted to them in the Maxubi tongue. We could not see them clearly for the shadows dappling their bodies, but it seemed to me they were large, hairy men, with exceptionally long arms, and with foreheads sloping back from pronounced*

eye ridges, men of a very primitive kind, in fact, and stark naked. Suddenly they turned and made off into the undergrowth, and we, knowing it was useless to follow, started up the north leg of the trail."

"In the morning, we went on, and within a quarter of a mile came to a sort of palm-leaf sentry-box, then another. Then all of a sudden, we reached open forest. The undergrowth fell away, disclosing between the tree boles a village of primitive shelters, where squatted some of the most villainous savages I have ever seen. Some were engaged in making arrows, others just idled--great apelike brutes who looked as if they had scarcely evolved beyond the level of beasts."

"I whistled, and an enormous creature, hairy as a dog, leapt to his feet in the nearest shelter, fitted an arrow to his bow in a flash, and came up dancing from one leg to the other till he was only four yards away. Emitting grunts that sounded like 'Eugh! Eugh! Eugh!' he remained there dancing, and suddenly the whole forest around us was alive with these hideous ape-men, all grunting 'Eugh! Eugh! Eugh!' and dancing from leg to leg in the same way as they strung arrows to their bows. It looked like a very delicate situation for us, and I wondered if it was the end. I made friendly overtures in Maxubi, but they paid no attention. It was as though human speech were beyond their powers of comprehension."

"The creature in front of me ceased his dance, stood for a moment perfectly still, and then drew his bowstring back till it was level with his ear, at the same time raising the barbed point of the six-foot arrow to the height of my chest. I looked straight into the pig-like eyes half-hidden under the overhanging brows and knew that he was not going to lose that arrow yet. As deliberately as he had raised it, he now lowered the bow and commenced once more the slow dance, and the 'Eugh! Eugh! Eugh!'"

"A second time, he raised the arrow at me and drew the bow back, and again I knew he would not shoot. It was just as the Maxubis told me it would be. Again he lowered the bow and continued his dance. Then for the third time, he halted and began to bring up the arrow's point. I knew he meant business this time and drew out a Mauser pistol I had on my hip. It was a big, clumsy thing, of a calibre unsuitable to forest use, but I had brought it because by clipping the wooden holster to the pistol-butt, it became a carbine and was lighter to carry than a true rifle. It used .38 black powder shells, which made a din out of all proportion to their size. I never raised it; I just pulled the trigger and banged it off into the ground at the ape-man's feet."

"The effect was instantaneous. A look of complete amazement came into the hideous face, and the little eyes opened wide. He dropped his bow and arrow and sprang away as quickly as a cat to vanish behind a tree. Then the arrows began to fly. We shot off a few rounds into the branches, hoping the noise would scare the savages into a more receptive frame of mind, but they seemed in no way disposed to accept us, and before anyone was hurt, we gave it up as hopeless and retreated down the trail till the camp was out of sight. We were not followed, but the clamour in the village continued for a long time as we struck off northwards, and we fancied we still heard the 'Eugh! Eugh! Eugh!' of the enraged braves."

Colonel Percy Harrison Fawcett.
Colonel Percy Harrison Fawcett in
1911

**Beastly Evidence:**

*Antagonistic Evidence:* Many researchers have cast doubt upon the marvellous discoveries of Percy Fawcett, preferring to imagine his claims as to the classic *'one that got away'* style of storytelling that appears to have been endemic among explorers during this period. Indeed, his stories, which include, among his encounters with the Maricoxi, stories of giant Apazauca spiders, a Bolivian dog-like cat called the Mitla, giant anaconda's (exceeding 62 ft. in length), bats so big they look like pterodactyls and an Amazonian Apatosaurus, among others, are what one would term, *'almost too good to be true'* and most likely fabricated due to the statistical improbability of one man encountering so many unique specimens, as much as any other extenuating aspects of the Colonel's faithful (or false) conveyance of the features born by these fantastical faunae.

However, in more recent times, one of the bizarre animals that Fawcett encountered in 1913, at a post on the Marmoré River, near Santa Ana, in East Bolivia; and described thusly: *"...Here we saw for the first and only time a breed of dog known as the Double-Nosed Andean Tiger Hound. The two noses are as cleanly divided as though cut with a knife. About the size of a pointer, it is highly valued for its acute sense of smell and ingenuity in hunting jaguars. It is found only on these plains..."* it was not only rediscovered but photographed, in 2005, by modern-day explorer Colonel John Blashford-Snell. While staying in a remote village in the same area where Fawcett originally reported his encounter, the Colonel was astonished, not only to see a dog exactly matching Fawcett's description but to also be informed by locals that this breed bore the very same name (the double-nosed Andean tiger hound) that Fawcett had recorded over a century before.

Whether or not this incidental validation of Fawcett's double-conked canine adds veracity to his other vociferous claims is for the reader to decide. What is certain is that apart from the booming rubber industry, this region was still largely underexploited and unexplored in Fawcett's time. Could the fallacious felicitations with which he presents his unique encounters, in fact, be a snapshot of the abundant animal life that once existed in the Amazon in the pre-industrial era?

Pachon Navarro: The Double Nosed Andean Tiger Hound:

## Beastly Theories:

*Undiscovered Amazons*: Could Fawcett have simply stumbled across an undiscovered tribe in the amazon and been overwhelmed by their strange appearance? Could the costumes worn by some tribes in mythical emulation of totem animals like the monkey, sloth, and jaguar, for purposes of war, stealth, or in honour of forest deities, have convinced him in a moment of panic and mortal fear that he was in fact, encountering some form or primitive human or semi-evolved ape?

*Favoured Races:* The racist ideology that some races were somehow 'genetically favoured' while others were disfavoured or even considered of a completely separate lineage to modern man pervaded nineteenth and early twentieth-century European thought about the world outside; and was popular among those keen to discover and classify those 'lower' than themselves, among the less industrialised/technologically advanced peoples of the world. This unfortunate philosophy, broadly capitalised upon in Robert Knox's 'The Races of Men' (1850), later indirectly implied in Sir Charles Darwin's *The Origin of Species by means of Natural Selection or the Preservation of Favoured Races in the Struggle for Life* (1859) and championed by his half-cousin Sir Francis Galton, who created the concept of Eugenics (well-born) in 1883, was sadly a product of its time and manifested itself in many pseudo-scientific methodologies; which themselves went on to influence aberrant characters to erroneously describe these unfamiliar peoples around the world as evolutionary sluggards or 'lesser apes'. Could Fawcett, upon discovering these strange Amazonians, clothed in skins and with faces distorted by tribal totems and ornamental modification, have presumed them to be something between man and ape? Or, did he encounter a true extant Neanderthal type, technologically adept at basic tool and weapons manufacturing, yet frozen in his march towards progress by the limited resources for industrial advancement in the dense forests of the Amazon?

*Fantasy Fatigue*: Sleep Deprivation and prolonged fatigue, as well as physically demanding environments, can on occasion cause hallucinations and perceptual distortions. Fawcett himself described the Amazon as *"a poisoned hell that could never be explored on foot..."* and said that it was populated by *"... 60-foot anacondas capable of picking a man out of a canoe, savage ape-men, an infested plain of deadly snakes, bats so big they looked like pterodactyls, ferocious black panthers, and swarms of biting bees..."* Could the terrible conditions and the mortal dangers that he and his team faced have exaggerated their perceptions, and if yes, are there any examples of such illusory affectations afflicting other persons in high-stress situations? COSR (Combat Stress Reaction), in military conflicts, for example, has been observed to cause panic, anxiety, depression, and hallucinations.

Additionally, some local hallucinogenic flora, like the Banisteriopsis caapi (ayahuasca) vine, the Jimsonweed, and the common Coca Leaf, could all have resulted in hallucinations akin to the strange experiences described by Fawcett.

*Amazon Ape-men*: The title *"Maricoxi"* has also been used as a generic term to refer to other hairy *"Wildmen"* of the Amazon, such as the *Mono Grande* and *Mapinguari*. Could the *Mari-Coxi* simply be a version of these other enigmatic Amazonian ape-men? While there certainly is some descriptive crossover between these types, they seem to retain fundamental physiological differences to one another that is sufficient enough to make one wonder if this region, similar to other regions in the world (like the caucuses mountains or Himalayas, might house several species, that correspond with the three wildman types – giant *Man-Ape*, *Neanderthaloid*, and *Relict Ape*, that this chapter is theoretically constructed upon?

## YOWIE

There are a great many *Yowie* stories preserved by various Aboriginal groups throughout Australia and even since the early days of European colonisation, encounters with these strange hairy Wildmen have been regularly reported. It is difficult for the European mind to conceive of the sheer unpopulated vastness of Australia's paradisiac wilderness. An empty land that is filled with unique species that have adapted to its myriad climates and strange topography. The bulk of its urban population resides in tightly packed cities in the eastern states of Queensland, Victoria, and New South Wales, with the population of the remaining states of Western Australia, the Northern Territory, and South Australia making up a paltry 18% of its total population. This sparsely settled island is replete with tales of mysterious animals and believed to be extinct fauna and it is here among them that we find the *Yowie*, a type of hairy 'Wildman' that may symbolise an antipodean variety of those other *Wildmen* types once regularly encountered in Europe and Asia.

**What's in a name?** -The name *Yowie* is a derivative of the Australian word *Yuwaalaraay* or Yuwi and has been used in one of its many deviations throughout the New South Wales coast since the 1930s and roughly translates means: *"dream spirit"* or *"ghost."* As one might presume in a 'continent' as spread out and tribally diverse as Australia, the Yowie also has myriad names throughout the land, such as *Australian Bush Ape, Bugaloo, Dulgal, Gooligah, Hairy Man, Jingara, Koyorowen, Makoren Koro, Mooluwonk, Moomega, Noocoonah, Quinkin, Wowee-wowee, Yahoo, Yaroma, Youree, Yowrie, Yowroo & Yuwi.*

*(Note: Aboriginal cultures, correspondingly with many other ancient peoples around the world, use the term Yowie and its many derivatives to describe a whole host of large hairy creatures that may include several different species or morphological types. However, in this section, we will focus primarily on those reports that appear to describe the wildman type that is common to most reports.)*

**Monstrous Measurements:** Bipedal. Body types range from long, slim and muscular, to that of a stockier build; however, shoulders are always wide, ranging from 3 – 4 feet in width. Height ranges from 5 – 9 ft tall, although most reports average 5-7 ft covered in brown, tan, white, grey, or black hair. It has black or dark grey leathery, gorilla-like skin, a dome-shaped head, a flat face with a low forehead and receding chin, and no (visible) neck. Several reports indicate that it has two large canine teeth. Its eyes are yellow or deep red, deeply set in the face, and appear to reflect light at night. (Curiously, several reports also indicate that the eyes can self-illuminate, often exhibiting an eerie yellow, green or red glow.) Breasts are not reported, either indicating that they are not present in this species or that *Yowie* encounters consist entirely of male specimens. Their arms reach almost to their knees and are covered in longer hair than that of the body. Hands and feet are often reported to exhibit sharp nails or claws. Their legs are long but with calves that are short in proportion to the thighs.

*(Note: There are other hairy man-like creatures reported at heights above 10ft. tall, but the author, theoretically, at least, considers these to be a different 'type' more closely related to the giant Man-Ape - Bigfoot or True Giant - Jogung!)*

**Terrifying Tracks:** 12 -18 inches long. Often *"turned backwards"*, a feature of many *Wildman* reports worldwide and possibly indicative of habitual concealment of their direction of travel, accomplished by walking in reverse. Toes are long in proportion to the foot and tracks often show only three to four visible toes, each about 5 inches long and lacking an opposable toe.

**Hairy Handprints:** Handprints show a semi opposable thumb and little finger. Several examples have been found left on vehicles and buildings in *Yowie* hotspots and often show signs of elongated fingernails or claws.

**Beastly Behaviours:** Although sometimes seen in daylight, the *Yowie* is primarily nocturnal and solitary. Sightings usually (but not always) involve single individuals, which, by the lack of obvious female sexual markers in nearly all reports, are presumed to be male. Walks with a shuffling gait run very fast but with a loping motion. Juveniles climb trees. Dogs seem particularly afraid of them. Can use a stick as a weapon to kill animals or for communication, or to throw at humans or vehicles (along with stones), usually when annoyed. Dislikes being seen and will often display an expression of extreme anger and rage upon its face. Territorial and aggressive, occasionally harassing rural homeowners, although physical attacks are rare and most aggression constitutes a form of threat display or bluff charge. Displays curiosity toward humans and will often follow or watch them. If seen, it will often lie flat on the ground, duck down behind an object or even stand statue-still behind a tree, or even out in the open, in the hope of not being seen. Believed to be a dangerous animal capable of attacking and killing humans and should be afforded the same caution as any large animal. However, for the most part, physical encounters are rare and the *Yowie* will choose to leave an area if seen.

**Deadly Diet:** Omnivorous. Grubs, wallabies, kangaroos, fish, shellfish, roots, vegetables, and roadkill.

**Hairy Habitat:** Prefers Mountains and scrubland. *Yowie's* (or some regionally named version of them) are reported in great abundance in the highly populated regions of Queensland, New South Wales, Victoria, and South Australia; and less so, in the sparsely populated regions of Western Australia, The Northern Territory, and Tasmania. According to the Australian *Yowie* Research Organisation, the most likely places to experience a *Yowie* encounter are The Mt. Kembla & Mt. Keira area, Illawarra region, New South Wales; Ormeau, Gold Coast, Queensland; The Antarctic Beech Trees area, Springbrook National Park, Gold Coast Queensland; Sassafras Gully, Springwood, Blue Mountains, New South Wales; and Tablelands Road, Wentworth Falls, Blue Mountains, New South Wales.

**Scary Sightings:** Although *Yowie* researchers are far less in number than those in North America, the few men and women who have dedicated their lives to this little known arena have successfully catalogued many hundreds of reports, creating a verifiable database that illuminates an encouraging continuity between, physical description, behaviour, diet, and habitat; that is an invaluable resource to researchers of the *Wildman* phenomenon worldwide. As with *Bigfoot* reports, *Yowie* reports are too numerous to recount in their entirety in a work as transient as this. I have, therefore, selected those significant reports that illustrate the contiguous characteristics of these creatures from both a historical and modern perspective.

<u>1871:</u> In April 1871, George Osborne allegedly saw an apelike animal climb out of a tree and run away on all fours near Avondale, New South Wales in April 1871. It was covered in black hair except for a tan streak from neck to abdomen. It had feet like an iguana's.

<u>1882:</u> On December 9th, 1882: Amateur naturalist Henry James McCooey. Encountered a strange man-like creature in bushland between Batemans Bay and Ulladulla. Recounting his experience in, The Australian Town and Country Journal, he wrote the following:

*"A few days ago, I saw one of these strange animals in an unfrequented locality on the coast between Bateman's Bay and Ulladulla. My attention*

*was attracted to it by the cries of a number of small birds which were pursuing and darting at it. When I first beheld the animal, it was standing on its hind legs, partly upright, looking up at the birds above it in the bushes, blinking its eyes and distorting its visage and making a low chattering kind of noise. Being above the animal on a slight elevation and distant from it less than a chain, I had ample opportunity of noting its size and general appearance."*

*"I should think that if it were standing perfectly upright, it would be nearly 5 ft high. It was tailless and covered with very long black hair, which was of a dirty red or snuff colour about the throat and breast. Its eyes, which were small and restless, were partly hidden by matted hair that covered its head. The length of the fore legs or arms seemed to be strikingly out of proportion with the rest of its body, but in all other respects, its build seemed to be fairly proportional. It would probably weigh about 8 stone. On the whole, it was a most uncouth and repulsive-looking creature, evidently possessed of prodigious strength and one which I should not care to come to close quarters with. Having sufficiently satisfied my curiosity, I throw a stone at the animal, whereupon it immediately rushed off, followed by the birds, and disappeared in a ravine which was close at hand."*

<u>*1885:*</u> William and Joseph Webb shot at a *Yowie* near Flea Creek in the Brindabella Range, New South Wales, in about 1885. Its head was set deep between its shoulders, and it was bellowing deeply. They didn't know whether they hit it because it ran away as soon as the gun went off. Its tracks were humanlike, with spreading toes and a long stride.

<u>*1912:*</u> On October 12th, 1912: George Summerell rode up close to a grey-haired *Yowie* that was drinking from a creek near Creewah, New South Wales, on October 12th, 1912; Australian poet and bushman Sydney Wheeler Jephcott visited the spot the next day and was able to make plaster-casts of hand and footprints.

<u>*1938/39:*</u> While hunting wallabies with a friend, Clyde Shepherdson encountered an animal standing next to a large tree. The creature stood 6ft tall, was covered in rusty-yellow hair, and resembled an ape. It had a short neck, a flat, broad face, and big ears that stuck out. On

seeing the two men, the animal raised its long arms and snarled. Both men then retreated.

*1970:* On August 10th, 1970: Rex Gilroy was eating lunch in a clearing near the Ruined Castle rock formation in the Blue Mountains, New South Wales, when a man-sized apelike creature with orange hair ran across the open ground and gave out a scream

*1974:* In the winter of 1974, at 3:30 pm, on a sunny afternoon, Alwyn Richards and his sister were riding up a hillside near their property, near Killawarra, New South Wales, when they saw a huge, 9 – 10 ft. tall, human-like creature standing in a firebreak and staring at them from around 30 metres away. The creature, which stood erect, was covered in long shaggy hair, which almost obscured its dark-skinned face, was muscular and broad-chested. The strange animal looked at them for what seemed like several minutes before walking away, stepping over a 4 ft fence in the process, without breaking a stride. A "terrible burning smell" permeated the area.

*1977:* On August 10th, 1977, a woman was awoken by high-pitched screaming and the sound of her dog yelping in her garden. On opening her back door to find the source of this commotion, she was confronted by the sight and smell of an odorous ape-like creature, covered in brownish hair, standing not more than 5ft. away and clutching her dog tightly against its chest. Upon seeing the woman, it promptly dropped the dog and began to back away while making short grunting noises and watching the woman intently before suddenly fleeing, its arms hanging loose, out into the street. The woman described the strange beast as being approximately 6ft. tall, with broad shoulders and chest, in the middle of which sat a comparatively small head. Its hips were narrow and its legs were strongly built. The creature was covered in brownish hair, which was short-cropped, apart from on its shoulders and had long arms that hung loose when it ran. Her dog (who survived the initial encounter but sadly died several weeks later) was covered in an oily substance that smelled terribly and took several antiseptic washes to get out. A single footprint 8.5 inches long and approximately 4 inches wide at the toes was discovered after the creature's visit, along with three strands of long, reddish hair, which were found on a fencepost.

*1996:* Emergency services were called to attend a 50-year-old woman that passers-by had noticed crying on a walking track in Barron River Falls, Cairns, North Queensland. The woman, who, they had assumed was suffering from an asthma attack, told her rescuers that she had regularly walked this same path every morning at exactly the same time for the past 7 years, but that this on this particular morning, she had been startled to see a large, hairy creature, with matted dark-brown hair and a black leathery skinned face, crossing the path ahead of her and disappearing into the bush. Realising that she was on her own, she had a panic attack. She emphasised to her rescuers that the creature was not any known Australian animal!

*1997:* Three builders driving through a rough four-wheel drive track in Delaney's Creek, Beerwah, Queensland. As they ascended a steep hill, they witnessed a tall, naked, hairy man step out of the bush behind them and cross the track. Just over a week later, a fellow builder who was always working at the site was jogging along the track when he heard some noise in the bushes beside him. Turning to see where the noise was coming from, he noticed a "big-hairy ape" jogging in the tree line adjacent to him (yet some small distance behind). The creature, seeing that it had been spotted, ran off into the bush.

*1997:* A group of children were playing in a small forest behind their grandparents' home in Camira, Queensland when they encountered a black and hairy animal that resembled a little gorilla. The animal, which was sitting with its back to the children and approximately 3 metres high up in a tree, according to the witnesses, was: "...*big, probably the same size as us, but it wasn't long or short and fat, just a bigger version of us.*" The children returned later with their father and found deep gouges, as if made by claw marks, ascending the tree as high as they could see.

*2000:* In June 2000, a woman with her children and newborn baby were driving between Gladstone and Blackwater, early one morning, when they observed a huge *Yowie*, beside the Capricorn highway, near the Gogango Range, which appeared to be running towards the hills, on the driver's side of the car. According to the woman, the creature ran on two legs, stood 7 – 8 ft. tall, had no neck, appeared broad and solid, had very long arms, and was covered in long, reddish-orange hair. She said of the creature's curious locomotion: *"he was side on to us... it wasn't really running, it was more like loping."*

*2001:* On March 2nd, 2001, at 11 PM, Aaron Carmichael was driving in heavy rain along a road near Hinze Dam, Queensland. He had just taken a bend at around 70kph when he noticed a large figure emerge from the bush to his left. The creature, which was 8 ft tall, twice the dimensions of a human male, solidly built and covered in thick brown hair, dashed across the road, causing Aaron to collide with it. The creature then fell beneath his car, causing the vehicle to become temporarily airborne and crash into the dirt wall on the left-hand side of the road. Leaving Aaron dazed and wondering what had just occurred. The creature was nowhere to be seen. Aaron's car sustained damage consistent with that of colliding with something solid and heavy over its entire front end.

*2003:* A school teacher witnessed a large *Yowie* while off-roading in a 4X4 through a thickly forested area of Middle Brother Mountain, North West Coast, New South Wales. The creature, which was approximately 10 ft. tall, was standing on the edge of the road and watching her vehicle's approach. She slowed her vehicle down to a crawl as she drew near to the creature and was able to observe that it was 10 ft tall and covered in hair, with arms that hung down near its knees. She stated, *"It seemed like a gorilla, but more upright."*

*2006:* A man was driving along a dirt road towards a campsite in the North of Mansfield, Victoria. Seeing that the sun was beginning to dip below the horizon, he pulled over to get his bearings in a map before proceeding towards his destination in what would soon be night. Suddenly, he became aware of something moving on the hill. He said, *"When I stopped to get the map out, it must have thought it had been identified... It was a big hairy, black man. It was quick, faster than a person. Built like a rock. It was a little bit taller than me and very stocky. All black."*

2008: A family of metal detectorists had two intense encounters with a *Yowie* while prospecting for gold in Redbank Victoria. The father, who had been prospecting on the hill, heard a noise and removing his headphones to ascertain its origination, noticed, just 32 feet away, a 7 – 8 ft tall, black, hairy, ape-man - that somewhat resembled a Neanderthal - peeking at him through the bushes. Running in terror down the hill to find his son and his son's wife, to whom he recounted his harrowing tale, they decided to check out the area in their car. The trio drove up the Bridal track and into a rocky, hilly area that was about 650 feet from where the father had seen the strange creature. Suddenly, they saw it cross the dirt track, not more than 160 feet ahead of them. The son described the creature, saying, *"...it looked to be about 7 to 7, ½ ft tall. I'm 6.6ft tall and it was at least a foot taller than me. It walked from the right to the left, looked up at the car, and then just kept walking. It was hairy, a very dark-brown to black. It had a weird walk, like 60% arms and only 40% leg movement. It was like looking at a Neanderthal, half-human and half man.*

2011: Two men, driving in opposite directions, both up and down a hill in Donnybrook, Western Australia, witnessed a large Orangutan-like creature, with long arms and covered in reddish-brown matted hair, running down the hill. One of the men, a Native American, said of the encounter, *"...Some movement caught my eye, it looked like an orangutan. I'm 5 ft 10" and it was a little shorter than me, but a hell of a lot stockier than I am. It didn't move like an orangutan, it ran like I would down the hill. The other guy stopped, so he must have seen it too. It ran, hooked on to a tree, and swung around it and then another tree. It used the trees to propel itself really fast into the bush. It was muscular and looked like an orangutan, but it didn't move like a monkey. There's no way it was human. I couldn't run down the hill like that. It flung itself around the trees before it landed. He was fast. You don't expect to see a monkey running in the bush!"*

2015: A man, who had lived in a house in Belobora, New South Wales, with his wife for 17 years, had two encounters with a Yowie that appeared to be hanging out on their property. The man said of his encounters: *"I went outside because our dog was barking and shone the torch down the driveway and there were two eyes looking at me and a dark figure. It was a big figure, it was bigger than me. It then ran about 100 metres and I could hear all the twigs snapping. Then it picked something up and was hitting one piece of wood against another. It did that for 10 seconds. It gave me a real fright. It was really loud and it was hitting it really hard. The next night I went back out there and shone the torch and there again was the figure. It had its back to me and turned and looked at me for about 10 seconds before turning away again. The next night I went out with a shotgun and let some shots off in the air to scare it off. We haven't seen it since."*

2016: On April 2016, at 4.30 pm, two men were returning home after a day of wildlife photography in a national park in Bellthorpe, Queensland. Just before dusk, as they were walking along a path called 'The Postman's Track', they spied a large form about 50 metres ahead, crouching down next to a tree, with its back to them. As they drew closer, the form stood up to reveal a creature that was 8 – 9 ft tall and 3 feet wide across its hunched shoulders; it had long arms and was covered in blackish-brown hair. The creature quickly disappeared into the bush. The witnesses were unable to find any footprints where the creature had stood due to the type of ground but did notice that a large area of grass had been flattened and that several trees, an inch and half thick, had been pushed over.

2017: A paleoanthropologist/archaeologist was surveying an indigenous heritage site in the Border Ranges National Park, near Tyalgum, New South Wales, when he had a strange encounter with a *Yowie* that may provide some insight into the evasion techniques used by these creatures when surprised by the sudden appearance of a human being. The witness of this strange behaviour said of his encounter: *"I decided to venture up a steep escarpment to view the area from above. Upon stopping to work out how to navigate a small waterfall, I noticed a crouched hominid with long reddish hair, sat on the other side of it. It had a grey, ape-humanoid face and large eyes like golf balls and was looking straight ahead. I got the distinct impression that it was trying to conceal its presence by pretending to be a tree or some other object. Like a child pretending you can't see them crouching right in front of you. It spooked the hell out of me, I pretended that I didn't see it, turned my back, and went down the mountain."* This highly qualified witness also had some significant theories about the possible origins of this creature and went on to say: *"This is not a hominin but a hominid and is possibly some other type, where no fossil evidence has been recovered."*

**Beastly Evidence:** Thanks to the continued efforts of several *Yowie* groups in Australia, trace evidence, such as tracks, handprints, and stick structures, etc., is plentiful. We will in this chapter cover only a few examples of these examples to provide an overview of the type and form of this ever-growing quantity of data.

*Tracks:* There are numerous track finds throughout Australia that range between 12 -18 inches long and which usually show 3 to 4 four visible toes, often lacking an opposable toe.

*Handprints:* Strange clawed handprints were found on top of a Bobcat on a farm in Gayndah in 2005.

*Witness Sketches:* The *Yowie* phenomenon is fortunate enough to have several correlating eyewitness reports that have produced remarkably similar sketches recorded by diverse and unconnected eyewitnesses.

*Audio:* In the early hours of March 23rd, 2019, two men claimed to have been stalked by a 9.8 ft tall *Yowie* in a popular Glow Worm Tunnel in Wollemi National Park near Lithgow, New South Wales. Although the men did not manage to capture footage of the beast, which they claimed was trying to conceal itself, and whose 'outline' they estimated to be 10 ft tall and 4 ft across the shoulders, they did capture audio of several loud, bark-like eerie howls that the animal made while attempting to drive them out of the cave. The men claimed that the creature was also making intimidating grunting noises behind them as it followed them out of the cave, which in their fright and urgency to leave, they did not manage to record. After exiting the glow worm cave, they ran the entire 1.2 miles back to their vehicle without stopping to see if they were being followed. *Australian Yowie Hunters*

*Thermal Image:* On May 4[th,] 2021, during an expedition to Springbrook National Park in the Gold Coast hinterland, Dean Harrison and the Australian Yowie Research team managed to capture a thermal image of what appears to be two 9 ft tall bipedal humanoids.

*Art & Archaeology:*

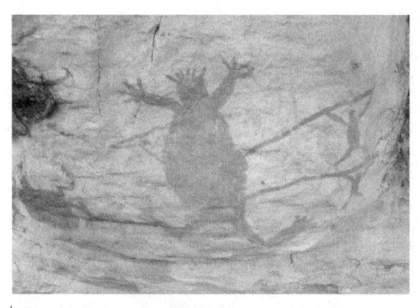

Although Indigenous stories of the Hairy Man are common, there appear to be relatively few examples of rock art that show Yowie-type creatures.

**Beastly Theories:**

*Hidden Homos:* Surviving Kow swamp people. The Kow Swamp people are believed to be an early population of Homo sapiens that inhabited Australia as recently as 9000 years ago. Some of their fossils exhibit robust features, large teeth and jaws, prominent brow ridges, and even sagittal crests. Although this could be from artificial binding. This rather hopeful theory may not sufficiently answer to the *Yowie's* purported dimensions, however. This in itself and the combination of their comparatively advanced civilisation, unfortunately, rules out any relation to the modern-day *Yowie*.

*Homo Naledi:* Could the *Yowie* be an extant form of ancient ape, like H. Naledi? Certainly, in life, this ancient ape may have shared some of the purported physiological characteristics that are attributed to the *Yowie*, such as its seeming to have 'no neck'. Whereas this is not technically true of H. Naledi (or the *Yowie*), the structure of its shoulder blades would have either obscured its neck from view or, depending on its hair cover, given its head the appearance of sitting atop its shoulders.

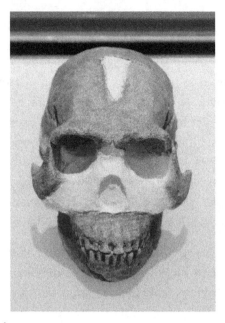

| Reconstructed Homo Naledi skull.

*Surviving Gigantopithecus:* Although only known from fossil remains in China, North Vietnam, and India. Gigantopithecus, with its scant fossil fragments, still enchants many Wildman researchers. Unfortunately, the fossil fragments that make up the entire body of Gigantopithecus evidence worldwide are little more than a few jaw fragments and teeth and offer nothing more than an opportunity for philosophical speculation about how these large terrestrial apes might have appeared, were they still alive today.

# RELICTS

*"Standing from 5 ft 6 in. to 7 ft 6 in. in height, these stocky apes, as opposed to the Man Apes and Wildmen, appear to occupy a position that is closer to that of true apes. And although they, too, like other Wildmen, are bipedal, they are also reported to walk quadrupedally and leave tracks that show a suspiciously ape-like, divergent medial toe. Something that may suggest an arboreal nature, suitable for climbing trees and rocky slopes."*

'View of Himalayas on a snowy day.'

## YETI

The Himalayas are an immense Mountain chain that stretches 1700 miles, from Afghanistan in the west to Assam in the south-east; straddling six countries and boasting diverse tropical valleys, alpine forests, bleak slopes, and glacier topped mountains, that, legend has it, among their enormous variety of wildlife, may also conceal a population of large, unknown apes, colloquially known as, *Yeti*.

**What's in a name?** The Name, *'Yeti'*, comes from a Sherpa word, whose meaning has been hotly debated and obscured over time. Pronounced, *"yeh-tay"*, it is generally understood to mean *"Rock animal"*; with *Yeh,* meaning *"Snowy Mountain"* or *"rocky area"* and *Teh,* meaning *"animal"*. While some interpretations claim that *Teh* has the same meaning as *Dred,* which means *"bear"*, others still conflate the modern Tibetan, *"dred pa"*, meaning, *"contempt/disgust"*, with this creature's most popular and certainly misplaced moniker – *"ABOMINABLE"* – as in: *"The Abominable Snowman"*.

As one might expect in the large and culturally diverse region upon which the Himalayas sit, the Yeti is known by many names. Some of which, like the *Dre-Mo* (almost certainly a bear!) and the *Dzu-Teh* (a type of giant *Man-Ape*, similar to *Sasquatch*), may, in fact, represent other species that inhabit a similar geographic zone but are, rather awkwardly, consigned a catch-all-category or flexible label, that can be interchangeably applied to several types of large animal! Nevertheless, it is vital when researching Yeti-lore to familiarise oneself with the many monikers that this abominable ape has earned for itself throughout its awe-inspiring precipitous habitat; such as *Banjhankri, Chelovek medvied, Chelovek Mishka, Chu-Mung, Dre-Mo, Dzu-Teh, Jungli-Admi, Khya, Metoh-Kangmi, Mi-Chen-Po, Mi-Go, Mi-Teh, Osodrashin, Pi, Rakshi-Bompo, Samdja, Snezhniy Chelovek, Sogpa, Yah-teh, Yeh-teh*, and of course, the eternally loved and forever fun – *Abominable Snowman!*

**Scientific Name:** The Yeti does indeed have a scientific name, or to be more precise – two scientific names! The first, *Homo Nivis Odiosus* that was conferred upon it rather flippantly by Harold T. Tilman in 1937, means *"the abominable snowman"*; and the latter, more gallantly named *Dinanthropoides Nivalis*, meaning, *"Big man in the tundra"*, which was given by the late, great, Bernard Heuvelmans in 1958.

**Monstrous Measurements:** Heavyset and muscular – the Yeti is described as being between 5ft 6inches to 7ft. 6 inches in height and weighing between 200 – 400 pounds. Its hair is thick, dark greyish–brown or reddish-brown, with the darker coloured varieties generally reported as larger than the reddish coloured ones. Whether this colour and size differentiation is due to age, maturity, or even representative of sexual dimorphism, is not known, as animals of both colours have been reported as having noticeably large breasts. However, if the *Yeti* is an undiscovered ape species, then one would expect the male of the species to be somewhat larger than the female.

The *Yeti* has a high, pointed head, with a gorilla-like sagittal crest, deep-set eyes, a flat nose, and a wide mouth with large teeth. It has less hair on the face, the skin of which varies, from white to black or dark in colour. Its arms, with their large hands and long fingers, are typically ape-like and reach to its knees, as are its ape-like bowed legs and plantigrade feet.

**Terrifying Tracks:** Plantigrade feet, which measure between 8 – 13 inches in length and 4-6 inches in width, with the large big toe being separate from four *(sometimes three)* smaller toes. It leaves a trail or trackway in a fairly straight line and has a stride ranging from 1.5 to 3 ft.

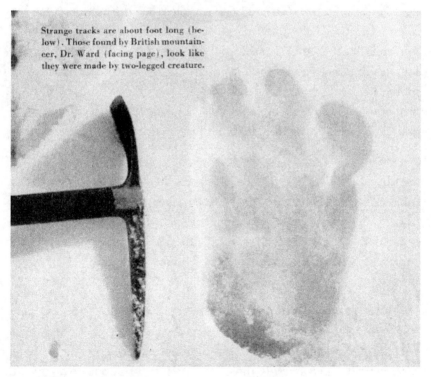

Strange tracks are about foot long (below). Those found by British mountaineer, Dr. Ward (facing page), look like they were made by two-legged creature.

*Photograph of an alleged yeti footprint found by Michael Ward, taken at Menlung glacier on the Everest expedition by Eric Shipton in 1951.*

**Beastly Behaviours:** The Yeti is believed to be migratory, solitary, and primarily nocturnal, but will, like many other ape species (known and unknown), make a temporary nest, usually comprising of dwarf juniper branches or any other similar materials that are close by. Although it makes loud calls, yelps, mews, chattering, and high-pitched cries, it does not appear to possess anything that could be construed as language; neither does it utilise tools or possess any technology. In another apogee of ape-like behaviour, it will destroy huts, tear up undergrowth, and 'bluff charge*' individuals. Females are said to throw their breasts over their shoulders when running on all fours. In this rural and time-frozen region, there are many stories of interactions between yetis and humans, even some that tell of intermarriage and hybrid children being produced. Or, of some isolated tribes being 'half-yeti'; and while there definitely appears to be a kernel of truth to some of these tales: i.e., the rumour that *Yeti* like to drink a locally brewed beer called 'Chang', or the inescapable universal legends of *Wildmen* abducting and breeding with human females in almost every country where these legends persist; it is far more likely that the tales of hybrid-human-wildman-children originate in the beliefs of superstitious locals trying to explain away and sadly, 'send away' or exile, children with certain birth defects from their communities.

**Deadly Diet:** The *Yeti* is omnivorous; its dietary regimen consists of pikas, rodents, hares, lizards, insects, eggs, moss, bamboo shoots, yaks, tahr, musk deer, and unsurprisingly, anything else that is seasonally and locally available. It is often said that the *yeti* will raid the occasional village potato patch or even empty a well of its water overnight.

**Hairy Habitat:** Contrary to popular belief, the *Yeti* does not reside on the high mountaintops of the Himalayas but instead is reputed to frequent the forests far below the snowline and, according to local lore, usually only ascends the snowfields, from 10,000 to 23,000 ft. during autumn, in search of food. Some form of the *Yeti* is reported, via its voluminous provincial appellations, throughout the Himalayan Mountains of Nepal, Kashmir, India, and Bhutan; the southern Tibetan Plateau; southern Xinjiang, Uygur Autonomous Region of China; and North-western Yunnan Province, China.

**Scary Sightings:** There are many notable *Yeti* encounters on record, and far too many to include in this short synopsis, yet a brief overview of some of the key features reported will enable us to paint the portrait of this enigmatic ape in our mind's eye:

*1832:* It is generally agreed that Brian H. Hodgson, British Minister to Nepal, was the first Westerner to write about ape-like creatures in the high Himalayas in 1832; nevertheless, his curious correspondence did not seem to garner any international attention and must have simply been put down to the over-imaginative superstitions of local inhabitants. And yet, from this period onward, these 'superstitious' encounters began to be shared in greater detail and with a greater frequency than had previously been recorded. Whether this 'spirit of openness' was a result of the culturally ingrained Buddhist philosophy of giving, or more likely, a way to enhance visits from curious tourists (both local and international) to the many impoverished rural monasteries dotted throughout the region, is not known. What is indisputable is that the Legend of the *Yeti* had started its upward ascent towards international infamy!

*1925:* While hiking, near the Zemu Glacier, in Sikkim State, India, at an altitude of almost 15,000ft. British photographer, N.A. Tombazi found fifteen small footprints at a spot where he had seen a naked, bipedal, human-like figure walking shortly before.

*March 1949*: A man named Mingmah was tending his yaks in Pangboche, Nepal; when he heard a loud call, looking in the direction from which the terrifying noise had emanated, he saw a *Yeti*. Fleeing in terror, he hid inside a stone hut nearby and, peering out from a chink in the stones, saw the creature only a few feet away, walking around on two legs. Seeing him inside the hut, it growled at him. Mingmah, in what can only be described as a moment of 'do or die' daring, attacked the creature with a smouldering stick from the fire, causing it to flee.

*December 1950:* A Sherpa named Sen Tensing was travelling to Phortse from Thyangboche when he observed in the moonlight a reddish-brown yeti walking along the road. Hiding behind a boulder, he watched as the animal passed by only 25 yards away!

*July 11ᵗʰ, 1974:* A young Sherpa woman named Lhakpa Dolma was attacked by a *Yeti* while tending her yaks near Tengboche, Nepal. The creature dragged her to a nearby stream, where it dumped her before proceeding to kill her yaks. In this case, an official report was even filed, the local police even finding tracks at the creature at the scene of the crime several days later.

September 22nd, 1991: a Russian biologist - Arkady Tishkov, who was a member of the Soviet-Chinese Glaciological Expedition, observed a *Yeti* for nearly an hour on the south-eastern slope of Mount Xixabangma, Tibet. Tishkov tried to capture the beast on film but realised that he was too far away. Attempting to move to a closer vantage point from which to document this extraordinary sight, the animal saw him approaching and, unfortunately, ran away.

**Beastly Evidence:** When a creature has been so thoroughly pursued as has the *Yeti*, one would expect a wealth of scientific evidence to lie beside the trail blazed by the plethora of explorers (none of whom were lightweights in the field of exploration or zoology) who have hunted it! Yet, as is often the case in cryptozoology, such 'evidence' is mired in dispute and sensationalism, along with a healthy dose of personal profiteering. Yet, in the case of this abominable media monstrosity, there is indeed material that can be examined and weighed against the available eyewitness testimony; to help ascertain whether it is correlation or coercion that has permanently cemented its name into the canon of cryptozoology:

*Yeti Scalps:* Historically, there were several 'alleged; *Yeti* scalps on display in Nepal, including the conical (sagittal crested, male) black-skinned, reddish-haired scalp at the Pangboche Monastery; the similarly sized 'female' scalp at the Khumjung Monastery; that was later borrowed by Sir Edmund Hillary in 1960 and examined by specialists at the Field Museum in Chicago and which turned out to be made from the skin of the Serow (Himalayan goat-antelope); and lastly, the obvious 'replica' scalp, which is kept at the Namche Bazar Monastery.

*A 'female' Yeti scalp that was discovered by Sir Edmund Hilary in 1960 and extensively examined by specialists at the field museum in Chicago turned out to be a fake made from the skin of a Serow (Himalayan – goat-antelope)*

*Mummified hands:* These mummified remains, similar to the yeti scalps, occupy a dual function in the life of the monasteries; acting as both holy relics and tourist attractions; generating much-needed income for the impoverished and often isolated monasteries and therefore, unfortunately, obliterating any possibility for genuine testimony as to their authenticity. In a way, they somewhat remind me of my first visit to Jerusalem, Israel, wherein, after walking into a catholic gift shop, I was horrified to see a wall full of holy relics, neatly packaged and for sale at very amenable prices. The wall itself was a contradiction in terms and contained small packets of *'fingernails of Christ'* and *'wood from the Cross'* without even the slightest hint of irony. As I visited more of these gift shops throughout Jerusalem, I was taken aback by the inexhaustible supply of these relics and the forethought that our *Lord* and *Saviour's* disciples must have had to have kept so many of *His* fingernail clippings and to have made sure that there was a regular changing of crosses during the *Crucifixion,* to enable future catholic merchants to keep up with the demand in holy relics! I accept as a universal truism (minor cultural variations notwithstanding) that human behaviours are pretty much the same the whole world over and that in this religious-superstitious mode of thinking and especially as far as the monasteries are concerned, the relics, such as Yeti scalps and mummified hands, can simultaneously occupy the character of genuine religious relics and consciously fabricated fakes; or more properly – religious replicas!

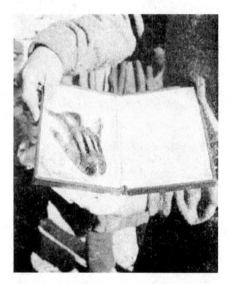

'The Pangboche Hand. 'In 1960, Sir Edmund Hilary examined the mummified hand of a 'yeti' at Pangboche monastery and declared it a mix of human and animal. However, it was later revealed by Peter Byrne that he had removed a phalanx and finger bone from the hand in 1959 and replaced them with human phalanges. Photo: Sir Edmund Hillary - Epitaph to the Elusive Abominable Snowman. LIFE Magazine. 13 January 1961.

When viewed from this perspective, the evidence as it is presented by those holy hermits in the high Himalayas seems less disingenuous, as does the religious significance that they attach to them. Of the acclaimed Mummified hands, most can be scientifically dismissed, such as the *Yeti Arm* at the Makula Monastery in Nepal, which consists of the paw and forearm of a Snow Leopard. However, The Pangboche Monastery hand is as unusual as are the sensational stories surrounding its examination. In 1959, Peter Byrne (financed by the infamous American Oil Tycoon – Tom Slick) was permitted by the monastery and, for a relatively sizeable 'donation', to remove a thumb and phalanx from the hand replacing them with human fingers he had brought with him. The story from here on takes on a Hollywood movie-like legend, as we learn the remains were then smuggled out of the country with the assistance of actor James Stewart and his wife, Gloria, who hid the bones in her undergarments in her lingerie case. Both a wise and shielding decision, as evidenced in her conversation with the British Customs official who checked her luggage; whom after she questioned as to why that particular case had not been opened said: *"Oh Madame, certainly not! A British customs official would never open a ladies lingerie case."* The real bones were then smuggled by the famous couple to primatologist W.C. Osman Hill in England. Hill initially declared them of human origin but then later concluded that they were Neanderthal-like. Zoologist Charles A. Leone, too, was baffled by the bones, while George Agogino thought they might be those of an ape. Later in 1960, when Sir Edmund Hillary examined the mummified hand at Pangboche monastery and declared it a mix of human and animal, he was blissfully unaware that he was viewing the hand that had been altered after Byrne's switch.

The bones analysed by Hill disappeared but later resurfaced in the collection of the Hunterian Museum of the Royal College of Surgeons, whose records show that it was bequeathed to them, by hill, in 1976. Later, in 2011, for the making of a BBC documentary, the finger was analysed by the Royal Zoological Society of Scotland at the request of journalist Matthew Hill, and its DNA proved human. A little-known portion of this parable of primate piracy is that Byrne also collected a skin sample from the Pangboche hand, although this, too, when tested, did not prove definitive. However, The US television show *Unexplained Mysteries* managed to obtain the skin sample decades later, but sadly, even with modern scientific methods, they were also unable to determine its source. One wonders what the wonders of modern DNA analysis might detect, were this sample to be tested today.

The hand at the modified hand at the Pangboche monastery vanished in 1991 after the story of the *yeti* relic aired and its current whereabouts are unknown; yet this story, too, has taken on a modern twist with a happy ending. In 2011, New Zealand adventurer, Mike Allsop, delivered a replica hand of the abominable snowman (crafted by the costumes and weapons makers of the *Lord of the Rings* movies, no less) to the monks of the Pangboche Monastery in Nepal, more than half a century after it (or a significant portion of it) was sold to Byrne/Slick; the ensuing attention this brought, according to the monks, inevitably leading to the theft of their other yeti relics. Upon delivering the 'new relic' to the monastery, Allsop told the BBC, *"I want to help the monastery have an income again — I want to help them out."*

*Tracks:* The popularity of this region with adventurers since the 19th century has left a wealth of anecdotal and physical testimony that attests to the existence of an unknown biped. In this matter, the long history of unexplained bipedal track reports, photos and film, work to establish a morphological blueprint of these alleged upright apes and attest to their mode of locomotion. Western reports date back, at least as far as 1889, when Laurence A. Waddell discovered large bare footprints at an elevation of 17,000 ft In north-eastern Sikkim State, India. Since that time and up to the present day, numerous notable *yeti-tracks* have been proffered, debated, and added to the annals of this intriguing hunt; yet all pale in comparison to those discovered by Eric Shipton on November 8th, 1951. Shipton, who, along with Sen

Tensing and Michael Ward of the Everest Reconnaissance Expedition, was ascending the southwestern slope of Menlungtse, west of Mount Everest, found (in a moment that would live on forever in yeti-lore) a mile-long trail of freshly made human-like footprints at 19,000 ft. Shipton's, now universally known photograph of an alleged *Yeti* track next to an ice axe, appeared in newspapers around the world and has since become the gold standard for photographing unknown tracks (i.e., a clear crisp, aerial photo, featuring a measurable object for scale!). The footprint, which was 13inches long and 8 inches wide, featured an enormous big toe and a second toe, nearly as large as the first. Next to these were three smaller toes, separated from the other two and, if genuine, certainly not anatomically comparable to any known animal species.

Additional *Yeti* tracks similar in shape to Shipton's were also discovered by Lord John Hunt, Sir Edmund Hillary, Frank Smythe, H.W. Tilman, and Peter Byrne. One has to wonder if the international attention these discoveries would have generated, as well as the possibility of expedition funding from rich financiers and scientific institutions, might have created a race for evidence, in which, not unexpectedly; some of the runners may have bent the rules of the race for the perceived greater good of further funded expeditions.

There have since been, undeniably, many alleged *Yeti* tracks discovered over the last few decades, some of which, like the series of 13 inches long, by 9.8 inch wide footprints found and cast by Destination Truth's – Joshua Gates in December 2007, certainly lends some credibility to the continuation of this mysterious phenomenon. While others, like the enormous, indistinct, 35-inch 'footprints' found by the Indian Army in 2019 (which were almost certainly those of a Himalayan black bear and her cub), are proof that the allure of the *Yeti* is still able to illicit belief and confirmation bias, even among persons as conservative and emotionally neutral, as professional soldiers!

*Yeti Droppings:* Today, animal scat is an important scientific resource, providing vital information on the variety of animal species present in an area, what their diet consists of, their relationship to other animals, their distribution, and astonishingly, even their population estimate. Animal scat also contains DNA and provides a way to study reclusive cryptid animals that have, thus far, managed to avoid capture. Although rare, some alleged *yeti* scat has been found and examined over the years; like the 'big bag' of *Yeti* scat collected at Lake Masumba on March 10th in 1954, by Sherpa Norbu, who was part of the Daily Mail's "*Yeti* Expedition" to Nepal; featuring mountaineer John A. Jackson, journalist Ralph Izzard, photographer Tom Biswas, and naturalist Gerald Russell. Russell later examined the scat and found that it contained a high percentage of Pika bones. More alleged *yeti* scat, along with tracks, was found on March 14th by Izzard and Russell above the Western fork of the Dudh Kosi. During the February to June 1958 Slick-Johnson Snowman Expedition, led by Gerald Russell and Peter and Bryan Byrne, expedition member Norman G. Dyhrenfurth and Sherpa Ang Dawa discovered many droppings with Pika bones and hair in a cave in the upper Dudh Kosi Valley that *Yeti's* allegedly used for shelter.

*Yeti Hairs:* in 2001, British zoologist Rob McCall claimed to have discovered *Yeti* hairs and claw marks in the hollow of a tree in eastern Bhutan. Intriguingly, McCall sent the hairs to geneticist Bryan Sykes *(RIP)* at the Oxford Institute of Molecular Medicine, who thoroughly examined the hair and said: *"We found some DNA in it, but we don't know what it is. It's not a human, not a bear, nor anything else we have so far been able to identify. It's a mystery and I never thought this would end in a mystery. We have never encountered DNA that we couldn't recognize before."* Sadly, later analysis revealed the hairs were from a brown bear and an Asiatic black bear. In 2008, primatologist Anna Nekaris and microscopy expert Jon Wells analysed alleged *Yeti* hairs that were collected in the remote Garo Hills area of North-East India. Although initially inconclusive, later tests revealed that the hair belonged to the

Himalayan Goral (a small ungulate found throughout the Himalayas).

*Yeti, Do's and Don'ts:* A letter written by Embassy Counsellor Ernest Fisk, on November 30, 1959, to US expeditions seeking permits to ascend the mountains, detailed explicit do's and don'ts for any persons encountering a Yeti. Significantly, the letter cautions that although photographing the *Yeti* and even capturing it was permissible, *"it must not be killed or shot at except in an emergency arising out of self-defense."*

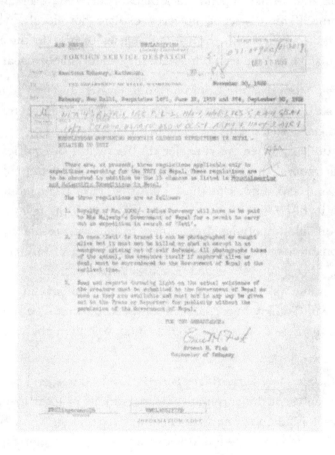

## Beastly Theories:

*Bear necessities:* Juvenile Asiatic Black bears spend most of their time in the trees to avoid attack by adult male bears. This temporary arboreal fixation tends to push their inner claw outward, allowing for an opposable grip whilst climbing trees. Some researchers have theorised that this unusual feature, in combination with the double imprint of the bear's feet, as it walks in its own fore tracks with its hind limbs, may produce the classic *yeti*-footprint; featuring an elongate, human-like, bipedal track that appears to have a hallux (big toe/thumb). This does not, however, explain how locals, who are more than familiar with the various species of bear in the region, could mistake a visual encounter with the yeti for that of a bear.

*Unknown anthropoid ape:* Could an undiscovered ape from the same genus as the orang-utan, or similar to the extinct Miocene ape – Sivapithecus, exist in this sparsely populated region. The possibility seems unlikely when we consider the zoological discoveries made thus far around the globe and especially in light of the concerted efforts and expeditions to the region that have been mounted to cement its discovery. Yet, our misconception about the region and its unfathomable unpopulated emptiness to hide and reside in; not to mention the largely intraversible nature of much of the terrain (as well as the *creatures'* alleged nocturnal habits), which create an impenetrable wall of shelter from our intrusive human endeavours to capture it! Frankly, against such odds, you would be far more successful in emboldening a *Yeti* to find you than the other way around!

*Holy Hucksters and Superstitious Sherpas:* Could the legend of the *Yeti* simply represent the corporatized superstitions of local Lamas and Sherpas, foisted upon impressionable western tourists who were only too keen to fetishize the folkloric overtones of their esoteric culture? Edmund Hilary's 1960 Himalayan Scientific and Mountaineering Expedition concluded that *Yeti* tracks were distortions of human footprints melted by the snow and that *Yeti* sightings made by

Sherpas were unreliable because they did not distinguish between the supernatural and natural world and that all of the scalps were probably fakes. And yet, could he have mistaken this traditional melding of the supernatural world and the real world as disingenuous, or did his western mind simply not understand the duality of habitation that these creatures occupy in a culture that believes that both worlds – the spiritual and the natural, exist simultaneously and often in conjunction with one another?

| *Montane Forests of Guatemala.*

## EL SISEMITE

Guatemala is a land whose beauty is matched only by its superstitions. Its people from the most ancient times populated their land with gods and demi-gods, demons, and spirits. The belief in *El Sisemite* is shared among all of the Indian tribes and the Ladinos who inhabit the area, who tells of a time when they were seen frequently until their number dwindled and they weren't seen anymore. In their legends, it was in ravines, springs, or rivers where the Sisimite appeared at night, making its way down from its home in the high mountains. These same high montane cloud forests and rain-soaked valleys of Guatemala, which receive 7 – 157 inches of annual rainfall and are covered in rich vegetation, support both high levels of biodiversity and endemism and harbour a diverse range of animal species, including several large predators, such as jaguars, pumas, and wolves. And, among these large predators is said to exist another, hairy, human-like animal known as *El Sisemite'*.

**What's in a name?** The word *'Sisemite'* comes from the Nahuatl word, *Tzitzimitl*, meaning *"diviner"*. Locally known as the *"Guardian of the* *forest";* It also has several lesser-known tribal aliases, such as *Chichimeque, Chichimicli, Chichinite, Itacayo, Li Queck, Quetcux* (a Chorti/Mayan, word meaning *"Abductor"*; *Sicimici, Siguanaba* (for the female), *Sirpi, Sisimiti, Sissimito, Suinta* (a Mosquito/Misumalapan word meaning: *"Spirit of the mountains"*), *Susumete,* and *Utcur witsir* (a Chorti/Mayan word meaning: *"guardian hill spirit"*).

(Note: El Sisemite' bares more than a passing resemblance to The Ulak (or Uluk), a bipedal, 5ft. tall, tailless primate, covered in black hair; reported along the Mosquito Coast of Central America; and possibly also, the Yoho, or Yuho, as it is known to the Rama and the Creoles, that is reported around the Garunta Mountains, north of the lower Rio Coco.)

**Monstrous Measurements:** *El Sisemite'* is large, upright, taller, and broader than the tallest man, with a human-like head, large eyes, and a heavily built, gorilla-like body covered in dark matted hair that reaches to the ground and which no bullet can penetrate. Its hands have four fingers and no thumb. In appearance, he is somewhere between a man and a monkey.

**Terrifying Tracks:** Footprints twice the size of a human and human-like in appearance, except for the big toe, which appears to be turned backwards. The stride is exceptionally long. Footprints are often found on the mountains but are impossible to track due to El Sisemite's ability to reverse his feet, baffling even the most adept tracker.

**Beastly Behaviours:** Primarily nocturnal. Walks bipedally but runs on all fours. Considered aggressive and dangerous. Has no language but emits terrifying howls and screams that the Guatemalan Chorti Indians call *"Marikonet"*, which means, *"We'll get you"*. Will kidnap unaccompanied women and children on lonely trails, the women are kept captive in its cave for mating (the female Sisemite is reputed to capture men for the same reason) but kills men, especially lone hunters, (according to some legends, to protect the wildlife of the forest) crushing their bones between its teeth in great enjoyment of their flesh and blood. Occasionally leaves little piles of twigs in the forest in an unsuccessful attempt to make fire and will sit next to an abandoned fire until the embers grow cold. Has incredible strength and can even break large trees.

**Hairy Habitat:** Lives in caves and uninhabited hills in the montane forests of North and west Cubulco, Guatemala; Nicaragua; Camasca Caverns and Pico Bonito, Honduras; southern Quintana Roo State, Mexico; and the Montanas Mayas, Belize. It is also regularly identified with another mystery primate that is believed to inhabit the area near the mouth of the Orinoco River in Venezuela and the Guiana Highlands.

**Deadly Diet:** Eats crabs and snails. Legend has it that if a Sisemite kills a man, he will feast upon his flesh.

**Scary Sightings:**

_1898_: Edward Jonathan Hoyt reported killing a large human-ape-like creature, which was about 5 feet tall, after catching it crawling across the end of his bunk, in Honduras, in 1898.

_1920s:_ Richard Oglesby March wrote in _"White Indians of Darien"_ that a man told him in the 1920s that he had killed a human-like _'creature'_ in Central America.

_Unknown Date?:_ Geologist Wendell Skousen said that the people of Cubulco in Baja Verapaz reported very big, wild men that were completely clothed in short, thick, brown, hairy fur, with no necks, small eyes, long arms, and huge hands lived in the mountains and that they left footprints that were twice the size of a man's. Several locals even claimed to have been chased down the mountains by the _'Sisemite'_. Skousen, upon hearing that the creatures travelled both on two legs and sometimes on all fours, initially concluded that they might be bears. However, upon questioning the natives carefully, he wrote: *"it looked like a bear, but it wasn't from the description they gave – no conspicuous snout and no ears."*

1912: The grandfather of Don Manuel Majia ran into a Sisemite on Pico Bonito, Honduras. It walked like a man and was tall and hairy.

1932: While leading an expedition sponsored by the British Museum, Thomas Gann glimpsed a large animal that ran on all fours in a marshy area near the Rio Azul, Quintana Roo State, Mexico. It had black, shaggy fur and a white mane that obscured its face. He thought that it resembled a large ground sloth.

1940s: A police complaint was made in Coban, Guatemala, by Miguel Huzul, who alleged his son-in-law was delinquent for allowing his daughter to be abducted by a Sisemite from their home while he watched helplessly.

**Beastly Evidence:**

As with so many ethno-known creatures believed to inhabit heavily forested regions, evidence, at least for the unprepared, is hard to come by. The leaf-littered forest floor covers the tracks of many animals and unless possessed of those particular skillsets, common to both hunters and zoologists, you are unlikely to be able to differentiate between a trail made by a Sisemite and a tapir. Nevertheless, even with this handy *'get out of jail free card'*, it is unusual that no trace evidence of the beast has been discovered (or reported)? Could there be a socio-superstitious reason for this dearth in physical evidence, or is its lack of international renown tied closely to the deficiency of any recorded evidence pertaining to its existence?

**Beastly Theories:**

*A Tribal Totem:* There is some archaeological evidence attesting to the existence of *El Sisemite'* (at least as a cultural phenomenon) at the ruin of Xunantunich, Belize. But is this Mayan carving, discovered by Cryptozoologist and explorer Lars Thomas, really a biological depiction of a flesh and blood *Sisemite*, or does this carving represent little more than an anthropomorphic forest deity from the pantheon of the god, tzultacah? Perhaps not! In his book, *'Kekchi Religious Beliefs and Lore regarding the Jungle, National Studies. Vol.3 [2]: 34-49'*, 1974; Anthropologist Michael Howard notes that the Kekchi Maya of southern Belize's Toledo District recognises three main classes of forest denizens. The third class consists of known animals that, although they are in a relationship with tzultacah, still belong in the physical world; moreover, along with the Jaguar and the Tapir, the *Sisemite* too, is viewed as a rare animal and not a supernatural being.

*Folklore & Fable:* Regional folklore maintains that as well as his wish to obtain the secret of fire from man, the El Sisemite will steal children to obtain the secret of human speech. And that when a person is captured by an *El Sisemite,* their close family relations are seized with a fit of shivering. Many folkloric fables are told of these kidnappings and their physical effects upon the, as yet unaware, family members of the unfortunate kidnapee.

Such a fable is told of a young couple named Felipe and Rosalia, who lived in a hut in the woods, from whence they could easily harvest maize. Having stepped on a thorn one day previous and being unable to accompany her husband into the field, Rosalia stayed home, with one of their two dogs as a guard, while her husband went to the field. Her husband, Felipe, had not been working long when he was overcome with a dreaded attack of shivering and hastily ran home to his hut to check on his wife. Arriving at their hut, Felipe found his wife gone and their dog cowering in fear. Immediately setting off for the village, he met his wife's family on the road, who had also experienced the shivers and set out to check on their daughter's wellbeing and seeing Felipe on the road, said, *"You have let the Sisemite steal our child, our feelings have told us so."* To which he answered, *"It is as you say."* Against the protestations of Rosalia's family, Felipe was arrested and jailed for the murder of his wife, but when asked what happened to his wife would only answer, "The Sisemite took her, no more than that I know." In a strange and almost unbelievable twist to this tale, several years later, a hunting party set out to capture a strange upright being with long flowing hair that had been spotted on Mount Karachal and ambushed them and captured the creature as it came to drink at a brook. After a violent struggle, they succeeded in subduing the creature and saw a *Sisemite* appear on the hillside flailing his arms wildly and carrying a monkey child on his back. The creature, in rage and desperation, to retrieve his 'bride' hurled great tree limbs at the party, but to no avail. The Wild woman had been captured. The Wild woman was then brought to Felipe to identify whether she could be his missing wife, to which he replied, *"My wife was young and beautiful; the woman I see is old and ugly."* The mysterious Wildwoman could not speak and made no sound. Refusing to eat, she died a few days later.

This tale, like many folktales, seems comprised of more fable than fact and it seems that local superstition was strong enough here to make Felipe's excuse of 'abduction by *El Sisemite'* a plausible defence for a likely marital homicide. The protestations of the 'abducted' woman's family to her husband's imprisonment for murder also support this assertion. It is important to remember that the legend of *El Sisemite'* is based on the folk tales of the Maya and predates the Spanish conquest of 1520-1540. It is also worthwhile noting that legends of male El Sisemite' kidnapping women, and female *El Sisemite'* kidnapping men for procreation, are woven into the fabric and legends of central America and were passed from the Indians to the conquistadors forming the legend as it exists in the cultures of the peoples who inhabit this region today. A region that is filled with towns, ravines, and hills named in honour of *'El Sisimite'* and whose omnipresent folklore is woven into the fabric of the very earth itself can only add a sense of superstitious bias to these extraordinary tales.

*Unknown primate/relict ape:* Similar to the physical ape-like appearance and behavioural characteristics that we have revealed with both the Yeti and the Skunk ape; such as the use of both bipedal and quadrupedal locomotion and in line with the theoretical outline of this chapter, I believe that a reclusive and as yet unknown anthropoid ape, from the same genus as orangutan; whose unfathomable, but not impossible, dispensation throughout Asia and the Americas, might account for these sightings.

Could the vast wilderness of the Florida Everglades hide the existence of an unknown species of Ape?

## SKUNK APE

The Florida Everglades is an ecologically rich and largely impenetrable wilderness, covering an area of approximately 7,800 square miles; comprised of coastal mangroves, sawgrass marshes, and pine Flatwoods that are home to a vast array of animal life. For 200 years, stories have been told by the Seminole Indians about the *Esti Capcaki* (Cannibal Giant), a foul-smelling, reclusive giant that was believed to dwell in the swamplands. A giant that may just have a modern-day descendent in the urbane embodiment of the *Skunk Ape*! And, although fisherman's tales and hunting stories have nourished the legend of this swamp ape since the 1920s, encounters with this pungent beast only started becoming commonplace in the 1970s, as human habitation began to encroach further into the Everglades. Perhaps even disturbing their ancient territories, whose once quiet and generationally walked paths, were now intersected with highways and homes. But, could such a creature remain undiscovered here in the third most populous state in the USA, and if real, is it a beast any different to the Bigfoot of the Pacific Northwest?

**What's in a name?** Named for its objectionable Skunk-like smell. Also known as *Abominable Florida Apeman*, *Abominable Swamp Slob*, *Bardin Booger*, *Sandman*, *Squatttam's Growler,* and *Esti Capcaki ("tall man")* that has been reported by the Seminoles since the 1800s.

**Monstrous Measurements:** Bipedal. 5 – 7 ft. tall. Broad and stocky. Weighing up to 300 pounds. Covered in hair that is longer on its upper body and short on its lower body. Its hair varies in colour, from red, muddy brown to black. Has an ape-like face, similar to, albeit larger than, an orangutan. Small 'hog-like' eyes that are reputed to glow red at night, and small, human-like ears. Sexual dimorphism is apparent in size, with the female being somewhat smaller than the male.

**Terrifying Tracks:** 2 types of tracks are observed; the first type is man-like, five-toed prints, 8-9 inches long, and the second type, exhibiting possible ectrodactyly, in its peculiar three or four-toed prints. Toes appear to dig into the terrain deeply when the animal is walking.

**Beastly Behaviours:** Stays close to the water. Prefers conservation areas, very possibly due to high food sources available at these locales. Uses levees to move about and will happily wade or even swim between islands, if needed. Shy and reclusive. Aggressive to dogs and humans and will even give chase if annoyed. Has a revolting odour that smells like a cross between rotting eggs and the spray of a skunk that is reputed to overpower the senses of anybody unlucky enough to encounter it. Unusually, for an ape, its eyes appear to reflect light, which may indicate that it is a nocturnal animal, although sightings have occurred with similar frequency, in both day and night. Makes distinctive calls that sound like hoots, whistles, and screams. It is fond of fruit and has been observed raiding orchards in human settlements. Will also peel away tree bark to get at the grubs inside. Has been reported to steal pots of unattended lima beans that have been left to soak overnight.

**Deadly Diet:** Omnivorous. Eats fruit, grubs, lima beans, and the livers of livestock and wild game.

**Hairy Habitat:** Reported throughout Florida, Georgia, and Alabama, in the areas bordering the Florida Everglades and Big Cypress National Preserve.

**Scary Sightings:**

*1942:* A man claimed to have encountered a large ape-like creature while driving in Suwannee County, east of Tallahassee. The creature, which came rushing out of the brush line on an isolated road, jumped onto the running board and decided to hitch a ride. The strange animal beat upon his running board and car door for approximately half a mile before leaping from the vehicle and racing back into the woods.

*1957:* Three hunters claimed that their camp was raided by an ape-like creature in the Big Cypress National Preserve, just east of Naples in southwest Florida.

*1963:* Several people witnessed an ape-like creature running across a field, on a ranch, just outside Holopaw. An (unnamed) prominent cattleman and citrus farmer, who was with the group, claimed to have seen the creature from just a few feet away, said that it was definitely some kind of ape.

*1970:* Nathan Russell was walking to a neighbour's house when he came across an ape-like animal sitting in a tree. The creature jumped down and stood staring at him, making a heavy breathing noise while its arms swung in front of it in an ape-like manner. Russell, frozen in fear, stood staring at the animal for about three minutes, and the animal stared back. Russell started to run and the beast gave chase, getting to within 6 feet of him as he reached the safety of his friend's house, upon which the ape-like beast broke off the chase and disappeared. Russell described the creature as being approx. 5 ft 8 in. tall with arms as long as his own. He said: *"It was bald and it had no hair on its neck. From the neck down, there was long hair, and then halfway down, the hair was short like a hound's. It had human-like ears and eyes, like a hog's."*

<u>1971</u>: In February 1971, H.C. Osborn was camped out near an Indian mound in the Fort Lauderdale area when he looked out of his tent and saw an 8 ft tall, 700 pounds, the ape-like creature standing a few feet away. It was covered from head to toe in light-brown hair and smelled dreadful. The following morning, he found five-toed footprints, approx. 17.5 inches long and 11 inches wide.

<u>1971</u>: Encounters with two smelly chimpanzee-like animals in August 1971 caused a local media frenzy in which everyone was talking about the comically nicknamed *'Skunk Apes'*. Later, Henry Ring, Broward County rabies control officer, who was assigned to investigate these strange ape-like appearances, said he found: *"nothing but a bunch of strange tracks, like someone, was walking around on his knuckles".*

<u>1974</u>: Just after midnight on January 9, 1974, Richard Lee Smith hit something with his car near the intersection of U.S. Route 27 and Hollywood Boulevard, on the eastern edge of the Everglades in Pembroke Pines. Smith later told the Florida Highway Patrol that what he at first assumed to be a tall man in dark clothing hauled itself up off of the road to reveal a seven to the eight-foot-tall, hairy beast, which charged toward his car, roaring. Terrified, Smith floored the accelerator and took off. Hours later, police received several reports from drivers who claimed to have seen a giant limping along U.S. Route 27. The officers who were dispatched to investigate the report at 2:12 am witnessed a huge, hairy man limping along the road near Hialeah Gardens, a few miles away from the scene of the accident. As they approached, the creature disappeared into the brush. The following morning, police searched the swamp by helicopter but found no trace of the strange creature.

*1974:* Palm Beach County Sheriff Deputy Marvin Lewis claimed that he and fellow deputy Ernie Miller had shot a tall, hairy creature just west of Lantana. Deputy Lewis described the large creature grunting before disappearing into the swamp and said: *"I know it exists!"*

*1974:* In June 1974, Lake Worth farmer Buddy Sterrett was terrified to witness a Skunk Ape lift up one of his hogs that weighed over a hundred pounds and rip it to pieces.

*1974:* In September 1974, Cary Kantor, a Security Guard in Wellington, near, Palm Beach claimed to have shot a Skunk Ape that approached him out of the woods and ignored his commands to stop. The injured creature ran back into the brush.

*1975:* In June 1975, twelve-year-old Ronnie Steves was awoken by sounds of a disturbance coming from his duck pen outside his home, east of Venice, Florida. Stepping outside to investigate, he was confronted with the sight of a 6ft tall, dark, ape-like animal running away. Later, 8 inch long tracks with a discernible arch were found on the property.

*1976:* At approximately 2:00 AM in July 1976, Martha Cowell witnessed a large hairy ape-like creature squatting beside the road while driving on Taylor Road in Port Orange, Florida. She said of her encounter with the beast:

*"...the headlights of the car I was riding in lit up a figure on the side of the roadway, which caught my eye. We were traveling quite slowly at the time and from the moment I first spotted the figure, my eyes didn't leave it. The closer we got to the figure, the slower we went. After realizing it was not a person, I had trouble comprehending exactly what I was seeing, but what I did see was a creature squatted on the side of the road, just at the edge of the roadway. It was squatted and picking something from the ground and placed what it was picking in its other hand folded up against its body. From time to time, it would taste or smell what it was picking. When the creature realized we were closely approaching, it lifted its head and looked directly at me. Our eyes locked and didn't break until we decided to move it*

*and get out of there. The creature didn't look angry or frightened; it looked more quizzical than anything else. It didn't attempt to move, walk or run away. I would estimate that if standing, the creature would have stood approximately 7 to 7 ½ feet tall and weighed between 400 and 500 pounds, although all of its hair may have made it look heavier than it was. It was covered with long, somewhat wavy and matted, Irish-setter red-colored hair. The hair on its chest wasn't as thick and long as on the rest of its body. Hair covered the face, but the hair on the face was short. No hair covered the palms of the hands. It had fingers and from what I could see toes as well. The head was round and the top of the head had long hair like on other parts of the body. After realizing what we were looking at, we quickly drove away, I think more confused than anything else. I am certain this couldn't have been a person. It was too real and too large!"*

<u>July 14<sup>th</sup>, 1977:</u> On July 14<sup>th</sup>, 1977, Vietnam veteran and former police officer Charles Stoeckman and his thirteen-year-old son Charlie were collecting bottles in the thick mangroves behind their home in Key Largo when they encountered an enormous ape-like creature, eight or nine feet in height. Stoeckman said: *"It had a huge head and shoulders. Long fur all over and it and stank like a dirty wet dog. The noise he made was a high-pitched wailing."* In an effort to discourage another visit from the creature, Stoeckman cleared the brush away from around his home, although he was unable to get rid of the terrible smell of the creature, which hung around for several nights. Later, the creature made another visit to the property and was seen by Mrs Stoeckman from her bedroom window, crouching just 30 feet away. Mrs Stoeckman, terrified, fled the property with her three children and called the police for assistance. Monroe County Sheriff Deputy Bill Haase, Florida marine Patrol Captain Jack Gillen, and Sgt Randall Chinn from the plantation Key Substation were later sent to investigate the strange occurrences at the property, said: *"There is definitely a problem there. These people are truly scared to death. "* Charles Stoeckman spent the following month alone at the house with his shotgun.

*1977:* Two workers notified Palm Beach County Animal Control that they had witnessed a seven-foot-tall, hairy, ape-like creature drinking from a lake on a golf course near Delray Beach.

*1982:* On a late afternoon, in the winter of 1982, Emma Carroll and her husband witnessed a skunk ape while driving along an isolated stretch of road in Montura Estates, Clewiston, Hendry County, Florida. The creature, which had emerged from a wooded area farther up the road on Hacienda Avenue, was travelling in the same direction as the couple, with its back to them. The couple, who initially had taken the figure to be that of a walker, was stunned to see, as they slowed to turn on Hunting Cub Avenue, a figure, approximately 6 ft tall, with a round head, around 300 lbs in weight and completely covered in dark hair, 4 – 6 inches in length.

*1983:* On a sunny afternoon in 1983, researcher Dan Jackson was hog hunting in Bayhead Swamp, Collier County, Florida, when he came face to face with a Skunk Ape. Jackson was tracking a group of hogs and, seeing a large, dark object in the distance, thought he had come across a bear. Stooping down low in the saw grass, he began stalking the animal and when he got within 20- 30 yards of the creature, he suddenly rose up to fire, only to see the creature rise up and turn to look at him. Realizing suddenly that he was not looking at a bear, but a hairy ape-man, Jackson, frozen solid and eyes locked with the creature, forgetting about his gun and watched the creature turn and walk back into the swamp, on two legs. He said, *"After I got my breathing back to normal, I went to the spot where he had been standing. There was a terrible odour like rotten eggs and sulphur and the grass was bent down where he had been. By looking at how low the tree limbs were and remembering where his head came to I was able to determine that he was approximately 6 and a half to 7 feet tall. I estimated his weight at 350- 400 lbs, solidly built. His head seemed to have a crest, I could not see the face well because of the sun."*

*1984/85:* Two friends were horseback riding alongside the Florida East Coast Railroad tracks when they noticed a dead animal smell and heard some branches breaking in the woods, which they dismissed as being a hog. Soon after, their horses started snorting and rearing and they were unable to calm them until they passed the tracks. Hearing the sounds of someone walking up the rocks at the side of the tracks, they looked back at the area they had just passed and were stunned to see a large, hairy figure standing in the middle of the tracks, just 150 yards away. One of the witnesses said: *"It was in sort of a crouched position but not all the way down, like it just saw us and froze and stared at us. What I saw was slim and covered in reddish-brown hair. It had long arms and I could see the eyes a little, it was at least 6½ feet tall and around 250 lbs. or better with no neck. It was getting dark out so we couldn't see any detail on the face. All the time that we saw it we had to fight with the horses to keep them under control. They didn't want any part of whatever it was, and neither did we. So we got out of there and I never went back riding there again. It wasn't a bear. And it wasn't a man unless he was covered in hair from head to toe."*

<u>1993:</u> On November 1993, at 4:00 AM Alan Mercier, was driving his paper route near the Econ River, Lake Underhill Road, Orange County, Florida when he observed a large figure going through some trash cans at the side of the road.

He said: *"It was trash night and the sides of the road were covered with people's weekly garbage. As I came down the highway heading east, I saw something to my right (the south side of the highway) Going through some trash cans. I don't drive that fast because I have to throw the papers from my pickup truck window. I saw this thing going through the garbage and it hears me coming, so it stops what it was doing, turns around, and starts to run across the road in front of me heading towards the woods on the other side, but it's not really running it's like taking these giant strides or something. I noticed that its wrists or whatever hang lower than humans do, like well below its knees. It almost looked like its arms were longer. I hit my high beams and it stops for just a few seconds, then continues across the road and disappears into the brush. I pulled over to give chase and then chickened out and left, but not before I made a mental note in my head of* the location so I could come back the next day to look for footprints, which I never found because of the rain the night before."

"...I got a fairly good look at the creature as it crossed the road in front of me. When I hit my high beams, it stopped like a deer frozen in headlights. It threw its left arm up in front of its face as to shield its eyes from the bright lights. That is when I noticed the breasts. It must have been a female. It was covered with long reddish/brown fur that looked matted like a wet dog is the only way I can describe it. I can only guess the height, but it didn't seem that tall, maybe 5-6 ft. tall. The thing that I remember most is that when it stopped in the middle of the road and turned towards me was, and this is strange - it didn't just turn its head it turned its whole body as if it wasn't capable of just turning its head - and that's when I saw the breasts and this is weird the fur on the front was either a lighter colour or not as dense as elsewhere; I noticed not only the breasts but the arm that was up shielding its eyes had no hair on its palm, You could see the skin or whatever. I guessed that it was either a female or a young girl because of its height and breasts. I wasn't the only one to see it. Other cars were pulling over and stopping to look at it. Out of fear of ridicule, I only told relatives."

1997: On Wednesday, July 16th, 1997, at 2 PM Steve Goodbread, a guide for Pelican Tours and thirty tourists witnessed a Skunk Ape along Turner River Road in Big Cypress, just east of Ochopee. Steve and his passengers saw, not seventy yards away, a large, hairy creature, around seven feet tall and covered in brown hair, standing on two legs behind some brush. The creature, which appeared agitated by their crowd of onlookers, was rocking back and forth and shaking the bushes. Goodbread tried to convince one of the passengers who had a telephoto lens camera to exit the bus and snap a photo, but she refused. All in all, Goodbread had observed the animal for 15 minutes before driving away, with the creature still in sight, partially hidden in the thick brush. Goodbread later admitted to having been quite shaken by the experience and refused to exploit the encounter to promote his tours.

*1997:* On July 18th, 1997, Everglades Day Safari tour guide Dow Roland and half a dozen tourists saw a reddish-brown Skunk ape near Turner River Road. Unconvinced by the behaviour and appearance of the creature, Roland and several of the tourists on board thought that it might have been a man in an ape suit.

*1997:* At 7:45 AM, on July 21st, 1997, Jan Brock, a real estate agent, saw an animal that she described as: *"Very shaggy looking, maybe six-and-a-half or seven-feet-tall..."* cross the road, while she was driving on Burns Road, Big Cypress. No more than fifteen minutes later, Ochopee Fire Chief, Vince Doerr, managed to capture a photo of the creature as it walked into the forest near his home. He said: *"At first, I thought it was a bear, but bears don't stay up on two legs the way this thing was."*

*1998:* Skunk Ape researcher, David Shealy, claimed to have taken 27 photos of a Skunk Ape after spending 8 months sitting in a tree in his backyard in Coolie County, Florida. Later, in July 2000, Shealy would claim to have captured film of the ape-like creature loping through a field near Ochopee, Florida.

*2000:* In July 2000, a 7-year-old boy and his brother were playing in their grandmother's backyard when they were frightened by the sight of a 'Bigfoot' standing in the old wooded orange grove that adjoined the property in Polk County, Florida. The older boy, who at first turned to his brother and said: *"run!"* Later, described the creature he encountered, saying: *"...the Bigfoot was very big and tall; hairy all over; looked human but it wasn't. No clothes, just hair all the way down to the ground. I couldn't see his feet. He or It stood there with its arms waving or moving about. Almost like he was mad about something. I only looked for a few seconds because I was too scared to look for long."* Later, accompanied by his Grandfather and his cousin, the young boy got up the courage to investigate the area where he had seen the creature, but apart from finding the remnants of half-eaten oranges, there was no trace of the creature that had frightened him.

*2000:* In September or October 2000, a woman took two photos of an orangutan-like creature seen in a kneeling position in her backyard, near the Myakka River, Florida. She estimated it was 7 ft tall. It had a strong odour and was making *"woomp"* noises. The photos were sent anonymously to the Sarasota County Sheriff's Office since the woman did not want anybody on her property.

2003: At 5:00 PM, in November of 2003, a dog walker out for a stroll by a pond near Old Moultrie Road encountered a terrible smell that was assumed to be coming from some dead animal nearby. This smell was followed by the sound of branches breaking in the adjacent woods and the dog, suddenly refusing to walk any further. Ahead on a dirt path that leads to a pond and train tracks was a figure, approximately 7 to 8 feet tall and covered in black or dark coloured hair. The upright beast appeared to be navigating its way through a muddy area and took no notice of the walker or the dog.

**Beastly Evidence:**

Photography & Film:

*Shealy Footage:* Dave Shealy claims to have seen one of the hairy manlike beasts as a child and again on three other separate occasions, including in the year 2000, when he captured video of the creature in an open field. Shealy said of the footage: *"I was actually looking for deer that day. I wanted to get some photographs for some hunting friends of mine. That's when I heard something moving in the water. It was running, it wasn't running like a deer or a bear,"* Many critics have pointed out that the footage, which due to its poor quality is at best ambiguous, looks like someone wading through the swamp in a gorilla suit.

*Myakka Skunk Ape:* On December 29th, 2000, the Sarasota Sheriff's Department received an anonymous letter with two enclosed photos taken by an elderly lady, who claimed to have photographed a large *'orangutan'* that had been stealing apples off her back porch. Her letter, which I have reproduced in full below, is quite likely, the single most important illustration of the invaluable contribution that the 'antagonistic witness' can make to the field of cryptozoology. Within its text, she has established that

1: she is oblivious to the term *Bigfoot*, or more importantly here, its local personification of the *Skunk Ape*.

2: That, by repeatedly calling the animal an 'orangutan', which it clearly is not, that she is using familiar features she has observed on the animal in conjunction with her own comparative mental library to identify an animal she has never seen before.

3: That, she is indeed an elderly lady and not some savvy cryptozoologist trying to hoax the local Sheriff's department.

This last detail is, in fact, the most demonstrable; she kvetches and complains like only an old person could, saying things like: *"...I'm a senior citizen and if this animal had come out of the hedge roll after me there wasn't a thing I could have done about it."* Or, *"...I'm concerned because my grandchildren like to come down and explore in my back yard."* And, *"...Why haven't people been told that an animal of this size is loose?"* And finally, my favourite, *"...I saw on the news that monkeys that get loose can carry Hepatitis."* If only every *Bigfoot* encounter was reported by an old lady who'd never heard its name... Cryptozoology would certainly be a nicer place!

*"Dear Sir or Madam,*

*Enclosed, please find some pictures I took in late September or early October 2000. My husband says he thinks it is an orangutan. Is someone missing an orangutan? It is hard to judge from the photos just how big this Orangutan really is. It is in a crouching position in the middle of standing up from where it is sitting. It froze as soon as the flash went off. I didn't even see it as I took the first picture as it was so dark. As soon as the flash went off for the second time, it stood up and started to move. I then heard the orangutan walk off into the brushes. From Where I was standing, I judge it as being about six and a half to seven feet tall in a kneeling position. As soon as I realised how close it was I got back in the house. It had an awful smell that lasted well after it had left my yard. The orangutan was making deep "woomp" noises. It sounded much farther away than it turned out to be. If I had known it was close to the hedge roll as it was I wouldn't have walked up as close as I did. I'm a senior citizen and if this animal had come out of the hedge roll after me there wasn't a thing I could have done about it. I was about 10 feet away from it when it stood up. I'm concerned because my grandchildren like to come down and explore in my backyard. An animal this big could hurt someone seriously. For two nights prior. It had been taking apples that my daughter brought down from up north, off of our back porch. These pictures were taken on the third night it had raided my apples. It only came back one more night after that and took some apples that my husband had left out in order to get a better look at it. We left out four apples. I cut two of them in half. The orangutan only took the whole apples. We didn't see it take them, we waited up but eventually had to go to bed. We got a dog back there now and as far as we can tell the orangutan hasn't been back.*

*Please find out where this animal came from and who it belongs to, it shouldn't be loose like this, someone will get hurt. I called a friend that used to work with animal control back up north and he told us to call the police. I don't want any fuss or people with guns traipsing around behind our house. We live near I75 and I'm afraid this orangutan could cause a serious accident if someone hit it. I once hit a deer that wasn't even a quarter of the size of this animal and totalled my car. At the very least, this animal belongs in a place like Bush Gardens where it can be looked after properly. Why haven't people been told that an animal this size is loose? How are people to know how dangerous this could be? If I had known an animal like this was loose, I wouldn't have approached it. I saw on the news that monkeys that get loose can carry Hepatitis and are very dangerous. Please look after this situation. I don't want my backyard to turn into someone else's circus.*

*God Bless,*

*I prefer to remain anonymous"*

*One of two photos of the creature that has since become known as the Myakka Skunk Ape. Even at first glance, it certainly becomes clear why our witness identified an 'orangutan' as the closest match to this curious beast. Yet, in its size, colouration, elongated fangs, and especially its glowing eyes, if genuine, it can only be representative of an, as yet unknown, ape species.*

*Bark breaking Ape:* On October 28, 2013, a video titled *"I think I saw a skunk ape, please help"* was uploaded to YouTube. It depicts a large, hairy humanoid creature crouching in the water and pulling bark off a tree with ease. Several expert debunkers and videographers analysed the footage and concluded that the humanoid figure, the back, arms, and head of which can be seen ripping bark off a tree in the footage, resembles superficially at least a large ape-like animal.

*Lettuce Lake Ape:* In 2015, kayaker, Matthew McKamey, captured video of an upright, ape-like creature wading through a cypress marsh at Lettuce Lake Park in Hillsborough County, Florida, The movement of the creature in his footage is remarkably fluid, as the swamp-like conditions, not to mention the alligator invested waters, make a hoax in this instance, highly unlikely.

*Tracks:* Over the years, several tracks have been recorded, and some have been cast, although perhaps due to the swampy conditions, they are found less frequently than those of their northern relative Bigfoot. And even though no tracks have been cast in the last twenty years or so, those samples that we do have, paint a peculiar picture of a three to four-toed bipedal animal, possibly descended from a limited family group with an inherited predisposition to Syndactyly.

*Bill of Rights:* Reported sightings of the Skunk Ape became so frequent that in 1977, state legislators introduced House bill 1664 (H.B.1664), which made it illegal to *"take, possess, harm or molest anthropoid or humanoid animals."* The bill, however, sadly failed to pass.

*Thermal Video:* In 2016, David Lauer of the Apalachicola Skunk Ape Project claimed to have captured the beast on thermal video at one of the project's habituation sites, where footprints had been found several weeks before.

**Beastly Theories:**

*Napes:* The term *'Napes'* meaning, *'North American Apes'*, was first coined by the cryptozoologist, Loren Coleman in 1962, inspired by a curious track he discovered (and cast) in a dry creek bed of Steven's Creek, near Decatur, Illinois. However, some researchers have doubted the veracity of this track, sighting several physiological red flags, such as the lack of dermal ridges and absent toe extension, even going as far as alleging that the cast is a composite of Coleman's own foot, with the big toe removed and his thumb inserted!

*Monkeying Around:* There's are several primate facilities in Florida, including one in Hendry County and a Sanctuary (The Centre for Great Apes) in Wauchula. Over the years, many rumours have circulated that several 'escapees' have made their way from centres such as these, private collections and the once-popular travelling circuses that frequented the state in the early 20th century, to the

Florida Everglades, where their occasional brief interactions with humans have generated the modern-day sightings of the Skunk Ape. Could the 'loss' of a large ape, like an orangutan or chimpanzee, have been covered up in the past to avoid bad publicity? With perhaps those responsible hoping that the animals would melt into the vast wilderness of the state? Florida is, after all, the invasive species capital of the World, and what's one more out of place animal against a multitude of the other troublesome types that have been released into this productive ecosystem?

*Black Bear:* Most sightings of the Skunk Ape, like Bigfoot sightings, can be dismissed as misidentification of the black bear. A black bear can stand upright and even walk on two legs for a short distance, and under the right conditions, even appear like another animal entirely. Bears are also known to rummage through garbage bins, which could explain the rotten smell that is so commonly associated with the Skunk Ape.

*Mercantile Monster Hunters:* It can easily be argued that many researchers have 'something to sell' and ergo' cannot be trusted to view evidence impartially due to their vested interest in its veracity. This certainly does pose a problem in the field of cryptozoology and is, sadly, not one easily solved. After all, cryptozoology isn't what one would refer to as a 'high paying profession' when or if it ever pays at all. And, since most great researchers are dedicated to the hunt, full time, the question of fiscal fortitude for those of us who are not 'men of leisure', so to speak, is often a troubling issue.

*Drought & Desperation:* Some researchers have hypothesised that the 'outbreak' of Skunk Ape sightings may have coincided with record drought conditions that the Everglades were experiencing in 1974. Could these conditions have led to less caution among the Skunk Ape population, prompting them to engage in risky behaviour in search of food? In India, for example, there are always higher recorded human confrontations with leopards during the worst drought years.

# LITTLEFOOT

*"The less common, smaller form, is a type of small upright ape or proto-pygmy, standing between 2 ft 6 in – 5 ft 6 in tall; some species of which, in the former, bear some resemblance to the ape-like Orang pendek of Sumatra and in the latter, the pygmy-like Ebu Gogo of Flores. Its feet are small and exhibit an ape-like divergent medial toe, with a rounded, tapered heel."*

Could small rivers and streams provide valuable protein sources like fish, lizards, insects, and frogs to feed a population of diminutive yeti-like creatures known locally as 'Teh-lma?'

## TEH-LMA
### (The Little Yeti)

Did the renowned zoologist and explorer Gerald Russell (and his Sherpa guide, Da Temba) discover evidence for the existence of a second, smaller *Yeti* species, called *Teh-Lma,* in the Choyang Khola Valley, Nepal, in 1958? Russell, who had been a member of the 1954 *Daily Mail Yeti Expedition*, was also recruited to the 1958 *Slick-Johnson Snowman Expedition*; along with big game hunters, Peter and Bryan Byrne, still-life photographer George Holton, Filmographer and mountaineer, Norman G. Dyhrenfurth, and Captain Pushkar Shamshere, of the Nepalese Government; and, when the group had split up to reconnoitre various *Yeti* hotspots throughout the region, Russell and his Sherpa, Da Temba, were assigned to explore the Chhoyang River (Khola) area. News of his subsequent discovery of tracks and his Sherpa's encounter with the creature caused great excitement within the zoological community, at that time, inspiring many pundits to predict that the *Teh-lma* would soon join the ranks of the Giant panda and Komodo dragon as a formerly ethno-known creature of cryptozoological folklore. But, could this animal really belong to an altogether distinct species of *Relict Ape*, living alongside the larger *Yeti*, or does the natural development that occurs in all species (i.e., – we start small and become big) explain away the occurrence of this diminutive snowman?

**What's in a name?** *Teh-lma* is a Sino-Tibetan (Sherpa) word, meaning *"little thing,"* Colloquially referred to as the *"Little Yeti"*. Also known as *Pyar-them* and *Thelma*.

**Monstrous Measurements:** Bipedal. 4-5ft tall. Stocky, with hunched shoulders. Covered in reddish-brown or greyish brown short hair. Flat, hairless face with large human-like teeth. Large head with a sloping forehead and a sharply pointed sagittal crest that has a slight mane.

**Terrifying Tracks:** 5 inches in length.

**Beastly Behaviours:** Nocturnal. Walks and runs on its hind legs. Makes a hooting noise. Constructs nests out of leaves and twigs on the forest floor.

**Deadly Diet:** It is a little-known 'fact' that there are thought to be two types of *Yeti*. A small dangerous variety that feeds on insects and frogs, small mammals, leaves (and *'allegedly'* humans), and a larger, more harmless variety that feeds on potatoes, saline moss, and occasionally, yaks. The *Teh-lma*, it seems, belongs to the more dangerous smaller variety!

**Hairy Habitat:** Occupies the forests below the snow line in the steamy mountain valleys of Nepal and Sikkim; eastern Nepal; Bhutan; south-eastern Tibet and Sikkim State, India.

**Scary Sightings:**

*1958:* In April 1958, having heard from a local man that a small Yeti was making nightly visits to a stream near Walung in the Chhoyang River valley, Sherpa De Temba, along with another Sherpa, organised a night vigil at the alleged locale. After finding a wet footprint along the river, they saw the creature about 30 yards away. When a flashlight was aimed at its face. The creature took a step towards the two men, who fled. The flowing morning expedition leader, Gerald Russell, checked the area and found small *Yeti* tracks.

**Beastly Evidence:**

*Hair, Scat, Tracks:* In 1954, The Daily Mail funded an expedition to the Himalayas with the express goal of capturing a specimen of the smaller species of *Yeti*, known as the *Teh-lma*, to determine whether this creature was, in fact, a missing link. Indeed, the confidence in the team they had put together for this expedition, which included - Gerald Russell (Zoologist and 'Discoverer' of the Giant Panda), Dr Biswamoy Biswas (curator of mammals department at the Calcutta Museum), Tom Stobart (Cameraman/Producer of *The Conquest of Everest*), John Angelo "Jacko" Jackson (intrepid mountaineer), Stanley Jeeves (wildlife photographer), Charles Stonor (anthropologist), and Ralph Izzard (reporter and reputed inspiration for Ian Fleming's world-renowned spy, James Bond) - was such, that they really believed that they might capture both a male and female specimen of this rare and elusive animal. Sadly, while the expedition certainly produced evidence, such as hair, scat, footprints, and sightings, a specimen was never obtained.

*Bumling Tracks:* Members of the 1958 Slick-Johnson snowman expedition encountered the small tracks of a *Teh-lma* at an altitude of 8,500 ft, near Bumling, in North-eastern Nepal.

*Byrne Tracks:* Peter and Bryan Byrne found a set of human-like footprints in the gravel next to the stream, near a half-eaten frog later in the spring.

*Scat the Species!* In 1959, A. Fain of the Antwerp Tropical Medicine Institute analysed the alleged scat of a *Teh-lma* (found by the Byrne brothers) but could not identify the species. A second sample (from the same find) was examined by Anne Porter of the Zoological Society of London, who found several hairs and tissue belonging to undetermined mammalian and invertebrate species.

**Beastly Theories!**

*The Hoolock Gibbon:* is a little less than 3ft tall when standing and could, especially when viewed in an erect posture at night, be mistakenly perceived as having some of the characteristics attributed to the *Teh-lma*. Although it should be noted that this gibbon has distinctive white brows and is only found in Lowland forests native to eastern Bangladesh, Northeast India, Myanmar, and Southwest China. The Hoolock Gibbon's diet is also inconsistent with that of the *Teh-lma*, in that it primarily feeds upon fruits, insects, and leaves. The species is diurnal, not nocturnal like the *Teh-lma,* and leads an arboreal lifestyle, in which it can be observed with its monogamous partner, loudly staking its territory while swinging through the trees.

*Could an unknown regional variety of Hoolock Gibbon have adapted to the environmental sparsity of the Himalayas?*

*The Sloth Bear:* The Sloth Bear is 4 – 5 ft. long and has black fur with a distinctive white mark on its chest, which forms the shape of a letter U or V. Its diet consists of insects, honey, carrion, fruit, flowers, and sugarcane. It is found in a wide range of habitats; throughout India, Nepal, Bhutan, and Sri Lanka.

*Unknown Relict Ape Species:* Researchers of unknown animals often fall into the trap of believing that only one unknown species could inhabit any geographic region or area of cryptozoological interest. And yet, what we find in nature, is that a habitat that is productive enough to support the needs of one species is often able to support that of another; either of a similar genus, as we observe with brown bears and black bears, or that has similar habitational requirements, like sharks and dolphins. And, it is this piecemeal common-sense approach to cryptids that we will use here. Theorising that where the large version of this species, the *Yeti*, has seemingly developed a diet that would seem most accessible at the elevated heights; i.e., potatoes, saline moss and occasionally, yaks, etc. Its smaller counterpart, the *Teh-lma's*, diet of insects and frogs, would be more readily available in its reputed river and forest haunts below the snow line.

The Nimbin Valley and Nimbin Rocks in the Northern Rivers of New
South Wales, Australia.

## NIMBINJEE

Nimbin is a village in the Northern Rivers area of New South
Wales and is an area of cultural and spiritual significance to
the Indigenous Bundjalung people, as well as being part of the wider
'Rainbow Region'. It is also an area where many progressive initiatives
such as permaculture and cannabis culture have been trialled among
its broadminded population before being imposed upon the rest of
Australian society. A place that has often been described in the
Australian media as a social experiment or 'hippie heaven.' The
name Nimbin comes from the Whiyabul clan whose Dreamtime epic
tells of the Nimbinjee spirit people protecting the area, and it these
spirit people with whom we are concerned in this chapter; as we seek
ripostes to the mysterious sightings of little hairy men throughout
Nimbin and the wider region. Are these little hairy men spirits that
have sprung from the Dreamtime or from a homemade bong?
Alternatively, could they represent a species of undiscovered primate

that was erroneously inculcated into the spirit world in a time when superstition and not science ordered the natural world?

**What's in a name?** *Nimbinjee* comes from the Aboriginal Whiyabul clan, who speak of the *Nimbinjee* spirit originating in the Dreamtime. Also known as *Njimbun, Njimbin, Nimbunj,* and *Junjudee,* which mostly correspond with the identification of a *"Little Hairy Man".*

**Monstrous Measurements:** Bipedal and quadrupedal. 3 – 4 ft tall. Gibbon-like appearance. Completely covered with dark brown or reddish hair, except for the area around its eyes. Roundhead with a flat face, round human-like eyes with a distinctive eye-brow ridge. Skin is grey-brown or red. Limbs are long. No tail.

**Terrifying Tracks:** Both 3 toed and 5 toed tracks have been recorded. 5 toed tracks appear similar to those of a 5-year-old child, except that every toe is equal in size to the big toe.

**Beastly Behaviours:** Runs on two legs, and also on all fours, like that of an ape knuckle-walking. Incredibly strong, considering its small stature. It is reputed to wrestle humans for fun. Makes calls or barks in groups of three that sound like: *"arroo, ARROO, arroo"* or *"gu-gu-gu-gu."* Also makes chirping noises like a bird and cackles like a chicken!

**Deadly Diet:** According to Aboriginal lore, the *"Little Fella"* (as opposed to the *"Big Fella" - Yowie*) is a meat-eater!

**Hairy Habitat:** Reported in one of its many appellations throughout the Great Dividing Range of New South Wales and Queensland, Eastern Victoria; Northern territory north of the Roper River and the Western Australia coast, between Shark Bay and Broome.

**Scary Sightings:**

<u>1968:</u> A man named George Gray was attacked by a *"Little Hairy Man"* while he slept in a small hut surrounded by bushland, in the rural saw-milling settlement of Kookaburra on the Carrai Plateau, in northern NSW. He awoke to find the creature pressing down on him.

Gray said that he was certain that the creature was not angry and that it *"just wanted to wrestle with him,"* which it proceeded to do for the next ten minutes, first on the bed, then the floor, after which it dragged him towards the door several times before releasing him and running out away. Gray described the creature as being *"broad and powerful"*, just over a metre in height, covered in grey hair with a hairless, copper-coloured face, a big flat nose, and round human-like eyes.

<u>1979</u>: In March 1979, Michael Mangan was parked at night on Tower Hill at Charters Towers in Queensland when a 3.2 ft tall animal smashed the window on the passenger side of his car and leered in at him. He described the creature to the police, saying he saw *"a black hairy face at the window...The face was small and drawn back like that of an ape"*.

<u>1994</u>: A retired timber worker named Paddy O'Conner claimed that two small hominins approached his camp at dawn, near Carnarvon Gorge in 1994, and chirped like birds while pointing at his billycan.

*Unknown Date:* Nathan Moilan reported a little hairy man encounter that his father and uncle had while working as timbermen. One night they were sleeping in their bush hut (comprised of 3 separate rooms) when a little hairy man entered the hut and attacked his uncle as he lay on his bed. Nathan's father rushed in when he heard cries for help and together, they wrestled with and finally overpowered the creature, which suddenly broke free and jumped straight out of the window. They both described the creature being as extraordinarily strong.

<u>1996</u>: Lynn Clark and her 12-year-old son Joshua were on their way to a birthday party on March 23, 1996, and had decided to walk up the 0.62-mile driveway to the house as they were concerned that their old car might not make the climb up the steep hill. Halfway up the driveway, 12-year-old Joshua was surprised to see what he assumed to be one of the children from the party dressed in dark clothing and dashing down the steep slope through the dep clumps of kangaroo

grass beside the concrete path. Expecting to see the child trip, he was surprised when it stopped suddenly, about 32 feet away, and stared. Joshua noticed that it had a black-skinned face and was covered in dark fur. The 'child' then dropped down onto all fours and continued to walk slowly downhill on its knuckles before standing up on two legs again and dashing off downhill. Lynn, Joshua's mum, described seeing a dark-furred animal with no tail, running on two legs, like a person.

Joshua Clark Eyewitness Sketch.

*1998:* A man named Damien encountered a little hairy man while prospecting alone for semi-precious stones along the headwaters of Wilson's Creek, on the eastern escarpment of Mount Jerusalem. Feeling as though he was being watched, he looked around and saw a little hairy man standing beside a tree, approximately 100 feet away. After they both spent a short period of time staring at one another, the little man stepped back behind the tree and disappeared. Damien described the creature as being 4 foot tall and covered in black hair, except for the area around its eyes, which had greyish-brown skin and distinctive eye-brow ridges.

*2000:* A woman and her daughter encountered an animal while riding their horses on Gwynne's Road at Jiggi. The creature, which was standing approximately 65 feet away, was 4 ft 9 inches tall, had a slim gibbon-like body, and was covered in thick, deep reddish-brown fur. It ran off on two legs, across a paddock, and disappeared into some trees.

*2018:* A man encountered three bipedal, gibbon-like animals with flat faces while herding cattle on horseback with his dogs in Crabbes Creek Valley. The three little hairy men varied in height, with the tallest standing at 3 ft 9 inches, the next 3ft 2 inches, and the smallest, 2 ft 9 inches. The tallest of the three creatures was covered in black fur, while the two smaller ones were covered in light brown fur.

*2020:* Gary Opit has been logging his experiences with the *"Little Hairy Man"* for several years, now; the first of which was an audio encounter that took place in 1996, behind a house that he was renting on the slopes of the Koonyum Range (at an elevation of 656 feet) at Main Arm in north-eastern NSW, and which may constitute one of the most detailed records of the territorial calls of the Nimbinjee, in which he heard 90 bark-like calls in succession, which sounded like, *"arroo, ARROO, arroo"*, followed by a guttural sound like, *"gu-gu-gu-gu."* An unbelievably distinctive and easily trackable behaviour trait, if the creature is truly territorial and one which the author hopes will, in time, reveal the true genus of this hidden Hylobatid. Most recently, during the Christmas of 2020, Gary's daughter and her fiancée had a visual and audio encounter with two Nimbinjee at his home. Gary said of their encounter: *"Our daughter and her partner when staying with us over Christmas saw a Nimbinjee or little hairy man jump up onto our roof at 2 am and from their description was exactly like a gibbon in all respects. Of course, there are no gibbons here and there have never been nocturnal and terrestrial gibbons known. They said that there were two of them calling quietly to one another. We have an audio recording of the calls and a coloured illustration of what they saw."*

| *Matteo Camelo: Eyewitness sketch:*

**Beastly Evidence:**

*Tracks:* On Saturday, August 9, 2008, Ray Westrap & Gary Opit found small child-sized footprints that intersected a wallaby onto the Jones Road track before crossing through a large puddle.

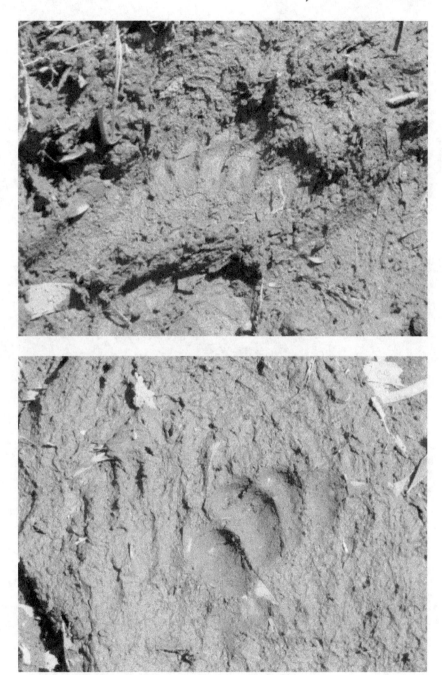

| Nimbinjee Footprints, Knuckle & Finger Prints. Photo by Gary Opit

*Tepee, Tracks, and a Handprint:* On September 12, 2008, Gary Opit found a small stick structure or tepee in the same area, where he had photographed the small footprints several days previous. Besides the small structure were more small 'footprints'. The tracks, which extended for approximately 9.8 feet and had walked in and out of a muddy rut several times, appeared to show a considerable amount of activity around the structure. The footprints were human-like, approximately 5 inches in length. Beside them was what can only be described as a hand-print.

Nimbinjee Footprints around stick structure. Photo by Gary Opit

Audio recordings:

*Blackbutt Calls:* Annett McClean recorded an unusual vocalisation recording at her property in Blackbutt, North Queensland, in what constitutes 50 acres of undisturbed dry sclerophyll eucalypt forest that abuts the rear of her property. Many wildlife experts tried and failed to identify the strange calls, which some have proposed could be the territorial calls of the *"Nimbinjee."*

*Opit Calls:* Gary Opit's daughter and her partner saw a gibbon-like primate at his property in Christmas of 2020 and managed to record the calls it was making with another animal that was hidden somewhere up in the trees.

**Beastly Theories!**

*Homo Floresiensis:* The discovery of Homo Floresiensis in a cave at Lian Bua, Flores, Indonesia, has led many researchers to conclude that the ancient legends and reports of little hairy men that are found around the globe have found a fossil friend in this comparatively recently extinct human *Hobbit* and one can see why they would be happy with its discovery. Standing at just 3.2 feet high and weighing approximately 55 pounds, this prospective pygmy form of Homo erectus represents a smoking gun in the search for Littlefolk and adds weight to what otherwise would have remained the forgotten folklore and fable of our superstitious forebears.

*Cave where the remains of Homo Floresiensis were discovered in 2003, Lian Bua, Flores, Indonesia.*

*Unknown Gibbon Species:* The little hairy man is often described as being like a large gibbon. Indeed, its territorial calls, which (apart from the fact that they are made at night) serve a similar function in their far-reaching, loud, and repetitive form and which are in effect a warning to other territory-holding adults, would seem to confirm this theory. Could a large, nocturnal, upright species of Gibbon exist in Australia? This vastly underpopulated country whose population centres comprise a paltry 0.25% of its landmass could certainly harbour several unclassified species. Of course, just because you have rooms available, that doesn't necessarily mean that you have tenants who want to rent; and while this imaginary monster imposter is a reasonable stand-in for the *Nimbinjee*, that doesn't automatically make it so.

*Opposites Attract:* When two closely related species share the same ecological niche, it is common for there to be a difference in size, which normally results in the size and weight of the smaller species being half that of the larger species to reduce competition between them. This can be observed clearly with species such as black and brown bears, whose territories overlap. Is it possible that this same particularity could apply to the hairy man, with the *Big Fella* and the *Little Fella*, both occupying a communally beneficial territory?

*Could an undiscovered species of bipedal primate inhabit the lush forested valleys of Kerinci Seblat National Park, Sumatra?*

## ORANG PENDEK

Kerinci Seblat National Park is the largest national park on the island of Sumatra, Indonesia. Covering an area of 5,324 square miles, it encompasses the provinces of West Sumatra, Jambi, Bengkulu, and South Sumatra and features some of the most remote primary rainforests in the world. The first recorded sighting of the *Orang pendek* is reputed to have been made by the famous explorer Marco Polo in 1295, whereafter, this cryptic primate remained ethno-known until the early 20th century when Dutch colonists began sending home stories of small human-like apes that walked on two legs. Europeans, who were ever hungry for tales of strange beasts in faraway lands at this time, were captivated and in the century or more that has elapsed since the first rumours emerged from this remote region, forest tribes, local villagers, colonists, scientists, and travellers, alike, have attempted to unravel the mystery of this mysterious ape and add it to the ever-growing zoological canon of former cryptid apes!

**What's in a name?** *Orang Pendek,* is a Malay word meaning ("Short Man.") Also known as *Atu pandek, Atu rimbo, Ljaoe, Orang Gugu, Orang Letjo* ("Gibbering Man"), *Orang pandek, Sedabo, Sedapa, Sindai, Uhang pandak.*

**Monstrous Measurements:** Bipedal. 2 ft 5 in – 5 ft 6 in tall. Covered with short dark-orange, chocolate-brown, black, or grey hair. Head hair extends into a slight mane down its back. Human-like face and eyes. Sagittal crest. High forehead. Bushy eyebrows. Broad nose. Long canine teeth. Thickset, square shoulders. Long arms. Short legs. Pinkish-brown skin.

**Terrifying Tracks:** 5 – 6 inches long. 4 inches wide. Some tracks are human-like, showing five toes that are all equal in size. Others show a semi opposed hallux (big toe). The heel is narrow and well-rounded.

**Beastly Behaviours:** Bipedal. Ground-dwelling, but also comfortable in the trees. Will run with arms outstretched or extended above its head if startled, or stand/lie motionless, pressed closely against a tree, in an attempt to camouflage itself. Makes noises that sound like whistling or mumbling and will emit a short bark that sounds like, *"Hu, Hu!"* if distressed. The creature's appearance has a strange effect on those who witness it, who often feel very distressed by the intensity of the experience.

**Deadly Diet:** Wild yams, Sugar cane, bamboo shoots, fruit, freshwater molluscs, snakes, and worms. Occasionally raids plantations or vegetable gardens.

**Hairy Habitat:** The Kerinci Regency of central Sumatra, especially within the borders of Kerinci Seblat National Park, Sumatra, Indonesia.

**Scary Sightings:**

*1910:* a Dutch colonist described two strange encounters with bipedal apes in the Barisan Mountains near Mount Sugirik. In his first encounter, he observed a group of the bipedal animals, who he described as short-legged and human-like, but with distinctly different faces, as they crossed his path. His second encounter occurred 4 days later in the same region, where he witnessed a significantly larger group of approximately 25 animals that were *"...definitely not Orangutans!"*

<u>1917:</u> In December 1917, a plantation manager named Oostingh encountered an *Orang Pendek*. Oostingh, who was in the forest near Bukit Kaba, Sumatra, said that when the creature noticed him, it stood up and casually walked away before suddenly swinging up into the trees.

<u>1923:</u> Dutch settler, Mr Van Heerwarden, was surveying land in 1923 when he encountered what he referred to as a female *Sedapa*. He said: *"I discovered a dark and hairy creature on a branch... The sedapa was also hairy on the front of its body; the colour there was a little lighter than on the back. The very dark hair on its head fell to just below the shoulder blades or even almost to the waist... Had it been standing, its arms would have reached to a little above its knees; they were therefore long, but its legs seemed to me rather short. I did not see its feet, but I did see some toes which were shaped in a very normal manner... There was nothing repulsive or ugly about its face, nor was it at all apelike."* Although Van Heerwarden had the creature in his gun sights, he felt that due to its human-like appearance, he would be committing murder if he were to shoot it.

<u>1925:</u> In his book, *'The 'short man' (Orang Pendek) of Sumatra'*, Gregory Forth details a 1925 account from a colonial officer named De Santy, who recorded the accounts of five separate Banjuasin villagers, including one from a fisherman who told him that he had once discovered a dead Orang Pendek. De Santy summarises his account, saying that *'...although the size of a child of about ten years, the creature was evidently mature for she had human-like breasts. The body was covered in hair about 20 centimetres in length, while the head hair, roughly the length of a forearm, was much longer. The hands, feet, and nails were like a human's, but the middle finger extended well beyond the others; also,*

*the heel of the small foot was much more pointed. The creature had 'long eyebrows' and lacked a cleft in the upper lip. In the previous night, before discovering the body, the informant had heard a sound like a human weeping. From its condition, particularly an abnormally swollen belly, the man inferred that the creature had died during a failed attempt to give birth.'*

*1994:* On September 30th, 1994, five years after finding and casting the tracks of an *Orang Pendek*, former-newspaper editor Deborah Martyr had a face-to-face encounter with the *Orang Pendek* in the Mount Karinci Area. The creature, which was striding through the jungle, approximately 200 yards away, stopped briefly to look at her before continuing on its path through the jungle. Martyr claims to have observed the creature on two other occasions since. She said, *"The most shocking thing about the orang pendek was that it seemed so human."*

*1995:* Claude Petit spoke to several local people in Liwa, who told him that they had observed several animals matching the description of the *Orang Pendek*, who had come running out of the forest during a recent earthquake.

*In 2011*: During a 2011 expedition to Kerinci Seblat National Park in West Sumatra, Dave Archer and guide Sahar Didmus observed an example of one of the evasion behaviours employed by the *Orang Pendek* to avoid human detection, when they encountered one of the creatures that had flattened its face and body against a tree, in an attempt to camouflage itself from them. Archer observed that the creature, which appeared to be in a clear state of distress, was blowing out of the corner of its mouth and rolling its eyes before suddenly moving off into the deep undergrowth. His guide Sahar, who had previously had a face-to-face encounter with a Tiger, found the whole experience so moving that he burst into tears. Later, Richard Freeman and Adam Davies interviewed an eyewitness called Pak Entis, who claimed to have seen an *Orang Pendek* in April of that year. The creature, which he described as being around three feet tall and tan coloured, with an ape-like face, massive shoulders, and chest, walked upright on two legs while swinging its arms. Suddenly becoming aware of Pak Entis, it became quite alarmed, raised its hands above its head, uttering a *"hoo-hoo"* sound, and moved swiftly away. He was able to watch the creature for around one minute. Another farmer in the same area told them that an *Orang Pendek* had broken into his shed one night to steal sugar cane, ripping away planks to get at the sugary crop.

**Beastly Evidence:**

*Tracks:*

On August 21, 1915, Edward Jacobson and his Sumatran guide, Mat Getoep, found strange 5-inch footprints at the edge of the Danau Bento swamp, southeast of Mount Kerinci, Sumatra. Jacobson's guide, Getoep, told him that the tracks had been made by the *Orang Pendek*.

Harry Gilmore and Otto Irrgang found small, bipedal, human-like tracks near the Kamooar and Siak Kecil rivers in Riau Province, Sumatra, in 1958.

In 1994, Deborah Martyr, a British travel writer, discovered strange tracks that were about the size of a seven-year-old child's in southwestern Sumatra, Indonesia. She cast one of the tracks, one of which she sent to the Indonesian national Parks Department. It has since, sadly, disappeared.

*Tracks and Hair:* A British Expedition led by cryptozoologist Adam Davies found Clumps of hair purported to belong to the Orang Pendek, as well as tracks with a semi-opposed hallux that did not match any known primate species. The hairs were sent off for DNA testing to Professor Bryan Sykes, Professor Todd Disotell, Dr Tom Gilbert, and Lars Thomas; and although not conclusive, yielded strange, almost contradictory results, with Lars Thomas concluding: *"The structural analysis point to either an orangutan or something very closely related to an orangutan... the DNA analysis on the other hand point to a human or something very closely related to humans."*

*Handprint: Orang Pendek* has been observed feeding off grubs that live in rotting logs. This handprint which was cast by Andrew Sanderson in 2011, was found next to a rotting log that had been ripped apart in the highland jungles around Lake Gunung Tujuhm.

*Ruse for Reward:* The early 20th-century European interest in the *Orang Pendek*, along with the reward money offered for its capture, 'Dead or Alive!', led to a rather poorly modified body of a Langur monkey being delivered to the national zoology museum in Bogor, Java. Indeed, even now, it is common knowledge among villagers that stories about the *Orang pendek* often come with a dollar value attached to them, adding an unfortunate element of doubt to these claimed encounters.

## Beastly Theories

*Unknown Gibbon:* Throughout this chapter, we keep returning to the hidden hylobatid hairy man explanation for several unexplainable 'Littlefoot' cryptids around the world. But could the *Orang Pendek,* too, be a large, unrecognised species of gibbon? Certainly, many of its physical attributes (for example, its long arms and shorter legs) seem to bear some morphological similarity to this species, and Gibbons are known to inhabit the same territory as the *Orang Pendek.* Behaviourally, however, although it does show some propensity for arboreal locomotion, this mystery primate is primarily a ground-dwelling animal, or at the very least, one in which terrestriality has become its primary mode of living; and unlike its alleged relative, it is not observed swinging from branch to branch in the forest canopy. Additionally, there is something to be said for the emotional reaction of the hunters and villagers who have encountered this animal, many of whom have felt too terrified to areas where they encountered the animal, in that its odd physiology and almost man-like appearance strike a relative chord in the human psyche, that of a sentient human-like being, too close, for comfort!

*Could an outsized Sumatran Lar Gibbon be a viable candidate for Orang pendek?*

<u>*Homo Floresiensis?*</u> It seems unlikely that the *Orang Pendek* is an extant descendent of Homo Floresiensis, as its foot structure, similar to those of other great apes, exhibits a divergent hallux (big toe); as opposed to Homo Floresiensis, wherein the hallux is abducted, sitting in line with the lateral toes. Australopithecus Afarensis, too, which is often wheeled out like a fossil forebear of the *Orang Pendek* and whose feet, like Homo Floresiensis, lack a divergent hallux (big toe), is a poor stand-in for this unidentified primate. There are stories throughout this region of a small race of people, standing around three feet tall, who are called *Orang kardil*, or *"tiny men"*. They are identified as being distinct from the *Orang Pendek*, and apart from their small stature, similar to humans in every other way. These groups were reputed to live deep within the forest, fashion poison bamboo spears and axes and hunt in small groups. They were also notorious for stealing food. Indeed, one such conflict wherein a hunter killed one of these 'little men' for stealing rice resulted in the

subsequent spearing to death of the offending hunter by five of his (presumed) relatives! Sightings of the Orang kardil have not been reported for decades, however, again making even their conflation with the *Orang Pendek* tenuous.

*Sun Bear:* Sun bears are the smallest of the bear family and can be found in southern China and throughout Indonesia. Undoubtedly, the Sun Bear may have contributed to some cases of mistaken identity, where footprints lacking claw marks have been observed, or where the animal has been observed in poor light conditions or at a distance in thick foliage; however, their long snouts, prominent clawed feet and distinctive white, U shaped markings make this animal an unlikely monster impostor.

Silhouette of a monkey at sunset in Yala National Park, Sri Lanka.

## NITTAEWO

S ri Lanka is an island country lying in the Indian Ocean and separated from peninsular India by the Palk Strait. The island has a varied topography, including forests, mountains, plateaus, and valleys, and is home to a diverse array of flora and fauna, including the Asian Elephant, Sri Lankan Leopard, Sloth Bear, Purple Faced Langur, and Toque Macaque. It is also home to several cultures (past and present) that have left an indelible impression on the superstitions and folklore of this island paradise. Like many South Asian countries, it is filled to the brim with 'beast-men' legends of every shape and size. It is here in the jungle tales of the Veddah people that we learn of the now extinct, *Nittaewo*. A fierce tribe of little hairy men, with whom the Veddha's lived in a state of perpetual conflict. The presence of this dwarfish race of hairy pygmies, which some have theorised may be a representative of Homo erectus, has been known on the island since the 4th Century BC, when Ctesias, a Greek physician at the Persian court, wrote about the *"little people"* who inhabited the island of Sri

Lanka, that was then known in the ancient world as Taprobane. But, could an extant population of this ancient human have survived until the beginning of the 19th century, or alternately, could the legends of the Nittaewo, represent a poorly understood ape species, misinterpreted as a competing tribe, whose animalistic barbarism and continued conflict with the ancient Veddha's eventually led to its demise?

**What's in a name?** *Nittaewo* comes from the Veddah word, possibly derived from the term *niya-atha* ("one who possesses nails"), or *Nishada*, an Indo-Aryan word to denote the early inhabitants they encountered when they conquered the island. Also known as *Nigadiwa, Nishadiwa, Nittavo, Nittawo,* and *Vinnara* ("man of the woods").

**Monstrous Measurements:** 3-4 ft tall. Covered in shaggy red body hair. Head hair is differentiated from that of the body and straight. Dark skin. Powerful short arms. Hands, ending in long talon-like fingers. Orangutan or gorilla-like appearance. Females are smaller than the males. No tail is present.

**Beastly Behaviours:** Bipedal. Does not wear clothes. Expert climber. Sleeps in caves or on platforms in the boughs of trees. Has a language that sounds like birds twittering, which was purportedly understood by the Veddah people. Lives in mixed family groups numbering 10 to 20 individuals. Does not fashion or use tools of any kind, choosing instead to utilise its talon-like nails to disembowel its prey and feed on their entrails. Fierce and aggressive, often attacking its human adversaries as a group and disembowelling them with its sharp nails. Forms raiding parties, often descending on hunters or villagers while they sleep to steal food stores and meat. Fears buffalos and dogs.

**Deadly Diet:** Omnivorous. Game, hare, squirrels, deer, lizards, tortoises, and crocodiles.

**Hairy Habitat:** Reputed to live in caves and the boughs of trees in the Yala national park; in the Tamankaduwa and Lenama regions of eastern Sri Lanka, as well as the forests around Pomparippu and Tantrimalai on the northwest coast.

## Scary Sightings:

<u>1984:</u> Spanish anthropologist, Dr Salvador Martinez, claimed to have seen the *Nittaewo* in Sri Lanka in 1984. He described the Nittaewo as having a human-like appearance, except that its body was covered in a coat of long hair, some areas of which were covered in scabs. Dr Martinez described the *Nittaewo* making unintelligible noises before suddenly fleeing toward the forest. Later, when seeking further information about his encounter from some local people, they insisted that he must have mistaken a member of a nomadic tribe for the legendary beast.

## Beastly Evidence:

<u>4<sup>th</sup> Century BC:</u> Ctesias, a Greek physician at the Persian court during the fourth century B.C., was the first person to write about the *"little people"* who inhabited the island of Sri Lanka that was then known in the ancient world as Taprobane. Ctesias wrote of these little men: *"whose clothes are the skins of wild beasts. They have no language; they bark like dogs ... Their teeth are larger than those of dogs; their nails are like those of animals, but longer and more curved."*

<u>1<sup>st</sup> Century AD:</u> Pliny the Elder also wrote of the existence of 'Beast-Men' who were reputed to live on the island of Ceylon during the first century AD.

<u>400 AD:</u> In 400 AD, Bishop Palladius, referring to the Veddah, described them as a race of primitive people living on the island of Ceylon, which was believed to have solved the age-old mystery of the Nittaewo. However, Veddah legend unquestionably depicts the Nittaewo as a distinct people with whom they were at war, and therefore it is likely that Palladius simply conflated the identity of the

two peoples, viewing them as primitive and indistinct from one another.

*Fourteenth Century AD:* In the fourteenth century, Moroccan traveller Ibn Batuta wrote after visiting the island, "*These animals are very numerous in the mountains.*" Although this is now generally believed to be a misidentification of the Purple Faced Leaf Monkey.

*1886:* In February 1886, Hugh Nevill, in his paper, 'The Nittaewo of Ceylon', narrates a folk tale about the Nittaewo, which he acquired from the Veddas: "*The Nittaewo were a cruel and savage race of men, rather dark, living in small communities at Lenama. They built platforms in trees, covered with a thatch of leaves, and in these, they lived. They could neither speak Vaedda, Sinhalese or Tamil, but their language sounded like the Telegu of pilgrims to Kattragam. They attacked any intruding Vaeddas, and no Vaedda dare enter their district to hunt or collect honey. Many years ago, the ancestors of the informants fought with these Nittaewo, and finally drove the remnant of them, men, women, and children into a cavern. Before this, they piled firewood, and kept up the fire for three days, after which the race became extinct, and their district a hunting ground of these Vaeddas*".

*1914:* Frederick Lewis wrote in his work, 'Notes on an exploration in Eastern Uva, and Southern Panama Pattu', in 1914, about a man named Dissanhamy whose grandfather had taken part in turning out a troop of the Nittaewo (that are also called *Mitto* -'dwarfs') in the Lenama country, north-west of Bargurey: "*They were a little people about so high (here the witness indicated a height of about 3 feet) who lived in small gangs of 10 or 20 or more. The legs of these people were hairy like wanduros (wanduro-wage), but the upper part of the body was human-like while they walked erect. They had no tails and were completely naked. Their arms were short, with strong hands and long, powerful nails with which they tore to pieces the animals that they caught. These consisted of small animals such as the mouse deer, the hare, squirrel, iguana, and tortoise. They could only capture animals by surrounding them, and for that reason, they lived in small troops. They lived in caves, hollow trees, and crevices. The females were shorter than the males. They spoke a language that was not loud – like the twittering of birds – but was understood by some of the Veddas. The Nittawo were very much afraid of dogs because they knew the Veddas used them, and also bows and arrows, against which they could not compete. They never came near the sea but confined themselves to the forest country. If they came on a sleeping Vedda, they fell on him in mass and disemboweled him at once with their 'talons' and for that reason, the Veddas spared them not".*

*1933:* R.L.Spittel, in his book *'Far-off Things' (1933)*, writes: "*These, according to persistent tradition among the jungle folk of south-eastern Ceylon, were a race of savage, hairy, long-nailed dwarfs feared even by the Veddas. They are said to have lived on platforms on trees, and eaten, crocodiles, tortoises, oysters, and crabs. On seeing a human being they attacked him and tore out his flesh with their long nails. They greatly feared the buffalo and the dog".*

*1940s:* British primatologist W.C. Osman Hill led an expedition into the region in 1945, where he found that a widespread belief in the existence of the Nittaewo still persisted on the island. In his report about the Nittaewo, he concluded that Dubois's Pithecanthropus erectus of Java, or Java Ape Man (now, Homo erectus!), was a close match for the descriptions of the Nittaewo.

*1958:* Bernard Heuvelmans' bestseller, *'On the Track of Unknown Animals,'* published in 1958, revived the popularity of the *Nittaewo*. In the chapter, *'Nittaewo, The Lost People of Ceylon,'* he writes: "*Asia may still hide unknown apes whose mental development is higher than that of the anthropoid apes. Or it may be inhabited by men more primitive than the Australian Aborigines, the Veddahs or the African Bushmen, and still at the Neanderthal stage.*"

*1963:* Captain A.T.Rambukwella led an expedition to the Mahalenama area in search of the Nittaewo in May 1963. During an excavation of a cave in Kudimbegala he discovered, the vertebrae of a monitor lizard and a piece of a carapace of a star tortoise, both assumed to be part of the Nittaewo's diet. During a further exploration of caves in Kudimbigala, he also discovered a man-made structure, which looked for all intents and purposes, *"reminiscent of the miniature Stonehenge"*. Later, he was reliably informed by the Veddhas in the area that the mysterious structure was *"the nittaewo altar,"* However, it was later discovered that it had been built by Veddah monks.

*October 2004:* In 1907, Drs Paul and Fritz Sarasin discovered microliths (small stone tools usually made of flint) in the Uva and Eastern Provinces. They believed that the tools were made to be used *"by small hands ... by a small-sized type of mankind".* Some researchers have suggested that these microliths, many of which can be found in the National Museum in Colombo, suggest that a race of pygmies once inhabited Sri Lanka.

**Beastly Theories!**

*The Little Genocide:* Veddah legend holds that the Nittaewo were exterminated by their ancestors at the end of the eighteenth century. The Veddah, who had become tired of the endless fighting between the two tribes and the cruel depredations of the Nittaewo, which included their brutal raids and even the kidnap of their children, decided that something had to be done. And, after trapping the remaining Nittaewo in a cave, they blocked the entrance with brushwood, which was set alight, suffocating the trapped fearsome nittaewo, over three days. Sightings are incredibly rare in modern times, suggesting that the species is now functionally extinct. But, could a small population of these 'little people' have survived, in much-diminished numbers, eeking out a more timid existence in the deep forests and lonely mountains of Sri Lanka?

*Short and Sweet:* Did island isolation and close marriage evolve a race of diminutive people, pushed out by stronger, larger tribes and forced to eke out a nutritionally deficient, hunter-gatherer existence in the forests and hills and on the fringes of the stronger civilisation. Researchers Osman C. Hill and Bernard Heuvelmans theorised that extant populations of Homo erectus, known from Southeast Asia, may once have been widespread throughout Asia before stronger, more technologically advanced tribes of human invaders drove them further southeast, where they finally reached Sri Lanka when the island was still connected to mainland India.

<u>Hidden Hylobatid</u>: Could the *Nittaewo* represent an unknown species of Sri Lankan gibbon? This candidate does conform to the *Nittaewo's* description in several ways, including its size, habitual bipedalism, opportunistic *omnivourism,* and propensity to live in troops. Perhaps, a regional variation of the Hoolock Gibbon, the only modern ape known from India, after entering the island when it was still connected to the Indian Mainland, pre - 5000 BC, could have evolved in that time into the fierce, razor clawed, *Nittaewo* that existed in Sri Lanka, until relatively recent times.

*Could an extant species of Australopithecus Afarensis dwell hidden somewhere in East Africa's vast landscape?*

## AGOGWE

Is there a small widespread race of unknown pygmies living in East Africa and its neighbouring regions? Could an extant species of Australopithecus Afarensis, that left traces of its presence in the Laetoli fossil beds in African prehistory, still be wandering the forests and hills of this ancient land; or has a large, unknown, terrestrial gibbon somehow managed to survive undetected in this densely populated region of East Africa? Certainly, we know from the example of the Bili Ape that distinct species can remain hidden in Africa's vast pristine countryside, but does that mean we can graft the Agogwe into the zoological canon, as an ethno-known species, likely to be found in the coming years of technologically magnificent and non-invasive animal observation techniques that might be applied to this region? Or, is an in-depth understanding of the sociocultural philosophies that permeate the African experience needed to pull apart fact from folklore in our hunt for this controversial cryptid?

**What's in a name?** *Agogwe* is a Kuria or Chagga (Bantu word) whose meaning is unknown. It also has several regional designees which seem to belong to animals of a similar species, such as the *Kakundakari* or *kilomba* in Zimbabwe and the Congo region; *Sehite* in the Ivory Coast; *Fating ho* in Senegal and *Agogure* or *Agogue,* in Tanzania and northern Mozambique.

**Monstrous Measurements:** Bipedal. 3 ft 3 in – 5 ft 7 in tall. Covered in long, woolly, brown, or russet-coloured hair. Human-like appearance. Rounded forehead, hairless face. Short canines, like a chimpanzee, but smaller. Yellowish-red skin, which can be seen beneath its hair.

**Terrifying Tracks:** 5 inches long, with 4 toes visible in tracks, of which the hallux (big toe) is longer and slightly separate from the other 3.

**Beastly Behaviours:** Bipedal. Travels alone or in groups of twos and threes. Has a horrible odour. Sleeps in caves, where it makes a bed out of leaves. Cannot climb trees or swim but will occasionally use logs to cross rivers. Sometimes travels alongside Baboon troops, with which it seems to have an affinity. Said to barter with local tribes for goods and will sometimes perform manual tasks in exchange for food and beer.

**Deadly Diet:** Omnivorous. Eats crabs, millipedes, snails, birds, and ginger-fruit.

**Hairy Habitat:** The *Agogwe* is reported on the eastern slopes of the mountains and forests of Mozambique and in the dense forests of North-Central Tanzania and Kenya.

**Scary Sightings:**

*1920s:* Captain William Hichens caught a glimpse of two hairy men as they walked upright across a clearing in the Ushur and Simbit forests, located on the western side of the Wembare Plains in Tanzania. Writing about his encounter in the December 1937 edition of

*Discovery Magazine*, he said: *"Some years ago I was sent on an official lion-hunt in this area (the Ussure and Simibit forests on the western side of the Wembare plains) and, while waiting in a forest glade for a man-eater, I saw two small, brown, furry creatures come from the dense forest on one side of the glade and disappear into the thickets on the other. They were like little men, about 4 feet high, walking upright but clad in russet hair. The native hunter with me gazed in mingled fear and amazement. They were, he said, Agogwe, the little furry men whom one does not see once in a lifetime."*

1924: S. V. Cook, the colonial administrator of Kenya, wrote of *"a race of little red men"* that were believed by the locals to inhabit the highlands of Kwa Ngombe, east of Embu in Kenya which were avoided by the local people. Cook's interpreter had even claimed that he and some others had been attacked in these very same mountains by *"scores of little red men hurling pebbles."*

1920/30s: Major Roger Courtney, big game hunter and 'father' of the British Special Boat Service (SBS) was reliably informed by his African Guide, Ali, that a race of little monkey-like people, covered in long black hair, had once captured his father near Mount Longonot, in the Mau Mountains.

1927: Cuthbert Burgoyne also wrote a letter to the *Discovery Magazine* in 1938 recounting his own personal sighting of a creature similar to that reported by Hichens in Tanzania. He said: *"In 1927: I was with my wife coasting Portuguese East Africa in a Japanese cargo boat. We were sufficiently near to land to see objects clearly with a glass of twelve magnifications. There was a sloping beach with light bush above upon which several dozen baboons were hunting for and picking up shellfish of crabs, to judge by their movements. Two pure white baboons were amongst them. These are very rare, but I had heard of them previously. As we watched, two little brown men walked together out of the bush and down amongst the baboons. They were certainly not any known monkey and yet they must have been akin, or they would have disturbed the baboons. They were too far away to be seen in great detail, but these small human-like animals were probably between four and five feet tall, quite upright and graceful in figure. At the time, I was thrilled as they were quite evidently no beast of which I had heard or read."* Burgoyne also claimed to have received a similar report from a friend, a Big game hunter, who, along with his wife and three other hunters, witnessed 3 of the creatures, which he had assumed to be a small family group consisting of father, mother, and child, as they crossed across a clearing. The native hunters who were with him forbade him to shoot the animals.

*1950s/60s:* Charles Cordier, a professional animal collector for zoos and museums, followed a set of 5-inch tracks that led to a cavern said to be the home of the *Kakundakari* in Zaire in the late 1950s or early 1960s. Cordier noted that the big toe was in the same proportion as that of a human print, except that it was lacking a visible fifth toe. Astonishingly, he even claimed that one of the animals had once become entangled in one of his bird snares, saying: *"It fell on its face, turned over, sat up, took the noose off its feet, and walked away before the nearby African could do anything".*

*1957:* A hunter came upon the body of a Kakundakari, which he described as being nearly dead, just south of Kasese near the Lugulu River. He brought it to a village and exhibited it in a cage where it was viewed by dozens of people, both black and whites, before escaping some time later.

**Beastly Evidence:** The *Agogwe* reportedly lives in the dense remote forest regions of Eastern Africa and no formal expeditions have been launched to locate this rare creature. Due to this paucity of scientific interest and owing to the tumultuous political nature of much of this region, there has been no physical evidence collected to support the existence of the *Agogwe*.

**Beastly Theories!**

*Surviving gracile Australopith:* Could the *Agogwe* and its numerous regional relatives represent an extant species of Australopithecus

Afarensis? Indeed, we know that this species once inhabited this part of Africa from the Laetoli fossil beds in north-central Tanzania, which contain the perfectly preserved examples of its footprints. This species, which stood between 3 ft 5 in and 5 ft tall and was believed to have had both ape and human characteristics would seem to constitute a perfect photo fit for the mysterious *Agogwe*; although the Australopithecine's somewhat diverged toe is far from what could reasonably be called, opposable.

Mary Leakey discovered bipedal footprints in volcanic ash at Laetoli, Tanzania, in 1978 that are believed to belong to Australopithecus afarensis.

_African Gibbon:_ A common theory to explain the presence of little hairy men around the world, at least those that are ape-like in appearance, is that of a large, unknown species of Gibbon. Indeed, in many reports, the described physiological characteristics could just as easily be applied to one of these lesser apes. However, the biggest problem with this theory is that Gibbons rarely walk on solid land and mainly use their arms to get about during their arboreal journeys through the forest canopy. However, if a gibbon was responsible for these encounters, it certainly would not be any species that we are familiar with and within that mystery, perhaps can be added, many other ill-fitting behaviours and characteristics that would seem out of place in an ordinary member of this genus? Nevertheless, gibbons are not known to live in Africa, instead preferring tropical and subtropical rain forests, and it would seem quite a stretch to transplant a largely unseen, highly territorial, exceptionally loud species such as this, without its presence being well known

_Happy & Hairy_: Could a closely related pygmy people, suffering from hypertrichosis (a condition characterized by universal hair overgrowth), which can be inherited as an autosomal or X-linked dominant trait, be responsible for the legends of the Agogwe? Perhaps even the ancestors of the Mbuti of the Ituri Forest in the Democratic Republic of the Congo may have made their way to east Africa and seeking to remain a distinct group, or perhaps keeping the larger and more aggressive tribes at arm's length, have suffered over time with low genetic diversity, which eventually accentuated several rare genetic disorder, that resulted in the pre-stone age, fixity of this tribes progress and development?

# MONKEY MONSTERS

*"Similar in appearance to known species of platyrrhines and catarrhines, in some respects, though massively outsized. Standing from 5 – 6 ft in height. These monstrous primates are usually highly aggressive and are just as comfortable on two legs as they are on all fours. Most types possess a tail. They have long, narrow, clawed feet."*

| *Puerto Ayacucho, Venezuela.*

## SALVAJE

A whopping 52.5% or 46,275,000 hectares of Venezuela is forested. This country sitting atop the heavily forested neighbouring nations of Brazil, Guyana, and Colombia, is a haven for wildlife and boasts 8,000 endemic species that are found nowhere else on earth. The indigenous tribes of Venezuela tell of an aggressive, man-sized cannibal monkey living in the isolated jungles and mountains, calling them *'Salvaje'*, a word meaning savage or wild. And although now largely bound to the past glories of 19th-century exploration, tales of this "King Monkey" persist throughout Venezuela and the neighbouring regions. Is the *Salvaje* simply a re-spun folktale deposited here by the Conquistadors hundreds of years ago, or could there be a hitherto unknown species of large, upright primate inhabiting Venezuela's endlessly abundant jungle paradise?

What's in a name? *Salvaje* comes from the Spanish, meaning *"Savage."* Also known as *Achi Conerre, Paudacota yege.* Possibly related to, if not the same as, the *Mono Grande ("Large Monkey"* or *"King Monkey"), Marimondas, Maribundas,* and *Didi.*

Monstrous Measurements: Large, monkey-like creature. 3ft - 5ft 6in tall. Covered in reddish hair. Thin physique. Long arms. Weighing approximately 80 to 100 pounds. Large lips.

Terrifying Tracks: Footprints are turned inwards. Heels face backwards.

Beastly Behaviours: Bipedal and quadrupedal. Emits eerie, human-like cries and yells. Travels alone or in groups of three or more. Has a strong odour. Makes huts. Said to kidnap and interbreed with women.

Deadly Diet: Eats fish, meat, fruits, roots, and sometimes, human flesh.

Hairy Habitat: Resides in the mountains, from where it travels to the rivers to find food. Reported in the Rio Orinoco and Rio Ventauri, Venezuela; Western Arauca Department, Colombia and Chiapas State, Mexico.

**Scary Sightings:**

*1536-1537:* Spanish explorer, Pedro Cieza de León, claimed to have encountered large apes that the natives referred to as *"Marimondas"*, during his expedition to San Sebastián de Buenavista and Urute, with Alonso de Cáceres, in 1536 to 1537.

*1769:* Dr Edward Bancroft witnessed 5 ft apes, which the local tribespeople referred to as *"didi,"* while travelling through Guyana and Suriname in 1769.

*1799 - 1804:* between 1799 and 1804, German naturalist Baron Alexander von Humboldt recorded stories of the *"Salvaje"* (wild/savage) hairy ape-men that would build huts along the Orinoco River and kidnap women, and that was even purported to prey on humans, occasionally. Humboldt also reported on the alleged kidnap of a woman from San Carlos, Brazil, who, according to locals, had been taken by a *Vasitri* ("Big Devil").

*1968:* Yugoslavian nobleman, Pino Turolla, claimed to have observed a large unknown ape twice while travelling in Ecuador. His alleged photograph, taken of the beasts, was never published. He also claimed to have received a harrowing tale from his guide, Antonio, who described how his son had been beaten to death with clubs/branches by three big *Mono Grande*.

*1980:* Hunter, Fernando Nives was sailing down the Orinoco River, about 25 miles north of the small town of Puerto Ayacucho, when he caught sight of a large hairy creature on the shoreline. Curious, he guided his boat toward the shore and became aware of a terrible odour seemingly coming from the animal, which became stronger as he approached. He then noticed that two other similar creatures were standing, partially hidden in the undergrowth. Whether Nives beat a hasty retreat or remained a short while to observe these imposing animals is not told. Nives described the creatures as being covered in reddish hair and standing on two legs at a height of 5 ft.

*1985:* A man who had been clearing forest to make way for a new road near Puerto Ayacucho reported hearing the call of the Salvaje. The man who had been using a bulldozer had decided to take a short break and was alarmed to hear a loud cry before being confronted with a 5 ft primate-like creature with red hair.

*1987:* Mycologist, Gary Samuels, had been given a grant by the New York Botanical Garden and had travelled to Guyana to study fungi. One day while out I the field with his Guyanese assistant, he heard footsteps approaching him and, expecting to see his assistant approaching, looked up, instead to see a large, bipedal, apelike creature, approximately 5 ft tall. The creature roared at Samuels before it ran away.

*1990:* In 1990, Marc and Khryztian Miller mounted an expedition to Venezuela in search of this legendary giant monkey and, although unsuccessful, managed to record many encounters with the strange beasts, including that of an Indian chief, from a small village on the Orinoco River, who had not only seen but killed a *Salvaje*, several months earlier. The Chief, who had been in the forest hunting with his blowgun, shot and killed the giant monkey but did not recover its carcass out of a superstitious fear that it might bring bad luck to the village. He described the creature as being 5ft tall and covered with red hair.

### Beastly Evidence:

*Racist Little Monkey:* As with all lies, the longer they are told, the harder it becomes to find the truth and the tale of the *De Loys Ape* is no exception to this rule. However, an overview of the case, including the author's own view, will suffice, I think, in this case, to elucidate a rather poor fraud, likely perpetrated, in this case by someone other than its progenitor. Between 1917 and 1920, Swiss geologist Francois de Loys had been part of an 'alleged' ill-fated oil expedition on the Colombia/Venezuelan border. In 1920, when apparently all but 4 of the original 20 members had perished, de Loys and his remaining team were camped on the bank of a tributary of the Tarra River, when they had a harrowing encounter with what they at first mistook for bears, but soon realised were two Giant monkeys (a male and a female); who appeared to be angry at the men and began howling, breaking branches and throwing their faeces. As the conflict with the animals escalated, the men opened fire on the pair, killing the female and wounding the male, who fled back into the jungle. Following the encounter, de Loys propped up the dead female (which was purportedly 4 ft 5 in tall) on a crate and took a (now infamous) photograph of the creature. The photo, skull, and skin of the animal were preserved for evidence, but due to the trepidations and terrors of their exit from the jungle, all but the photo were lost en route.

*By Francois de Loys - Montadon, George (1929 apparence anthropoïde en Amérique du Sud&quot. Journal de la Société des Américanistes*

This story, however, would not even be known if not for an anthropologist friend of de Loys, named George Montandon, who found the photo among de Loys belongings and published it in the journal *Comptes Rendu* in 1929, with a description of the ape, even going so far as to give it the name: *Ameranthropoides loysi*. Montandon, who had been trying to find a few 'missing pieces' to promote his theory of evolution called *"Polygenism"*, claimed to believe that the existence of this American anthropoid proved his theory that different races evolved from different apes and championed de Loys discovery as proof of the origin of the Native American race. There is much about Montandon that indicates a man of unscrupulous character, not to mention the fact that he was executed in his homeland of France after the war as a traitor.

In 1999, damning testimony regarding de Loys ape encounter, from an eyewitness who had been part of the same expedition was exposed in the Venezuelan scientific magazine *Interciencia,* when they republished a letter, sent in 1962, from Doctor Enrique Tejera to the editor Guillermo José Schael of the magazine *Diario El Universal:*

It reads:

*"...This monkey is a myth. I will tell you his story. Mister Montandon said that the monkey had no tail. That is for sure, but he forgot to mention something, it has no tail because it was cut off. I can assure you this, gentlemen, because I saw the amputation.*

*...Who is speaking here in 1917 was working in a camp for oil exploration in the region of Perijá. The geologist was François de Loys, the engineer Dr. Martín Tovar Lange. De Loys was a prankster and often, we laughed at his jokes. One day they gave him a monkey with an ill tail, so it was amputated. Since then, de Loys called him "el hombre mono" (the monkey man).*

*Sometime later, I and de Loys went in another region of Venezuela: in an area called Mene Grande. He always walked along the side of his monkey, who died sometime later. De Loys decided to take a photo and I believe that Mr. Montandon will not deny it is the same photograph that he presented today.* (Ref: to a public lecture in which Montandon presented Ameranthropides in 1929.)

*More recently, during a visit to Paris, my astonishment was great visiting the Museum of Man. On top of a monumental scale, filling the back wall, there was a huge photo with the caption: "The first anthropoid ape discovered in America." It was the photograph of de Loys, beautifully modified. The plants were no longer visible in the background, and it was not possible to understand on which kind of box the monkey was sitting. The trick is done so well that within a few years the monkey will be over two meters high....*

*Finally, I must warn you: Montandon was not a good person. After the war, he was executed because he betrayed France, his homeland.*

*Sincerely, Your friend Enrique Tejera."*

Tracks:

<u>1876:</u> In 1876, explorer Charles Barrington Brown reported that on several occasions he had heard the cries and even found the tracks of a strange bipedal creature which lived in the forests of British Guiana. According to Brown, the creature was a type of wildman, known locally as the *Didi*.

<u>1988:</u> A well-known jungle pilot named Rodriguez found strange footprints belonging to the Salvaje on his airstrip. He reported oddly that the creature's footprints were turned inwards and estimated from the depth of its tracks that the animal weighed somewhere between 80 to 100 pounds. Later, a group of locals followed the tracks into the forest but found nothing.

<u>Tall Tail:</u> In 1931, inspired by de Loys' discovery, three Italians mounted an expedition to Venezuela in search of this *"Big Monkey"* but disappointingly returned with a few spurious eyewitness reports that seem to have been given by the natives in a manner of mockery, perhaps indicating the fairy tale feeling that such tales had even within the local population. Later, an American scientist named Phillip Herschkowitz retraced de Loys' route only to conclude that the *Mono Grande* was indeed a hoax. There have been many other hopeful expeditions launched along Guyana's Maruzuni River since, none of which, sadly, have captured any evidence of the elusive – *King Monkey*.

<u>Fortune & Glory:</u> de Loys' ape continued to capture the interests of adventurous types and those who seek to profit from various curios and knick-knacks, even inspiring one American millionaire to offer a reward of 50,000 dollars to anyone who could find a specimen. Later, in 1951, Frenchman Roger Courteville, a civil engineer, who claimed to have crossed South America by canoe, claimed in his 1951 book, *Avec Les Indiens Inconnus de l'Amazonie,* that he had encountered a large ape in the same area as de Loys' and even went on to offer a photograph of the creature, allegedly taken by a Dr de Barle in 1938. Unsurprisingly, the animal featured in De Barle's photo is none other

than de Loys' original photo, crudely doctored – a hoax of a hoax, no less!

**Beastly Theories:**

*Spider Monkey:* Brown Spider Monkeys live in lowland forest at the very top of the canopy. They are endemic to northern Colombia and some smaller sites in Venezuela. In the case of de Loys' ape, at least, they would seem a perfect fit for the animal that is y represented in his now-legendary photo. We also have the testimony of de Loys' expedition team member, Doctor Enrique Tejera, who testified in writing that de Loys' had a pet spider monkey, which he photographed after its death and subsequently became the world-renowned, *Ameranthropoides loysi.* However, the other numerous accounts of the *"Big Monkey"* in its many designees and appellations throughout this region cannot be so easily explained by this conspicuous monkey monster impostor and we are left with some rather large monkeys, exhibiting physical characteristics and behaviours outside of any known primate species in the new world.

*Giant Monkey:* Surviving Protopithecus brasiliensis, an extinct, Pleistocene spider monkey from eastern Brazil that was twice as large as any extant species. It should be noted that although due to its size, it is assumed to have been primarily terrestrial, the skeleton of Protopithecus does not show any adaptations that would be favourable to terrestrial locomotion.

*Hidden Tribes:* The Yanomami are a large group of Amazonian Indians that had remained relatively untouched by modern civilisation until the 1970s. Their diminutive population of 38,000 people, which occupies an area of 9.2 million hectares in Brazil and 8.2 million hectares in Venezuela, consisting of fragmentary village outposts, where men hunt and fish and women garden plantains and cassavas, is widely feared. Known for their violent intertribal wars and wife raiding parties (they will even resort to kidnapping foreign women and travellers), endocannibalism (ritual eating of their dead), and endemic first cousin marriage; they could easily be mistaken for the raging *Salvaje* ("*Savage*"), whose hut building, flesh-eating, wife kidnapping ways, may have engendered the characteristics of this legendary beast!

The Yanomami are the largest relatively isolated tribe in South America. They live in the rainforests and mountains of northern Brazil and southern Venezuela

*Foreign Folklore & Fable:* The 19^th-century German naturalist, Alexander von Humboldt, who heard stories from the Orinoco about furry human-like creatures called Salvaje ("Wild"), was convinced that these myths had entered into the lexicon of South American folklore through European colonists. Indeed some remnant of this phenomenon is present in the tribal folklore of both North and South America, leaving one to ponder whether any of the legends that European explorers pursued during the eighteenth and nineteenth centuries may have originated a little closer to home than they would have expected. Another common theory is that many of these monstrous tales grew out of Arthur Conan Doyle's book The Lost World (1912), egged on by locals in the area, who exaggerated local stories to encourage a type of rudimentary adventure tourism.

| Kenyan Tealands.

## NANDI BEAR

Western Kenya's Nandi District is home to a ferocious creature that appears to have the power to change its appearance depending upon the observational biases of the persons who witness it. This apparent changeling has been described as resembling a giant baboon, a lion-sized hyena, a bear, and a hybrid anteater. Indeed, as far as cryptids are concerned, their multifarious forms and identities are somewhat perplexing, but, in keeping with the symmetry of this chapter, we will here indulge its possible primate character, not foregoing, of course its other possible identities. For centuries before European passions for the Nandi bear were kindled (in the early part of the 20th century), the majority of Nandi Bear encounters were reported by members of the Nandi tribe. Encounters, they say that still continue to this very day.

**What's in a name?** *Nandi Bear*, named after the Nandi People, who inhabit the area around Kapsabet in Kenya's rift valley. It is known by a multitude of names in the various tribes that inhabit this area, such as *Booa, Chemisit, Duba, Engargiyar, Geteit, Giant Forest Hyaena,*

*Kabiniro, Khodumodumo, Kichwa Mutwe, Koddoelo, Mubende Beast, Ngargiya, Ntebarganyar, Rwujigar, Sabrookoo, Shivuverre* and *Too*.

**Monstrous Measurements:** Like a thickset baboon or large hyena. 6 ft in length, with a shoulder height of 4 – 5 ft. Long, shaggy, Dark Brown, reddish-yellow, or tawny coloured fur. Long head with a stumpy, bear-like snout. Large canines. Small rounded ears. Short neck with a thick mane. Downwards sloping back. Thick forelegs. Thick front paws with long claws. Tail, 18 in long and 4 in wide.

**Terrifying Tracks:** five-toed with one deep claw mark. 5.5. Inches in length and 3.5 inches in width.

**Beastly Behaviours:** Nocturnal. Walks on four legs, occasionally on two. Often seen sitting on its haunches. Cannot climb trees but can leap over tall fences. Extremely savage. Raids sheep pens and other livestock and kills them by tearing open their heads and feeding on their brains. Will attack solitary humans on sight, dispatching them in a similarly grotesque way to cattle. Also, raids rural huts at night, killing their occupants. Has a terrifying call or howl.

**Deadly Diet:** Feeds on the brains of livestock and people, which it accesses by tearing open their heads.

**Hairy Habitat:** Uganda; the highlands of western Kenya; Southern Kenya in East Africa to the coast.

**Scary Sightings:**

*1905:* Geoffrey Williams glimpsed a strange dark beast while on safari at Sergoit Rock on the Uasin Gishu tableland of Western Kenya. The creature, which was no more than 30 yards away, was sitting 'bear-like' on its haunches and shambled away in a sideways canter. Williams described the creature as being approximately 5 ft tall, with a long head and small pointed ears. Its fur appeared to be thicker at the front and somewhat smoother at the back. Its tail was short or non-existent.

*1912:* A Major Toulson observed a long-haired, black beast on the Uasin Gishu shortly after it had attempted to raid his camp's kitchen. The thickset creature, which stood 18 – 20 inches at the shoulder, produced a peculiar moaning cry and shambled off.

*1913:* At 9 AM on March 8th, 1913, railroad engineer G.W. Hickes observed a shaggy-haired, Hyaena-like animal on the Magadi Railway in southern Kenya. He got a good look at the animal that was standing 50 yards away and realised that it was no ordinary Hyaena. He said:

*"It was almost on the line when I first saw it and at that time, it had already seen me and was making off at a right angle to the line... As I got closer to the animal, I saw it was not a hyena. At first, I saw it nearly broadside on: it then looked about as high as a lion. In colour, it was tawny--about like a black-maned lion, with very shaggy long hair. It was short and thickset in the body, with high withers, and had a short neck and stumpy nose. It did not turn to look at me but loped off--running with its forelegs and with both hind legs rising at the same time. As I got alongside it, it was about forty or fifty yards away and I noticed it was very broad across the rump, had very short ears, and had no tail that I could see. As its hind legs came out of the grass, I noticed the legs were very shaggy right down to the feet and that the feet seemed large..."*

Hickes, who suddenly realised that this animal could be the strange "bear" which had been reported several times throughout the area, could still see the animal in the distance and momentarily considered whether to stop and pursue the animal, but remembering that the other engineers were still waiting for him, decided to press on and check for tracks and signs of the animal on his return journey. Sadly, heavy rainfall washed away any evidence before he could return.

*1914:* A suspected Nandi Bear was ambushed by the residents of Kapsowar, Kenya after it had killed several people. The villagers, who had placed a dummy of a man in the doorway of a hut, shot the creature to death as it attacked their clever decoy.

*1925:* Government agent William Hichens went to investigate the animal's depredations in a Kenya village. His tent was attacked at night by something that gave out a horrifying roar and carried off his pet dog, leaving enormous clawed tracks behind.

*Unknown date:* Charles T. Stoneham was awoken one night by a lion-sized animal with a square head, a pig's snout, large circular ears, and a thick tail at his trading station in Sotik, Kenya. Stoneham ran indoors to get his rifle, but the creature was already out of range when he returned. Stoneham later became convinced that he had probably seen a hybrid ant-eater, although some of Stoneham's friends said that he had encountered a Nandi bear.

*1930s:* Capt. F. D. Hislop saw a bear-like animal at night that was 3 ft high at the shoulder, with a small, pointed head as it ran off on all four legs, near Kapsabet, Kenya.

*1936:* A settler claimed to have been attacked by something that looked like an 8ft tall grey polar bear, which broke into his hut in Trans-Nzoia.

*1958 & 1981:* Douglas Hutton shot two animals that stood 3ft. high at the shoulder, with rearward sloping backs and heavy manes at the Chemomi Tea Estate, Kenya, in 1958. The bodies were stored in the factory and seen by several staff members of the staff before being sent to Coryndon Museum, Nairobi, where they were identified as "giant forest hyenas", although no such species has ever been classified. In July 1981. Some locals around the estate claimed to have seen a *"nyangau"* (Swahili: "dirty dog") which they described in similar terms to the animals shot by Hutton 23 years previous. The locals insisted that the animal was not a hyena, baboon, or pig.

*1962:* A lion-sized, hyena-like animal with large teeth was shot in Kenya by a big game hunter in 1962

*1960s:* Engineer Angus McDonald told of a terrifying encounter he had with a 7ft tall ape-like animal that chased him around his hut in

Kipkabus. During his encounter, he observed the creature running both bipedally and quadrupedally.

_1998:_ In February 1998, engineer Dennis Burnett and his wife observed an enormous, hairy, bear-like hyena on a road running along the base of the Nandi Escarpment.

**Beastly Evidence:**

_Hutton Trophies:_ Douglas Hutton shot two animals at the Chemomi Tea Estate, Kenya, in 1958. They stood 3 ft high at the shoulder, had rearward sloping backs, and had heavy manes. The skeleton, skin, tracks, and photographs of the animal were sent to Coryndon Museum, then on to the Natural History Museum by sea. Mysteriously, all the evidence disappeared en route.

_Fritz Schindler Track:_ Although the Nandi bear's tracks have frequently been described, no known casts were ever made, and only one image exists: a rough sketch made by Fritz Schindler of a track found in mud near the Magadi Railway. Bernard Heuvelmans suggested that this track was, in fact, two honey badger footprints, one superimposed over the other.

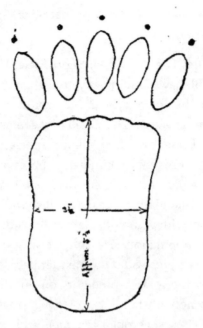

Sketch of the track found by F. Schindler found near the Magadi Railway

*Gunnar Anderson Tracks:* Gunnar Anderson investigated reports of an unknown animal that had killed a forest pig at Kaimosi, Kenya. The Nandi villagers who had observed the animal said it had long, black hair and a long tail. Later, in his report to the Kenya Game Department, Anderson said that although he hadn't seen it, he did find a few ambiguous leopard-like tracks nearby.

## Beastly Theories!

*Giant Baboon:* Could the *Nandi Bear* be an extant species of the prehistoric *Dinopithecus*, a large, baboon-like primate that lived in South Africa as recently as the Pleistocene? Or, perhaps, *Therapithecus oswaldi*, an extinct baboon, the size of a male gorilla, that lived in Kenya during the same period? A surviving species of one of these believed to be extinct primates may be somewhat supported by the testimony of the Mau, Nandi, and Wa-Pokomo people, who also categorise the primate-like *Chemosit*, *kerit*, and *Koddoelo* as types of *Nandi Bear*.

*Short-Faced Hyaena.* The lion-sized, Short-Faced Hyaena had a short muzzle, formidable jaws, and massive teeth, giving a more bear-like impression than that of a hyena? But, could such a conspicuous species survive undetected? The possibility seems unlikely. It would have to be both a nocturnal and solitary species to avoid detection and this would require that each individual occupies a large territory, which in turn would increase the dispersion of the species and consequently, exponentially increase conflict with humans (farmers, etc.) and predators with whom it shares its territory. Additionally, the minimum viable population size rule of 50/500, even at the very bottom end of this scale, would dictate that people would be coming into contact with these large predators on an almost weekly basis. That being said, notwithstanding 1 or 2 sightings in the 1980s and 1990s, the Nandi Bear has not been regularly reported for several decades now. It has been suggested that the Nandi Bear was more common in this area before the rinderpest epidemic at the end of the nineteenth century. Might the overt encounters with this creature, catalogued in the 20th century, have been the functional extinction of this dwindling species being played out in real-time?

Giant short-faced hyena (Pachycrocuta brevirostris) could this species be responsible for some sightings of the Nandi Bear? Cast of the holotype skull at the Musée Crozatier.

<u>*Chimaera:*</u> The Chimaera was a monstrous fire-breathing creature of Greek mythology. The superstitious embodiment of several nightmarish creatures rolled into one. Throughout human history, it has been common practice to assign an unidentified beast with the physical characteristics of those animals that are most familiar to us. And it seems likely, at least in part, that this is what has occurred with the Nandi Bear. Bernard Heuvelmans, in his book, *On the Track of Unknown Animals*, proposed that the *Nandi Bear* was a non-existent composite animal, a modern-day chimaera, created from the descriptions of several different animals, and with this theory, I am inclined to agree.

| Yanachaga–Chemillén National Park, Peru.

## (THE) ISNACHI

Peru holds the 10th-most-forested area of any country in the world, which amounts to 260,000 square miles, just over half the country! This rich ecosystem is home to 500 species of mammals, 300 species of reptiles, 1,800 species of birds, and, importantly, 32 known species of New World monkeys. Yet within the endless canopy of the cloud forests of Peru, there is talk of another mysterious monkey, a giant of the forest, known to the local Indians who inhabit the forest as *Isnachi*. Though rarely encountered, this secretive simian leaves evidence of its powerful herbivorous predation, in the form of the torn-off tops of the Chonta palm tree, on whose shoots it feeds. But, are the legends of this cryptid colossus any different to those of boogie men found in every culture around the globe, or could there be fossil confirmation that several creatures matching its description once inhabited this region aeons before human recollection began?

**What's in a name?** *Isnachi* comes from the Quechua, meaning ("Strong Man".) Also known as *Camuenare* ("Father of the Monkeys") and *Maquisapa maman* ("Mother of the Spider Monkeys") in Spanish; or, *Majero, Ma jero,* and *Maemi.*

**Monstrous Measurements:** Bipedal and quadrupedal. 4 ft tall. Resembling a giant baboon with a body as large as a chimpanzee or a cross between an ape and a sloth. Muscular body. Black skin. The snout is shaped like a mandrill. Long fangs. Barrel-chested. Thick arms. Hands have flat nails, not claws. Huge thighs, larger than a man's. Short, thick tail, 6 inches in length. Covered in short, matted, black or dark brown hair. Occasionally seen with patches of caiman-like skin interspersed among its body hair (possible scabs?)

**Terrifying Tracks:** Feet and claws are turned backwards.

**Beastly Behaviours:** Primarily arboreal. Lives in the mountains, in pairs (presumably monogamous), but is sometimes seen in groups of 20 or more. Careful and stealthy. Moves noiselessly, using the forest to camouflage its presence. Ambushes trespassers on its territory, emitting a blood-curdling shriek, before suddenly rushing upon them; or if threatened, will quickly descend from the trees, fiercely attacking intruders while running on its hind legs Afraid of water. Has an odour so foul that it can cause dizziness and fainting. Can also expel a stream of pungent gas at its enemies. Occasionally travels alongside spider monkey troops.

**Deadly Diet:** Vegetarian. Eats wild fruits and the shoots of the inner parts of the Chonta palm, which it reaches by tearing off the top of the tree. (Its presence can be confirmed by trees damaged in this way and local Indians will avoid any areas where these damaged palm trees are seen.)

**Hairy Habitat:** Lives in vegetation-rich mountain forests, at altitudes of 1600 – 5000 feet, where it makes platform-like nests. Known from the Loreto Department in the north through to the Yanachaga-Chemillen National Park to the Cordillera Urubamba, in Peru.

**Scary Sightings/Beastly Evidence:**

_1985:_ A forestry official in Lima told Peruvian cryptozoologist, Dr Peter Hocking, that an Ecuadorean botanist Benigno Malo had once encountered a large black ape in a forest near the Peruvian/Ecuadorean border. Malo, who had been collecting orchids at the time, saw the strange, out-of-place "ape" moving towards him through the trees and managed to capture one photo of the creature before disappearing into the forest. It should be noted that Malo always dismissed his sighting as being that of a probably escaped circus animal. Nevertheless, Hocking and several other researchers have proposed that Malo's offhand dismissal of his sighting was likely due to a lack of knowledge of local encounters with the Isnachi. Hocking, encouraged by this sighting and the discovery of several totally new monkey species in South America, believes that the Isnachi may constitute an example of a large unknown species of monkey, still awaiting classification. The location of the photo is currently unknown.

_Historical restoration of Protopithecus brasiliensis, an extinct genus of large New World monkey that lived during the Pleistocene._

**Beastly Theories!**

*Outsized Spider Monkey:* Could an outsized species of spider monkey be responsible for the legends of the Isnachi? Certainly, many of the behavioural characteristics of the Isnachi match those of this arboreal species. Perhaps a form of insular gigantism, a phenomenon in which the size of an animal species, usually isolated on some far-flung island increases far beyond that of its mainland relatives, has taken hold of a remote and genetically limited mountain group, which over time has replicated this rare phenomenon within its closely related family group. Or perhaps even a rare form of Acromegaly, a condition wherein a tumour of the anterior pituitary gland that leads to excessive secretion of growth hormone causes rapid growth.

*Monkey Magic:* Although evidence of fossil primates was once thought to be sparse in Latin America, there are now three large new world monkeys that are known from the Late Pleistocene - *Protopithecus brasiliensis*, *Caipora bambuiorum*, and *Cartelles coimbrafilhoi*, and although their fossils are currently only known from the cerrados of Eastern Brazil, their discovery should caution us against dismissing the possibility that a new or extant species of large monkey could still be awaiting discovery in the dense forests of Peru and the heavily forested neighbouring states of Ecuador, Colombia, Bolivia, and Brazil.

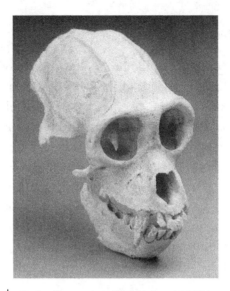

| *Protopithecus brasiliensis, Lund 1838*

*Spectacled Bear:* The name Isnachi (which means "strong man" in Quechua) in terms of the elusive cryptid monkey was coined by Dr Peter Hocking, as it was the most universally applied appellation used for this mysterious primate. However, just as in other remote communities around the world, a descriptor such as this often has several applications and this seems especially true when dealing with large mammals. Thus we find that in Peru that Isnachi is also used to refer to the spectacled bear (Tremarctos ornatus.) This animal, which is found in the Andean cloud forests of Peru, Bolivia, Ecuador, Colombia, and Venezuela, is present in the same areas the Isnashi is purported to inhabit and, to make matters even more complicated, is even adept at climbing trees, where it finds its favourite fruits. Additionally, in Bolivia, the Spectacled Bear is referred to as a monkey. Physically, however, with its distinct white eye patches and tailless body, it is a match for the Isnachi in name only!

| Town Hall, Danville, New Hampshire:

## DEVIL MONKEY

When visualising some of the far-flung regions of the world that could harbour a hitherto unknown species of terrifying monkey monster, Danville, New Hampshire, is not the first place that springs to mind. Yet, for 2 weeks in September 2001, this small New England hamlet was the scene of several scary encounters with a giant baboon-like beast that has since become known as, *The Devil Monkey of Danville*. Tales of this terrifying primate have been around since the 1930s and sporadic reports seem to pepper diverse locations, along with both the east and west coasts of the United States and Canada. But, what is the zoological significance of such sightings, and do their *'gelada-like'* proportions indicate a baboon-like escapee, or perhaps even that a small feral population of these aggressive primates has become established in parts of the United States and Canada?

**What's in a name?** Name coined by Mark A. Hall. Also known as *Giant Monkey* and *Nalusa Falaya*.

**Monstrous Measurements:** Bipedal and quadrupedal. Resembling a large baboon or dog. 3-8 ft tall. Covered in light brown to black hair. Sometimes has a patch of white fur extending from its neck to its belly. Pointed ears. Baboon-like or Dog-like muzzle. Large canines. Strong chest. Short forelegs, with claws. Muscular, almost kangaroo-like, hind legs. Large feet. Has a long bushy tail that is sometimes hairless

**Terrifying Tracks:** Three-toed tracks (toes appear rounded). 12 – 15 inches in length.

**Beastly Behaviours:** Very aggressive to humans and dogs. Walks bipedally and quadrupedally. Can leap long 20 ft. in a single bound. Very vocal, possibly territorial, emitting a range of barks, cries, and screams, often heard echoing through the Appalachian mountains region and that bear a resemblance to the territorial calls of other known primate species. Strong jaws, long canines, and razor-sharp claws, which it uses to bring down its prey, often attacking its torso, face, and other vulnerable areas.

**Deadly Diet:** Said to kill livestock, pets, and small game.

**Hairy Habitat:** British Columbia, Appalachian Mountain region of the United States. Devil Monkey sightings have also been reported in Kentucky, New Mexico, Utah, and Colorado.


**Scary Sightings:**

*1930s:* Kentucky is reputed to have experienced a rash of Devil Monkey sightings as far back as the 1930s.

*1934:* Several eyewitnesses described seeing a mysterious beast that could *"leap across fields with lightning speed."* in South Pittsburgh, Tennessee.

*1959:* The Boyd family were driving through the mountains near their home in Saltville, Virginia, when their vehicle was attacked by a monkey-like creature that rushed at the car, grabbing at it with its front paws. The Boyd's daughter, Pauline, described the terrifying attacker, which left three claw-like scratches on their car, saying, *"It had light, taffy coloured hair, with a white blaze down its neck and underbelly... it stood on two, large well-muscled back legs and had shorter front legs or arms."* She went on to tell of another similar encounter that occurred shortly after in the same region, saying, *"Several days after this incident, two nurses from the Saltville area were driving home from work one morning and were attacked by an unknown creature who ripped the convertible top from their car."*

*1973:* A Devil Monkey was thought to be responsible for the slaughter of several cattle in Albany, Kentucky, in 1973.

*1979:* Several Devil Monkey encounters occurred in rural Georgia, in 1979, with one female eyewitness describing it as: *"The ugliest looking thing I've ever seen... it had a tail like a beaver's, but it's bushy...and a face like a dog."*

*1997:* On June 26th, 1997, Debbie Cross saw a 3 – 4 ft tall, hairy animal with long arms and a short tail outside her rural home near Dunkinsville, Ohio. It walked on its knuckles as it moved away from her.

*2001:* In 2001, nine locals reported seeing a strange primate, while others reported hearing its eerie cries in Danville, New Hampshire. A local fire chief, who spotted the ape-like animal in the pre-dawn hours one night in September, said: *"It jumped out of the trees. As soon as he hit the ground, he took a giant leap and went back where he came from. The first thought I had was: That's nothing that's native to here."* He described the creature as being like a primate with a reddish-brown coat, razor-sharp claws, and a dog-like muzzle. Over the following 2 weeks, parents kept their children home after sunset. After several search parties failed to find the animal, the sightings stopped and the creature was not seen again. It was generally assumed that it was an escaped animal that had likely been recovered by its owner.

<u>2006</u>: An anonymous witness claimed that he returned to his Chicago home, with his family one evening to find a *"devil-like creature violently attacking my 6-year-old Labrador dog* and stated that the animal was *"an unusual combination of a monkey, wolf, and devil,* with *"long fangs, a monkey-like tail, and extremely bright glowing eyes."* The man, who snapped a photo of the beast, which apparently frightened by the flashbulb of the camera, *"sprang to its hind legs and ran,"* escaping through the open door behind them, also claimed that his numerous pets had gone missing from his neighbourhood leading up to his sighting and that another individual had seen an identical beast hanging from a local tree by its tail.

**Beastly Evidence:**

*Deridder Roadkill:* In 1996, Barbara Mullins was driving down a hot and dusty asphalt Louisiana highway called Highway 12. When she noticed a strange creature dead on the side of the road. Pulling over to get a closer look at the animal, she was astonished to see a recently deceased animal, about the size of an adult Saint Bernard and covered in thick brown hair, curiously she noticed that what she at first had taken to be a dog, possessed ape-like feet extending from its bulky body. It had small pointed ears and a very simian-like appearance. Luckily she was equipped with a camera and took a picture of the bizarre beast. On September 5th, the Dequincy News published a story about Barbara's strange find, speculating that it could be a Chupacabra or even a Devil Monkey. The Louisiana Department of Wildlife and Fisheries later examined the photos stating that they believed that the deceased beast was a small breed of domestic dog called a Pomeranian. Many were quick to point out the size differentiation between this breed and a Saint Bernard, although the photo is seemingly lacking in anything, apart from the patchy clumps of grass surrounding the animal, which could provide a reliable object for scale, which, sadly, does nothing to aid us in ascertaining the size of this alleged cryptid carcass.

**Beastly Theories!**

<u>*Napes':*</u> The term *'Napes',* an abbreviation of *'North American Apes',* was first coined by the cryptozoologist Loren Coleman in 1962, inspired by a curious track he discovered (and cast) in a dry creek bed of Steven's Creek, near Decatur, Illinois. This assumed American ape is tailless and thought to belong to an as yet unclassified genus that may include cryptids like the Florida Skunk Ape and the Yeti. However, the descriptions of the Devil Monkey, with its baboon-like muzzle and tail, do not match the ape-like physiology of the *Nape'* or any known ape species, and it is far too large to be any known species of monkey.

<u>*Therapithecus oswaldi:*</u> Could an extant (related) species related to Therapithecus oswaldi (a 220lb, gorilla-sized ancestor of the modern gelada baboon that lived in east Africa during the Pleistocene) be roaming the Appalachian Mountains? It seems unlikely. Besides the ancient date of its demise, likely brought about by human conflict/predation, this fossil gelada, despite its widespread distribution in southern, East, and North Africa, Spain, Italy, and India, is not known to have existed in the New World.

*Gelada (Theropithecus gelada gelada) is the only living member of the genus Theropithecus, "Beast Ape."*

<u>*Feral Monkey Colonies:*</u> Many people believe that the Danville Devil Monkey, in particular, was an escaped primate, most likely a baboon. Certainly, the numerous public encounters with this beast followed by its sudden disappearance seem indicative of an escaped pet running amok for a few weeks before being quietly recovered by its owner. However, several eyewitnesses remain unwavering in their convictions that the animal they encountered does not correspond with any known primate species. There have been several examples of escaped monkeys forming feral colonies in parts of the US. Indeed, Florida, the unofficial invasive species capital of the world, provides a more extreme example of this phenomenon, with its established colonies of Squirrel monkeys, Rhesus Monkeys, and even troops of Capuchin monkeys which have become endemic in the state within the last few decades. Who's to say whether small groups of other species, like baboons or even the odd Mandrill, might not have escaped and are perhaps living, undetected, in other parts of the US?

<u>*Killer Kangaroos:*</u> It has been suggested that escaped Kangaroos could be responsible for Devil Monkey encounters and that there may even be feral populations living in several US states. Kangaroos are great escape artists, their powerful hind legs and feet giving them the ability to jump 10 feet high or to cover 25 feet in a single leap. Phantom Kangaroos have been reported quite regularly in the US since the 1930s, and this steady stream of escapees could certainly explain several purported Devil Monkey encounters.

| Gosainkunda Pass, Nepal.

## KRA-DHAN

G osainkunda pass lies directly north of Kathmandu and is a
popular trekking route for tourists due to its close proximity to
the capital and the popular pull of Gosainkunda Lake, which draws
Hindu and Buddhist pilgrims from far afield to see the place where
Shiva pierced a glacier with his trident to obtain water after
swallowing a poison that threatened to destroy the world, thus,
parenthetically creating Gosainkunda Lake in the process. Nepal is a
well-travelled country that has been on the western bucket list of
must-see nations since the late 19<sup>th</sup> century and its many legends,
including that of the *Yeti*, are well known. And yet, this mysterious
nation may also harbour another mystery species in the form of a
ferocious, giant monkey the locals call, *Kra-Dhan*. And, although
sightings of these terrifying creatures are seemingly rare, what is
certain, is that those who survive an encounter with this imposing
primate are left convinced that they are lucky to have escaped with
their lives!

240

**What's in a name?** The name *Kra-Dhan* name comes from a Bahnar word whose origins are uncertain. Also known as *Bec-boc, Bekk-bok,* and *Con luo iuo i.*

**Monstrous Measurements:** Resembling a large, upright monkey. Approximately 5 ft tall. Black face. Yellow eyes. Long, yellow fangs. Well-built but sinewy, grey-haired body. Long-tail. Long, thin legs.

**Terrifying Tracks:** Large tracks – 18 inches long, 8 inches wide, with a 4 ft stride.

**Beastly Behaviours:** Walks on its hind legs. Very aggressive. Reputed to be able to change colour like a chameleon. Has a ferocious call that sounds like an insane laugh, a raucous roar, or aggressive chattering. Organised. Groups are led by a large dominant male and consist of several individuals of mixed ages and genders. Territorial. Ambushes humans and animals in groups of 7-8.

**Hairy Habitat:** Gosainkunda Pass, Nepal; Annam Highlands, near Kon Tum and Pleiku, Vietnam.

**Scary Sightings:**

<u>1953:</u> Entomologist George Brooks, and Physician, George Moore were ambushed by seven to eight hairy, five-foot-tall, upright, monkey-like creatures while travelling through the Gosainkunda Pass, Nepal, en route to Kathmandu. Moore, who at the time had assumed that they had encountered the infamous, *Yeti,* recounted their harrowing experience in the article titled, *"I Met the Abominable Snowman (A True Story)"* in the May 1957 issue of *Sports Afield,* where he described himself and Brooks, being assailed by the animals after becoming separated from their porters, who were further back along the trail. Moore said of the creatures that were led by a large male, who announced his presence with a raucous roar, accompanied by the angry chattering of the group:

*"...a hideous face thrust apart the wildly thrashing leaves and gaped at us. It was a face that seemed to extend from ear to ear and long, yellowish teeth were chattering. But those eyes, beady, yellow eyes that stared at us with obvious demoniacal cunning and anger. That face!!!... A hand pushed through the leaves. Then a quick movement and a shoulder... As the creature emerged through the dark leaves, we strained to make out his form...The creature was about 5 feet tall, half crouching on two thin hairy legs, leering at us in undisguised fury. Claws or hands seemed dark, perhaps black, while his bedraggled, hairy body was gray and thin. It shuffled along with a stoop the way a Neolithic caveman might have walked. Well-built and sinewy, it could prove to be the most formidable opponent. Teeth bared, it snarled like an animal. Two long fangs protruded from its upper lip... Suddenly, a sharp flicking movement behind it caught our eyes, a tail... Other figures were approaching now from several directions. We could make out 6 or 7 of them through the mist. One appeared to be carrying a baby around its neck. They seemed to mean business as they growled at each other. The one that had pushed through the foliage first was the leader. There was little question as to his authority as he led the attack..."*

The two men, who were indeed in dire straits, decided to fire their guns over the heads of the enraged beasts in the hope of frightening them away, which, after three gunshots per man, seemed to have driven the creatures back, albeit temporarily. The two men could now hear the angry chattering of the beasts, hidden somewhere in the undergrowth, preparing for another surprise assault. Trapped, they knew that their only hope of escape lay in the arrival of their porters, which duly happened, when Shiva (the Gurkha boss of the porters), having been panicked by the sound of gunfire, came hurrying along the trail, searching for his employers.

<u>1943</u>: A Kra-Dhan killed a man near Kon Tum, Vietnam. In his book Abominable Snowman – Legend Come to Life – Ivan. T. Sanderson writes of the incident: *"There is a report that one of these creatures either committed murder or was responsible for a murder near Kontum in 1943. Unfortunately, the matter was tried by the local native court, of which no records were sent to the central French Authority."* He goes on to add:

*"This is not by any means the only report of these Kra-Dhan to be made to foreigners, and we have heard of similar entities in areas far to the west of Kontum."*

## Beastly Theories!

*Extant Orangutan Population:* Could a surviving mainland population of Orangutan, A species that is now limited to the islands of Borneo and Sumatra, explain the legend of the Kra Dhan and Bekk Bok? It seems unlikely. Neither the physiological proportions nor the behaviour of the Kra Dhan matches those of the Orangutan, which, while not docile, is neither an actively aggressive species and is also not territorial, thus making an organised troop ambush on perceived intruders somewhat out of character. Orangutan fossils have been found in Laos, Vietnam, and China. However, not unexpectedly, there is no evidence of their presence in this region beyond the early Pleistocene.

*Giant Mountain Macaque*: Abbe' Pere David, the discoverer of the Giant Panda, noted that a giant mountain macaque (a baboon-like monkey) was believed to exist in eastern Tibet. Could a phenomenon like insular gigantism, wherein the pressure of an isolated and limited environment causes a species to become outsized, have taken effect in an isolated population of mountain macaque, forcing them to become large and more aggressive in order to survive in the unfertile mountains and foothills of Nepal?

*Could an unknown subspecies of giant mountain Macaque be responsible for the legend of the Kra-Dhan?*

<u>*Unidentified Giant Monkey*</u>: Loren Coleman and Patrick Huyghe write in *'The Field Guide to Bigfoot and Other Mystery Primates'* of Giant Monkeys that may inhabit the temperate regions of Asia and the Americas. The Giant Monkey is described as being 4-6 ft. tall, with a doglike or baboon-like face and pointed ears. It has dark piercing eyes and shaggy black or red hair and would seem a perfect match for what both Brooks and Moore encountered in the Gosainkunda Pass, Nepal, in 1953.

# DOGMEN

"A large, muscular, wolf-like or dog-like humanoid, standing from 5 – 8 ft tall, that was once widespread throughout the ancient world but is now rare. Perhaps related to the monkey monsters still seen in Asia, Africa, and South America in the present day. Its feet are dog-like or wolf-like and leave large clawed tracks."

'Welcome to Elkhorn, Wisconsin'

## THE BEAST OF BRAY ROAD

Forty-six per cent of the state of Wisconsin, roughly 16 million acres, is covered in forest. It is home to a thriving grey wolf population, numbering almost 1000 individuals, 40,000 black bears and approximately, 1.9 million white-tailed deer. The rest of the state is punctuated with dairy farms that have earned the State the nickname *'America's Dairyland'* or *'The Cheeselands'*. With its thick forests and profuse prey species, this largely rural landscape makes Wisconsin a perfect home for any number of large, elusive predators to thrive in. It is against this background of rural isolation and environmental abundance that a strange Werewolf-like beast started appearing to people on Bray Road; a quiet rural farm road, which starts along Highway 11, east of Elkhorn and winds west to Highway NN and I-43, just outside of Elkhorn Area High School. Hearing about these strange reports, a local newspaper, *The Walworth County Week*, sent one of their reporters, Linda Godfrey, to investigate these peculiar encounters. Godfrey, who was admittedly sceptical at first, found herself swayed by the sincerity of the witnesses and wrote a series of articles about the creature, which would later morph into her first book, 'The Beast of Bray Road: Trailing Wisconsin's Werewolf.' Since then, the Beast has become part of Wisconsin folklore, spawning numerous books, documentaries, and films. But could there really be anything more to this story than the small town tales that are common to most rural communities?

**What's in a name?** Named after the location of its most infamous sighting, on Bray Road, in rural Wisconsin. Also known as *"Bear-Wolf"*, *"Manwolf"*, *"Indigenous Dogman"*, and *"The Werewolf of Wisconsin"*. Some researchers consider the creature to have been mistaken for a 'Dogman' and say that it is actually a type of Wisconsin Bigfoot, known as the *"Bluff Monster"* or *"Eddy"*.

**Monstrous Measurements:** Height 5 ft 7 inches to 7 ft tall. Weight, 250 – 700 pounds (estimated). Covered in thick, shaggy, Brownish-silver hair. Bear-like or wolf-like head. Long muzzle. Protruding canines. Humanoid shape. Wide chest and shoulders. Clawed fingers. Muscular forelegs. Hind legs are oddly shaped, like a dog's, but longer. It has a tail like a German shepherd or a husky. Bipedal and quadrupedal. Resembling a classic Werewolf.

**Terrifying Tracks:** Dog-like, clawed tracks, 4 inches wide and 4 – 5 inches long.

**Beastly Behaviours:** Nocturnal (although occasionally seen in the day). Can stand on two legs but walks awkwardly. Runs on all fours. Sits on its haunches and kneels like a man. Holds its food, as a man would, with palms facing up. Growls at humans. Aggressive. Will chase people and attack/scratch their vehicles but does not attack humans physically. Has been observed eating/scavenging roadkill and chasing deer. Appears to be intelligent.

**Deadly Diet:** Carrion. Road kills. Wild game (several witnesses claimed to have observed an unusually large wolf-like creature running on all fours through cornfields and pursuing deer).

**Hairy Habitat:** Bray Road, Elkhorn, Wisconsin.

**Scary Sightings:** Stories of mysterious hairy humanoids go all the way back to the very first settlers in Wisconsin, who described canine creatures that would attack before quickly vanishing without a trace. However, most of the detailed reports of the alleged Beast of Bray Road have occurred since 1989.

*1930s:* A man driving through Jefferson County saw what he believed to be a man digging in a field and slowing down to watch him was astonished to see, not a man, but a hair-covered creature that resembled a cross between a dog and an ape rear up to its full height and stare at him. The shocked driver got a good enough look at the monster to see that its hands were shaped like human hands.

*1964:* Dennis Fewless was driving in Jefferson County when he saw a tall, brown-hair-covered man with a head like a dog's, run across the road in front of his car before leaping the fence on the other side of the road and disappearing into a field. Fewless said that the creature 'ran like a man'.

*1980s:* Several witnesses reported that their vehicles were damaged by the Bray Road Beast, which threw tree trunks at them and left long scratch marks on the doors and trunks of their vehicles.

*1989:* In the fall of 1989, Lorianne Endrizzi saw an unusual wolf-like creature kneeling by the side of Bray Road. It seemed to be eating something which had been hit by a car. The creature ran into the woods as she approached it in her vehicle.

*1989:* An 11-year-old girl saw a dog walking on two legs across her family's property near Bray Road.

*1989:* Dairy Farmer, Scott Bray, encountered a *"strange-looking dog"* that left tracks in his cow pasture in September or October 1989.

<u>1997/98:</u> Another werewolf-like creature was encountered by three people in the town of Franklin, Wisconsin, in a partially developed neighbourhood that backed on to old farmland and where their home, was at that time, the only occupied property on the lot. The witness said of their encounter: *"I lived in the town of Franklin, WI. This was about 1997-98, we had just moved into a brand new subdivision and were currently the only house that was built. The rest of the area for a long distance was empty lots on what used to be the adjoining farm's old land. Our backyard had a running creek. On the other side of the creek was some brush and a single-lane road with an old wooden streetlight that gave off an orange hue about 30 yards or so away. It was a warm summer night, and I was having a sleepover with one of my friends. We had all the lights off and were playing hide and seek in the dark. I went back into our sunroom and saw something crouched over illuminated through the brush and the orange streetlight. I'm not sure how to describe its body posture. You know how when you're about to throw up, and you hunch over on your knees and palms? It was similar to that. Its breaths were so deep and heavy that you could see its chest heaving from that distance. We had a 140lb Akita who stood 6 ft. tall on his hind legs. I could easily tell that whatever this was dwarfed my Akita. I also know that it wasn't any type of dog or wolf. Its hind legs were thick and muscular like a man's, but its body tapered at the abdomen and it had a head like a wolf or canine. I called out to my friend who came over and just said "what the fuck is that!?" to me, trying not to make much noise. We sat there as it was hunched for a good 30 minutes. My dad (who was a hardass Vietnam Vet) came out to see what the hell we were doing up so late. We asked what it was and he just said, "I.....don't know." He then went outside as we stayed in, scared for my dad. He had one of those old "megalights" that had "the power of 1000 candles" and took it with him. He stood in the driveway and shined it onto whatever we were watching. It looked back at us and I honestly don't remember its eye colour. What I do remember is that when it took off into the brush it took off upright, like a sprinter from the on all 4's stance. My dad heard it splash through the creek and hightailed it in. It was one of those f****d up moments you don't really talk about because people will think you're crazy. When I heard about it so many years later, I immediately knew I'd seen it too."*

*1999:* Along Bray road on the night of August 13<sup>th</sup>, 1999, a woman and her family saw what they at first took to be a deer. As it steadily approached their car, they could see that it was about 5 ft tall and had glowing red eyes. It came to within 50 ft of their vehicle, before, becoming unnerved by the creature's appearance, they decided to get out of there and drove away.

*1999:* On October 31<sup>st</sup>, 1999, Doristine Gipson was driving along Bray Road when she unexpectedly hit something with her car. Exiting her vehicle to check what she had collided with, she was terrified to see an angry wolf-like creature running towards her. Junming back into her vehicle, she sped away. The werewolf-like creature jumped onto her car but could not hold on, leaving claw marks in the rear passenger door. Gipson later filed a police report in which she described a tall, hairy monster with the face of a dog, prominent fangs, and glowing yellow eyes! The story made its way to local reporter Linda Godfrey who covered the incident, and impressed by the veracity of the witnesses, went on to write her now legendary book, 'The Beast of Bray Road: Tailing Wisconsin's Werewolf.'

*2018:* At about 10 PM on January 27<sup>th</sup>, 2018, Danny Morgan encountered a strange wolf-like creature in the Town of Spring Prairie while driving from Lake Geneva to his home in Menomonee Falls. Morgan, initially seeing the creature walking on all fours in an adjacent cornfield, took it to be an ordinary wolf, and having never seen one in the wild, decided to slow down and take a picture. To his surprise, when the wolf approached the roadside, it suddenly stood up on 2 legs and walked quickly across. Danny said: *"It walked just like any human would...didn't stumble or look awkward. It was swinging its front legs like a human walking. Who knows, maybe it was a werewolf."*

*2020:* In May 2020, Lake Geneva resident, Ron Rice, observed a large, hair-covered bipedal creature while picking up fertiliser to deliver to a farm on Highway 36 just west of Church Road, near the town of Lyons. Ron had stopped to load up his truck with fertilizer at a location in Burlington that is surrounded by deep woods and was sitting in his truck when he noticed a figure about 150 feet away from the driveway. He said: *"This thing was huge, it was over 7 feet tall, and it was brown and hairy with coarse hair. It walked out and picked something up, then turned its back toward me and went back into the woods."* Two weeks later, Ron observed the creature again at the same location as it walked out of the woods before quickly returning to the cover of the trees.

## Beastly Evidence:

*Animal Kills:* Animal mutilations have been reported in the area around Bray Road with animal remains, including deer and livestock that have been partially eaten. However, it should be noted that Wisconsin has a high population of Grey Wolves, and it would not be unexpected to find animal kills in various states of predation in areas in which this species is endemic.

*Wolfman Walking:* On January 29th, 2018, Danny Morgan claimed to have captured a photo of the beast responsible for the Bray Road legend whilst driving on a rural road east of Elkhorn, Wisconsin.

## Beastly Theories!

*Wisconsin's Wolf Problem:* It has been said that Wisconsin has a *'wolf problem'*, with the species being estimated at up to one thousand individuals at the end of 2019, which led many farmers and local people to demand that the hunting quota be doubled from one hundred and fifty to three hundred individuals, a request that was summarily approved in the fall of 2021. However, many have pointed out that since the Chippewa nations legally have the right to claim half of that number, yet, refuse to hunt the wolf, which they consider as a sacred animal and a 'brother', it is doubtful that their population will see any serious decline. Could this unusually high wolf population explain some of the Beast of Bray Road sightings? Could a spinal injury, maybe even caused by an unsuccessful hunt, have produced the awkward bipedal gait of the beast? Certainly, its bipedal and quadrupedal mode of locomotion would indicate that bipedalism is not its natural state!

Could an animal like this, if observed, albeit temporarily, on its hind legs, give someone the impression that they had encountered a werewolf?

*Black Bear*: Wisconsin has an estimated population of 24,000 black bears and although primarily located in the north of the state, they are not generally found in this area and could therefore constitute a good monster impostor candidate. However, that an eyewitness, upon seeing a black bear (even when unexpected), would interpret this creature as a werewolf seems unlikely. It is therefore hard to imagine that these sightings were inspired by an out-of-place bear encounter. Some have proposed, however, that an emaciated bear suffering from mange, if encountered unexpectedly at night, could explain some of the purported behavioural characteristics and physical dimensions of the *Bray Road Beast*.

*Hoax:* The Bray road beast has become something of a golden goose and it would make sense that some details of these alleged sightings might be embellished to further the commercial life of this story. It is also possible that hoaxes and media mania have caused a few attention seekers to enter the fray or for unusual encounters with normal animals (grey wolf, black bear, etc.) to be artificially lumped under the same label. Unfortunately, as is often the case, the creatures of cryptozoology, especially those on the fringe, like the werewolf, offer an endless attraction for commercialised clickbait journalism and those mercantile monster hunters seeking a financial return for their fakery.

*Unidentified Giant Monkey:* Some have theorised that werewolf sightings could be the result of people encountering the remnants of an unknown species of Giant Monkey. Certainly, in a country like the United States, that is historically saturated in European werewolf lore, the natural response would be to identify the *Bray Road Beast* with this superstitious hand me down handle; yet, this identification, lacking in any zoological credentials, only serves to close any investigation into the flesh and blood nature of these creatures; relegating them to the world of the supernatural. But, what if historical werewolf sightings around the world could be explained by the presence of a large upright monkey species, one that may have inhabited many areas of the world, including Europe, up until the medieval period, and perhaps even until the present day? Still, many locals consider the *Bray Road Beast* to be a bonafide werewolf. However, considering the high proportion of Western European descendants that inhabit the state of Wisconsin, this assumption represents more of a cultural twitch than a conclusion.

## OLD STINKER - THE WEREWOLF OF HULL

I n the winter of 2016, Britain's national newspapers were abuzz with reports that people had seen a terrifying, werewolf-like creature prowling around Barmston Drain, a man-made channel near the town of Beverley, in the East Riding of Yorkshire. Some locals were quick to associate the sightings with the legend of Old Stinker, notorious for its characteristically bad breath, which was reputed to roam the Yorkshire Wolds in the 18th century, and soon, the story and the legend garnered attention on the international stage, even rousing rock legend, Alice Cooper to ask, *"So there are suddenly several reports of a werewolf-like creature near a small town in the UK. Do you think it could be real?"* Investigators and pundits alike were out searching for evidence of the mysterious beast and supplying all manner of outlandish theories from Alien visitors to escaped mental patients to explain it. A few weeks later, when the newspapers lost interest and the story eventually faded, encounters with the beast also mysteriously stopped. What could this beast have been and why has no one ever seen it since? In contrast to its Celtic neighbours, English folklore is rather barren of werewolf stories, making the cultural triggers that often cause such kneejerk misidentifications unlikely. Furthermore, Britain has not had a population of wolves for over 400 years and it is unlikely that a missing Malamute would be enough to convince several scared witnesses that they had witnessed something 'paranormal'.

**What's in a name?** *"Old Stinker"* is named for its famously bad breath and is also known as *"The Beast of Barmston Drain"*, which is undoubtedly the same creature or same type of creature, is named after the drainage channel that runs through the countryside. It is also known as *"The Flixton Werewolf"* and *"The Werewolf of Hull."*

**Monstrous Measurements:** Bipedal and quadrupedal. 8 ft tall. Dog-like face (some accounts describe it as being dog-like, but with a human face.) Long snout. Tail. Covered in dark or creamy-beige hair.

**Beastly Behaviours:** Eats dogs, capable of great feats of athleticism, such as jumping 30 ft across a drainage ditch or leaping 8ft. vertically over a fence. Can run on two legs and all fours. Has very bad breath.

**Deadly Diet:** Domestic dogs (observed), Livestock (sheep), and game animals such as deer, grouse, etc.

**Hairy Habitat:** Roams the rural landscape of Yorkshire, England's largest county. May use the deep drainage ditches (such as its infamous haunt of Barmston Drain) to traverse more populated areas after dark.

**Scary Sightings:**

A woman who sighted the *'potential werewolf'* in December 2016 said: *"It was stood upright one moment. The next, it was down on all fours running like a dog. I was terrified. It vaulted 30ft over to the other side of the drain and vanished up the embankment and over a wall into some allotments."* She said that it both ran on two legs and on all fours, having the qualities of both a human and a wolf.

Another couple said they saw something *'tall and hairy'* eating a dog next to a drainage channel, which runs through the countryside. They added that it jumped over an 8 ft-high fence with the animal in its mouth.

Yet another woman, who was walking her dog one evening, spotted something she described as being *'half dog and half-human.* She said that her dog adamantly refused to go any further along the path they were walking.

Jemma Waller, an animal rescue worker, described the moment she came face-to-face with the notorious werewolf *'Old Stinker'* as she was driving through the East Riding village of Halsham. The 24-year-old said the beast looked like *"a big dog with a human face".*

Ms Waller was with two friends at the time of the sighting and said: *"We were driving down this country lane on our way to get some pizza and my friend in the back seat said that he had seen a fox. I looked on my driver's side and saw this beast on all fours, who started to walk straight towards my car on two legs. It looked like a big dog, probably bigger than my car, but it had a human face. It also had this cream and grey fur. My automatic reaction was to keep on driving, but thankfully it didn't keep coming towards me. It just turned around and ran off diagonally. Everyone in the car was really shaken. We'd never seen anything like that before."* The party stopped their car at a nearby petrol station to calm themselves down. When concerned staff asked what was wrong, the friends described what they had seen, only to be told by the staff about the legend of the Beast of Barmston Drain.

Ms Waller said: *"We had never heard about it before, but when we started reading up about it, it was exactly like what we saw. It just made us more scared, to be honest, and I didn't get any sleep that night. It was just like a horror movie."*

*A police sketch of the creature, an animal rescue worker described as being like, "A big dog with a human face." Seems to have a suspiciously Bigfoot-like appearance (Sketch by Andy Rawlins.)*

**Beastly Evidence:**

*FOI Request:* The sightings led to a freedom of information request to Hull Council, which confirmed it had *"No policy on werewolves!"*

*Government Intervention:* The sightings were taken relatively seriously in the local community, with Local Labour Councillor Steve Wilson even offering to *"keep a diary of sightings by people around here and report them to Hull Council."*

*Newspaper reports*: Several newspapers reported on the sightings as they happened, which could reasonably have led to other witnesses using these descriptions to explain their own unusual encounters:

*The Express*: '...Residents in Hull claim to have seen a werewolf in the area. Seven separate eyewitnesses claim to have spotted the 8ft tall creature lurking in an abandoned industrial area outside the centre of Hull. Residents and folklore experts believe the mythical beast, said to turn from a human to wolf at a new moon, is Old Stinker. According to a centuries-old legend, the foul-breathed creature prowls the Yorkshire Wolds.'

<u>The Daily Mail</u>: '...Over the past months, witnesses have come forward to speak of spotting a huge, hairy creature around the Barmston Drain, a man-made channel near the town of Beverley. Some locals believe the sightings are evidence of a mythical Yorkshire beast called 'Old Stinker'... A woman who sighted the potential werewolf in December told the Express, *"It was stood upright one moment. The next, it was down on all fours running like a dog. I was terrified. It vaulted 30 ft over to the other side and vanished up the embankment and over a wall into some allotments."* She said that it both ran on two legs and on all fours, as if with the qualities of both human and wolf. Another couple said they saw something *"Tall and hairy"* eating a dog next to the channel, which runs through the countryside. They added that it *"jumped over an 8 ft-high fence, with the animal in its mouth."*

**Beastly Theories!**

<u>British Bigfoot:</u> Could werewolf sightings simply be misinterpreted encounters with the British Bigfoot; with witnesses, unfamiliar with the bigfoot/wildman phenomenon, simply mistaking these hairy humanoids for the more familiar legends of the werewolf. Certainly, if one thinks back to Lon Cheney's legendary portrayal of 'The Wolfman,' the 1941 Universal Studios picture, his appearance would fit our modern portrayal of Bigfoot far better than any Werewolf. In the last decade, there has been something of a resurgence of wodewose and green man legends in the U.K., which has led to a modern-day phenomenon of British Bigfoot believers. And, although the edifices of our ancient holy architecture and the standards and tapestries of our noble families certainly attest to our ancient cultural knowledge of such a beast in Olde Britain, unfortunately, apart from anecdotal testimony, most of which has coincidentally come to light since the international popularity of *Bigfoot* hunting shows like, *Finding Bigfoot* landed upon our shores in 2011, there is little evidence to suggest that such a beast still haunts our forests and hills.

*Publicity photo of Chaney in full make-up: By Horror Monsters.*

<u>Hoax:</u> Newspaper hoaxes are not a regular occurrence in the UK, but in strange and outlandish subjects like cryptozoology and especially in regards to some of its fringe elements, like werewolf lore, mistaken identity, or indeed, intentional hoax, should always be the default setting for researchers investigating such reports. '*Old Stinker*' and other related Yorkshire werewolves (*The Beast of Barmston Drain, The Flixton Werewolf, The Werewolf of Hull*, etc.) Certainly have a relevant pedigree in the folkloric history of the area, but like so many other reports these days, they are hijacked by journalists who produce articles that are filled with sensational accounts crafted to capture an audience increasingly addicted to clickbait culture. And, in light of

such pervasive embellishment, it would be prudent to entertain the notion that this was simply a big aggressive dog that scared a couple of walkers in 2016.

*Collective Guilt:* In England, most wolves were wiped out by the Anglo-Saxons, although there were areas of England that maintained a remnant population up until the 15th century and Scotland, up until the 17th Century; and Yorkshire certainly held on to its population for far longer than other English counties. Could then the stories of *Old Stinker*, including its modern-day apparition, be a collective hallucination brought on by the cultural guilt we inherited from our ancestors for exterminating the wolf from our landscape hundreds of years ago. Somehow, I think not. Most modern Brits do not even know that their country once had an indigenous population of wolves, bears, and many more animals besides... No, it is far more likely that the sightings began with a case of mistaken identity, which was seized upon by others eager to share in the attention the revival of the legend was receiving, and some who were perhaps, simply too impressionable to second guess what might have been on any other occasion, an easily explainable encounter.

*Missing Malamute:* More than ever before, wolf-like breeds of dogs are being kept as pets in the UK. One only has to think of the Amerindian Malamute, for example, which would certainly give the impression of a wolven creature if encountered at night in one of England's lonely, unlit country lanes. These breeds are fiercely independent and prone to wandering. Could the sudden explosion of Werewolf sightings followed by their cessation in late 2016 simply have been the knock-on effect of a careless owner, losing and later recapturing one of these exotic breeds?

*Unidentified Giant Monkey:* Loren Coleman and Patrick Huyghe write in 'The Field Guide to Bigfoot and Other Mystery Primates' of a Giant Monkey that may inhabit the temperate regions of Asia and the Americas. Known as kra-Dhan and Bekk Bok in Asia and as Salvaje and Isnashi in South America. The Giant Monkey is described as being 4-6 ft. tall, with a doglike or baboon-like face and pointed ears. It has dark piercing eyes and shaggy black or red hair. It is also reputed to be aggressive towards humans and dogs, which draws a parallel with several 'werewolf' reports in western nations. Surely, if a relict population of these animals had survived in small numbers in Europe and North America, then they would be convincing contenders for the fearsome werewolf?

Could this be the view that the ancient Inuit beheld as Norse settlers reached their lands from across the sea?

## THE ADLET

The Inuit are a hardy group of indigenous peoples that inhabit the Arctic regions of Greenland, Canada, and Alaska. Their rich culture abounds with cautionary tales of mythical monsters that represent something of a deified pantheon of dangers inherent in the arctic wastes, which the Inuit inhabit. Among these monsters is the *Adlet*, a werewolf-like entity borne from an unholy union between an Inuit woman and a dog, whose voracious, half-human, half-dog offspring were sent to live on a remote island. But is this legend anything more than a symbol of the creation myths and superstitions common to all cultures, or does the Adlet represent an allegory of the Inuit's cultural interactions and conflicts with an intelligent yet ravenous culture from across the sea?

**What's in a name?** The meaning of the name *Adlet* is uncertain, with some proposing that it is derived from the Inuit stem, *Ad* meaning *below* and therefore might denote, *"those below."* Or *"those that come from below."* Alternatively, others have proposed that the stem *Agdlak*, meaning *"striped"* or *"streaked,"* could be rendered as *"the striped ones,"* a possible reference to the painted faces of the American Indians. It could also come from the word, *"Atlat"* which means *"others,"* which could be a derogatory term used to describe the American Indians. Other names: *Erqugdlit, Erqigdlit*.

**Monstrous Measurements:** Bipedal and quadrupedal. Taller than Inuit and white people. Wolf-like face. Log snout. Dagger-like teeth.

Pointed ears. Piercing yellow eyes. Has the upper body of a man (except for its wolf-like head) and the lower body of a wolf. - Covered in fur, which can be red, black, brown, or white. Sharp claws on its hands and feet. Long-tail.

**Terrifying Tracks:** Wolf-like and clawed.

**Beastly Behaviours:** Fast runner. Superhuman strength. Superhuman eyesight (can see in the dark), hearing (can hear the approach of a hunter from far away) and smell (can smell a fresh corpse from a mile away). Ferocious predator. Strong, bone-crushing jaws. Will attack humans on sight. Hunts in large packs. Extremely cunning. Can paralyse its prey with its piercing howl. Impervious to conventional forms of weaponry and can heal its wounds quickly. Allergic to silver. Afraid of fire. Alpha males are significantly larger and more aggressive than other individuals. If the pack leader is killed, the rest of the pack will flee.

**Deadly Diet:** Carnivorous and, like many predators that inhabit barren environments, will feed on pretty much anything that crosses its path. Inuit legends state that the Adlet prefers human flesh, especially the warm blood of a freshly slain human, over other animal prey. It also enjoys cracking the bones of its prey to get at the marrow inside. Although fully carnivorous, it will eat vegetation if its preferred food is unavailable.

**Hairy Habitat:** Alaska, Northern Canada, and Greenland, especially around the Labrador and Hudson Bay coasts of Canada.

*Wolf killed by Inuit hunter, March 29, 1914, near Schei Island, Greenland:*

**Beastly Theories:**

<u>*Culture Clash:*</u>

The *Adlet* comes from an Inuit legend that seeks to explain the origins of other peoples and also serves as an allegory for the interactions the Inuit had with American Indians and Europeans during their expansion west and south, during the period of the little ice age and also after that, and seeks to provide a creation story for these competing peoples. One version of this tale (there are many) is known as the *'The Girl and the Dog'* or *'The Dog Husband,'* in which a woman who lives with her father and refuses to marry, marries a dog. The union bears issue and the woman brings forth 10 children, some of which are human, some which are dogs, and some which are a mix of both human and dog and are called - *Adlet*. The children are

ANDY MCGRATH

ravenous and are sent to live on an island with only the daily meat provided by their grandfather to sustain them. The meat, which must be collected by their father, is placed in boots that are bound around his neck as he swims between the mainland and their island home. One day, the grandfather, who hates the *Adlet*, places rocks into the boots instead of meat and drowns the dog father. The mother, fearing for the lives of her children, sends some of them inland (The *Adlet*) and some across the ocean (The Dogs) and from them, the numerous peoples with whom the future Inuit's would have contact (namely the American Indians and Europeans) are born.

There are other folk tales, too, in which the *Adlet* are represented as a savage tribe and clearly representative of non-Inuit tribes whom the Inuit perceived as uncivilised. One of these tales, called 'The Tornit and the Adlet', which was published in the Journal of American Folklore, came from a man who was known as the "*Smith Sound Eskimo*", who spent some time in New York City during the winter of 1897-1898, where he told of an Eskimo (Inuit) tradition where Two *Tornit* (*Bigfoot*-like creatures) were captured by a tribe of murderous Adlet. The *Tornit* managed to escape one night by sabotaging the sleds of the *Adlet*, cutting the thongs attached to their dogs; and, as the *Adlet*, woken by the barking of their dogs, mounted their sleds to give chase to the *Tornit*, they fell, allowing the Tornit to make their escape. Here again, The *Adlet* seems to be more of a symbol of conflict with uncivilised (possibly cannibalistic) tribes, and of the clever Inuit, in this case, represented by the Tornit, forever outsmarting their savage enemies.

Indeed, in many of these tales, it would seem that the *Adlet*, which are sent inland, are identified with the savage and marauding tribes that needed to be kept at bay, and the dogs that were sent across the ocean, are identified as Europeans, who would later return and bring beneficial gifts with them to aid the Inuit in their daily travail.

266

| An American Indian medicine man. Oil painting.

## SKINWALKER

The legend of the *Skinwalker* originates from the Navajo people, a Native American tribe primarily located in the American Southwest states of Arizona and New Mexico. In Navajo culture, it is generally believed to be a type of corrupt medicine man, who in contravention of Navajo religious custom, has become a witch. This process usually occurs through a secret initiation into a heretical sect, wherein the initiate offers a human sacrifice in exchange for supernatural abilities, such as the power to transform into an animal like a wolf or bear, which goes some way to explaining the multifarious forms and assignations that Skinwalker reports take, and why some Navajo may even construe an unusual encounter with a known animal-like, a dog or a fox, as being with that of a

Skinwalker. The identity of this beast seems to have undergone something of a transformation since its public expose' in the mid-1990s when a team of scientists descended upon a Utah ranch to investigate a succession of strange phenomena, and since then has morphed into several unexplainable marvels. And, although largely relegated to the status of hoax, there is something of the real in these legends which makes one wonder if they may represent an as yet undiscovered animal.

**What's in a name?** *Skinwalker* is an English rendering of the Navajo, *"Yee naaldlooshii"* which means *"those who trot about with a wolf skin"* or *"by means of it, it goes on all fours"* and belongs to a family of different types of Skinwalkers called *'ánti'jhnii.*

**Monstrous Measurements:** Not quite human and yet, not fully animal. Height 3 - 5ft. 7 in. Black hair. Blazing orange or reddish eyes. The face is marred or featureless (although the skinwalker can steal faces from people). Long arms. Deformed, animalistic body. Sometimes four-legged with a human-like face.

A skinwalker is a person with the ability to transform into any different type of animal at will. They are most frequently seen as coyotes, wolves, foxes, eagles, owls, or crows.

**Terrifying Tracks:** Leaves large tracks, larger than any known animal.

**Beastly Behaviours:** Runs on all fours. Faster than a car. Can traverse vast distances in a single night. Sometimes turning into a fiery ball when running, leaving a trail of colour behind it. Makes fiendish cries like a baby. Can mimic animal sounds and human voices to lure its victims. Wears animal skins (but is otherwise naked) and skulls of the wolf, coyote, cat, dog, or bear, and can also transform itself into one of these creatures. Animalistic in appearance, even when assuming human form. Impervious to death and can only be killed with a bullet or knife that has been dipped in ash. Obtains transformational powers and other supernatural abilities after killing a close family member, usually a sibling. Can read minds and even control the thoughts and behaviour of anyone it locks eyes with. Can bring about misfortune and ill health. Stalks and harasses homes, peering through windows, banging on walls, and scratching its fingernails on the roof. Will sometimes appear suddenly in front of a vehicle on the road to cause an accident. Has power over nocturnal animals, such as owls and wolves. Robs graves to collect ingredients for use in black magic and to make poisons out of their corpses. Can even reanimate corpses to do its bidding. Lives on the expired lifeforce of its victims in a vampire-like fashion and must continue to kill to survive.

**Deadly Diet:** Cattle. Pets. Corpses. Possibly even humans.

**Hairy Habitat:** Commonly encountered near native reservations in Arizona and New Mexico, although encounters are also reported elsewhere in the USA, in states like Utah.

**Scary Sightings:**

*The Running Man:* From 1965 to 1970, people started reporting harrowing accounts with hairy bipedal creatures in New Mexico that local Indians attributed to Skinwalkers, culminating in an incident that occurred in January 1970, when four youths in a car were chased by a hairy man, near Whitewater, New Mexico. The hairy man-like creature, which was approximately 5 ft 7 in tall, managed to keep pace with their car, even when they increased their speed from 45 to 60 miles per hour. Finally, one of the terrified teenagers shot the creature and it fell down, allowing them to escape.

*Skinwalker Stalkers:* In the 1980s, a family driving through the Navajo Reservation in Flagstaff, Arizona, observed a black, hairy figure wearing a shirt and pants (trousers) jump out of a ditch as they slowed to navigate a sharp bend in the road. A few days later, they were awoken by the sound of drumming and chanting outside their home. Standing outside, just beyond their fence, were the three dark man-like figures outside their fence. Who, seemingly unable to navigate the barrier, turned and left.

*Battling Bipedal Dogs:* "So, this happened about twelve years ago. My family owns a farm in the heart of an Indian reservation. One winter, I was home for Christmas taking care of the farm while my parents were away from Christmas shopping. As I was home by myself, way late in the night and I heard all our cows freaking out. I knew it had to be the wild dogs that were rampant in the area. So I throw on some boots, grab a shotgun, load it up, and head out to the field. This was a perfect scenario for a horror movie, it was cloudy, but there was a full moon, and it was breaking through the clouds just right to light up all the snow. I ran out into the middle of the field, and just in time, I see two dogs, they were standing up facing each other and fighting. I think, *"perfect, two for one!"* So I pumped a shell into the chamber of Mr. 12 gauge and then it happened. The two dogs heard the rack, they both stopped, looked over at me, and ran away on their back legs. Immediately I froze, and every ghost story about Skinwalkers and all the other Native legends I grew up with flew through my mind. Keep in mind I am a white guy, and up until then, these were all just boogie man stories the Native kids like to tell to scare us. That night, they became real to me."

*Dogged Dogkiller:* "I was spending a month with my cousins at my grandma's house. It was August and my cousin's ages ranged from ten to fifteen, and I was the oldest (being fifteen). I was staying with a ten, thirteen, and fourteen-year-old. We stayed up telling scary stories often, but one night a few weeks in, we decided to make a campfire outback. My grandma's house is in a rural suburb, the neighbours aren't too far when you're driving down the road to her house, but in the backyard, it's a thick forest with manmade paths through it. Each house is on a hill, so only part of the basement was actually underground. That isn't important until later, though. So, we're towards the east side of her yard, in a smallish patch of open land. You couldn't see the neighbouring yards from there, and there were probably three-quarters a mile to each side of us that belonged to my grandma.

It was maybe eleven at night, and we were playing truth or dare after telling scary stories, and my fourteen-year-old cousin dared me and the thirteen-year-old to go walk through the paths for ten minutes or so. I said yes right away, as I wasn't easily scared and rather level-headed, but my younger cousin was a bit more hesitant. We didn't bring a flashlight because it wasn't pitch dark yet, and we could see enough to not die. We were walking through the paths for about five minutes and could barely see the fire through the trees when we decided to turn. In the middle of the path was a large dog-like creature, hunched over with its front hands an inch from the ground.

What I remember most was how its eyes were so fucking bright white, and it was humanoid-dog shaped with a human-like head but a dog-like body but human hands and feet. It looked right at us and I know I was paralyzed with fear as it dashed away from the opposite way from us, towards a creek that ran through the yard. Eventually, my cousin and I screamed bloody effin murder, and the other cousins and my grandma ran to us. I don't remember much here because I was really disoriented and I couldn't think properly, but I did wake up in bed, so I assume that I was brought up to the house. All the kids slept in the basement, in a big room with sliding glass doors to the outside, as the room was on the side that wasn't underground. My bed was pressed against a big glass window, and I could see my cousins playing outside down below. The house is in Michigan, so it gets slightly chilly even at the end of August, and there was a slight breeze, so I put on a jacket and ran to join them outside, skipping breakfast, not wanting to miss out on anything fun.

When I got down, I could tell they weren't playing but rather running to get my grandma. Her dogs–both of them–were dead, ripped up. That night we went to bed early. I woke up at maybe two in the morning because I felt something hit my head. My cousins were all sitting on the double bed opposite me on the other side of the room.

There was one bunk bed and two double beds, the double beds for me and my fourteen-year-old cousin. They were being quiet and staring at me. The thirteen-year-old nodded his head toward the window. I froze. They all looked afraid. I turned my head slightly to the side and I saw a really messed up-looking face pressed to the window with gaping eyes looking down at me. I screamed so fucking loud, and it bolted. My grandma called the police after I told her what happened and they found nothing. I went home after that and I have never been there during the night again."

*Beauty and the Beast*: "In July 2004, near Gallup, New Mexico, I had my first and only encounter with a Skinwalker. Before this, I used to say, *'I'll believe it when I see it.'* Well, I'm a believer now. What I saw was not full human nor full animal. I was moving and had just completed the cleaning and was with my 10-year-old son. We had called it a night and were headed to our new place. As we walked out the front door, I saw a figure move from behind my neighbour's car to a nearby tree that stood between our apartments. It didn't have red glowing eyes, snarling teeth, or a rotten smell. It did move quickly, but not quick enough to avoid the light from a nearby light post and the porch lights. It didn't look at me or come toward me. It moved as if trying to avoid being seen. I was within fifteen feet of it, but I did not look back to fully inspect it. What I saw was a wolf-like animal that sort of resembled the beast in "Beauty and the Beast", just not cartoonish. It had brown fur that completely covered it, it wasn't a pelt, and it was a very large wolf. It didn't have any human traits except that it walked on its hind legs. It cowered behind the tree as we got into our vehicle. When we got in, I asked my son, *"did you see that??!"* Thankfully, he hadn't. My brother-in-law insists that it wasn't a Skinwalker because I would have never seen it. To this day, I can picture what it looked like, know they exist and pray I never encounter one again."

*Buckskin Pants:* "This didn't happen to me but a very close friend of mine. I've heard a lot about coyotes and Skinwalkers and had a weird experience or two with coyotes (creepiest was waking up to my sleeping bag being surrounded in paw prints without ever hearing them during the night) but never anything paranormal, so to speak. Patrick's story, however, kept me from going back to a favourite backcountry secret stash.

He was leaving the area one morning, had been camping there a couple of days, and said there was a coyote that always seemed to be close by, like in his peripheral vision but never overt. He loaded up his truck and started to drive down the washout to the fire road. At the end of the wash, he could see the coyote following him. When he pulled onto the road, it was running next to him. Now he was freaked out, so he sped up. He said he was going 35 or so, and it was running alongside him. Definitely not possible. When he looked back, the coyote was running on two legs and was wearing what Patrick said looked like buckskin pants. An instant later, it was a person wearing coyote fur keeping pace with his truck. When he looked again... It was gone. We never went back to the grove after that."

*Friendly Faces:* "This all happened about 5 years ago. One night, a few of my friends decided after a night of hanging out that we'd go on an adventure at about 3 am. We took a ride about 50 miles to this old Spanish ruin called *Quarai* in New Mexico that was once the seat of the Inquisition. I can't for the life of me remember what the place is called. So we jump the front gate to the place and start exploring.

One of my friends brought a flute with him and he started playing it and about 30 seconds into his (mediocre) playing, something started screaming really loud on the tops of the long-destroyed walls of the place. It was going from wall to wall quick, screaming the most blood-curdling scream you've ever imagined. We got the fuck out of there (one of my friends pissed his pants) and drove for a few hours to Bandelier National Monument, where we planned to camp out at for the rest of the weekend.

We got to Bandelier at probably like 6 or 7 am and set up our camp. After a few hours just talking about what the hell happened at the ruins, I went to take a piss, probably only like 300 feet from our camp.

This is where everything starts getting a little fuzzy. I remember seeing two dust devils coming my way and when I turned around again, two of my friends were there and they were motioning me to follow them. I couldn't help but to follow them like I was being pulled behind them in shackles.

I followed them for what seemed like 10 or 15 minutes and then I snapped out of it. These weren't my friends; they had bright red hair, with my friends' faces and cat eyes. Both of these friends were brunettes. I stopped walking and they looked at me with the most terrifying gaze I've ever seen. Monsters in movies are nothing compared to this. I turned around and ran as fast as I could back the way I came from. After like 5 minutes of a full sprint, I got back to that rock that I pissed at and found our camp. Everyone was there, still sitting around talking, and didn't even notice that I was gone. I told them what happened with the look-alike Skinwalkers and we packed up everything and left probably within like 10 minutes and got the hell back to Albuquerque."

**Beastly Evidence:**

*Skinwalker Ranch*: The legend of the Skinwalker first came to public attention in 1996, when the Desert News ran a piece titled *"Frequent Fliers?"* chronicling the strange experiences that a Utah family named Sherman had experienced around their ranch. Over an 18 month period, they witnessed cattle mutilations, even finding some of their cows hung in trees, while others disappeared without leaving a single track. Terry Sherman, the father of the family, even claimed to have heard queer voices on the wind while walking his dog that sounded like words spoken in an unfamiliar language and that seemed to be emanating from the darkness. These experiences culminated in Terry's encounter with a big wolf, three times the size of an ordinary specimen, and with glowing red eyes while walking his dog around the ranch in late 1996. Terry, terrified at the spectacle before him, unloaded his shotgun into the creature, which stood there unfazed.

The property, which was sold to Las Vegas realtor and UFO enthusiast Robert Bigelow in 1996, became the location of a long-standing television series and the headquarters for the National Institute for Discovery Science.

*Cryptok Craze!* On TikTok, a trend emerged in 2020 that saw people searching for and photographing 'alleged' Skinwalkers. Most of the clips are poorly staged or doctored with some low-budget CGI. The trend returned again in 2021 and yielded similar results, with some users claiming to have captured a bizarre creature with human legs and a coyote-like body and another clip that claims to show a pale creature running through a patch of long grass towards a group in the car, who 'coincidentally' have that particular area illuminated with their torches and also, 'coincidentally', cut the footage long before the creature can be identified... the results, of course, are predictable and the likes and shares come flooding in. Yet, there is something invaluable in the idea that teenagers are spread out across the country, phones in hand, just hoping to capture something worthy of sharing on their social media; in that, at some point, they may unintentionally do so.

**Beastly Theories!**

*Shamanic Shape-Shifters and Cults of the Wolf!* There is some evidence that the Greco-Roman cult of the wolf existed and was even present in Britain in the first century AD. The roman emperor Nero, too, was reputed to carry out the most brutal atrocities against sacrificial victims in the skin of a wolf, likely in part, as an offering to this abominable religion! There are rumoured to be modern cults that carry out similar practices and whose devotees believe themselves to be the embodiment of or to be possessed by a wolf! Could this practice have also been secretly widespread among a heretical cult of Navajo medicine men, hoping to attain magical powers through the medium of human sacrifice in the semblance of a wolf?

In Navajo culture, witches are anathema and seen as evil. It is also taboo to wear the pelt of any predatory animal, which explains why the Skinwalkers common appearance as a medicine man clothed in the skin of a wolf is such a sacrilegious personification of apostasy. It is also commonly believed that the Skinwalker is capable of transforming itself into an animal, most commonly, the coyote, wolf, fox, cougar, dog, and bear; which goes some way to explaining the large number of Skinwalker reports that consist of nothing more than an animal hanging around a person's property, or exhibiting unusual behaviour.

The confusion surrounding the true enormity of the number of sightings of this beast is compounded by a general reluctance and superstition surrounding the taboo of even mentioning the Skinwalker, and the Navajo will not speak with outsiders about these creatures for fear of reprisal. Dr Adrienne Keene, Native American academic, writer, and activist, sums up this stubborn cultural exclusivism when she says about the Skinwalker, *"These are not things that need or should be discussed by outsiders. At all. I'm sorry if that seems 'unfair,' but that's how our cultures survive."*

A Navajo Medicine Man: by Edward S. Curtis. USA, 1900. The picture is housed in the Wellcome Collection and is on display.

<u>Lost in Translation:</u> The ancient Navajo stories that we are being told today may simply be rehashed versions of the original culturally modified tales told to the original Europeans, aeons before. And, that in those antique times, an attempt to express these beings in a way that the original European settlers would understand may have inspired the Navajo to incorporate elements of European folklore to better convey their meaning to an audience unfamiliar with their religious beliefs. For example, anyone who has travelled to far-flung corners of the world would have had the experience of elucidating one of their own cultural customs or ideas, using, sometimes awkwardly fitting local examples! Could the wolf-man-like attributes of the Skinwalker have their route in European legends of the Werewolf?

<u>Unidentified Giant Monkey:</u> Loren Coleman and Patrick Huyghe write in '*The Field Guide to Bigfoot and Other Mystery Primates*' of a Giant Monkey that may inhabit the temperate regions of Asia and the Americas. Known as *Kra-Dhan* and *Bekk Bok* in Asia and as *Salvaje* and *Isnashi* in South America. The Giant Monkey is described as being 4-6 ft. tall, with a doglike or baboon-like face and pointed ears. It has dark piercing eyes and shaggy black or red hair. It is also reputed to be aggressive towards humans and dogs, which draws a parallel with several 'werewolf' reports in western nations. Surely, if a relict population of these animals had survived in small numbers in Europe and North America, then they would be convincing contenders for the fearsome werewolf?

| Rural Village in Ethiopian Highlands

## HYENA MAN

The *Werehyena* is the cultural embodiment of the many dangers that lurk in the rural landscape of the Horn of Africa. Each day, before the sun sets, local farmers can be seen racing home to lock their cattle indoors. Market stalls hurriedly shut up shop and anxious mothers call their children home. Here, superstition occupies a primary place in the lives of the local people, many of whom believe that evil spirits like *Jinn* and shapeshifting *Buda* (witches/wizards) like the *Werehyena* roam the towns and countryside after dark. Certainly, the dangers are very real, with savage hyenas, packs of wild dogs, lions, and even wolves inhabiting the region, making a cultural bogeyman a much-needed monster to warn the foolish away from venturing out unaccompanied into the night. But, does this legendary being constitute any more than a cautionary tale; or is there a real flesh and blood animal, inextricably melded into the myth of this sub-Saharan therianthrope?

**What's in a name?** The name, *Werehyena* is an analogy of the more commonly known *Werewolf*. Also known as *Bouda*, or *Buda* ("Witch" or "Wizard") in Ethiopia, Sudan, Tanzania, and Morocco; *Kaftar* in Iran; *Qori Ismaris* ("One who rubs himself with a stick") in Somalia; and *Bultungin* or *Kabultiloa* ("I change myself into a hyena") in the Kanuri language of the Lake Chad region.

**Monstrous Measurements:** Bipedal and quadrupedal. Resembling a giant hyena, a human-hyena hybrid, or a hairy human. Hairless, except for a tuft of hair on its upper back. Large golden or red eyes. Has two mouths with which it can talk and eat at the same time.

**Terrifying Tracks:** Hyena-like.

**Beastly Behaviours:** Nocturnal. Solitary but also hunts in packs. Man-eater attacks people at night and sucks blood from their necks. Massive appetite. Buries its victims alive to feed on later. Robs graves. Shapeshifter. Can transform between a man, human-hyena hybrid, or giant hyena. Possesses superhuman strength. It can mesmerise its prey with its eyes or pheromones. Nasal voice. Haunting laughter-like cry, similar to a hyena. Imitates human voices and calls people by name to lure them to their doom. Has the power to heal when in human form. Understand the art of blacksmithing. Can be identified in human form by its hairy appearance and foul odour.

**Deadly Diet:** Blood and flesh of animals and humans.

**Hairy Habitat:** Arabian Peninsula, the Levant, North Africa, the Horn of Africa, and the Near East, as well as some adjacent territories.

**Beastly Evidence:**

Ancient Literature:

1376: A Persian medical treatise written in 1376 tells how to cure people known as *"kaftar,"* who are said to be *"half-man, half-hyena,"* and who have the habit of slaughtering children.

<u>*1406:*</u> Al-Doumairy, in his Hawayan Al-Koubra (1406), wrote about vampire-like hyenas that would fall upon people in the night and suck the blood from their necks. Arab folklore from around this period also tells of these vampire-like beasts that could hypnotise victims' with their eyes or their pheromones.

A hyena as depicted in a medieval bestiary.

## Beastly Theories

*Unidentified Giant Monkey:* These cryptozoological creatures are generally described as being 4 to 6 ft tall, with muscular bodies, barrel chests, thick arms, strong legs, and a thick tail. Their faces are often described as doglike or baboon-like, with prominent fangs, dark piercing eyes, and pointed ears. They have a heavy hair or fur coat and large flat feet, between 12 – 15 inches in length that narrow as they lengthen. Many researchers have theorised that many Werewolf/Dogman-like sightings might be based on a mistaken identity of this, as yet undiscovered, giant monkey. A species that would likely correspond with the familiar *'dog-like'* features that are described on these creatures in diverse countries around the world.

*Hyena Men:* There are, in the Ethiopian town of Harar Jugol, men that perform a most peculiar form of public service. These men, who gaze daily into the jaws of death, are called 'Hyena Men' and as their name implies, they have managed to nurture a relationship of a most unusual kind with the local hyena population; wherein, they have taken to feeding the animals at several established locales on the outskirts of town, which the hyenas repay by chasing out, or consuming all of the invisible Jinn (evil spirits) in the town and even more helpfully, by not attacking any of the townsfolk. The custom, which is believed to have started during a famine in the 1890s, has had a profound effect on Hyena predations in the area, although local legend professes that the people of this region have continued this practice in some form or another for over 200 years; during which time, there have been no hyena attacks on the local population. Indeed, these Hyenas are so used to seeing people as feeders instead of food that there is a nightly show for tourists, where, for a fee, they can watch the 'Hyena Men' feed these savage beasts by hand. And, if brave enough, even try the age-old custom themselves! Could the legends of these hyena whisperers have spread throughout the region, their character transforming with each telling, from men who feed hyenas to men who are hyenas.

*Hyena Men of Harar, Ethiopia: By Karoline Piegdon.*

*The Legendary Language of Discrimination:* In Ethiopia, it was commonly believed that Blacksmiths were particularly prone to turning into Werehyenas. This superstition later became focused on the countries Jews, for whom blacksmithing was a common hereditary profession. This early form of antisemitism seems to be contingent on the cannibalistic blood libels that have so often been lain at the door of this ostracised group. The Ethiopians (who referred to blacksmiths as Bouda - witch/wizard) believed that these blacksmithing Jews were capable of transforming into Hyenas and that they would regularly dig up the corpses of the dead and consume them. The unfortunate Jews, being excluded from schools and prohibited from working in most professions, were often trapped in blacksmithing or woodcutting, which required no formal education. They often found themselves relegated to being scapegoats for any misfortunes that may befall their superstitious neighbours.

# AMPHIBIOUS ANTHROPOIDS

*"These semi-aquatic, anthropoidal forms are always described with both arms and legs and with ape-like or sometimes, reptilian characteristics. Unlike the Merbeings of old, they do not have tails and prefer rivers, lakes, ponds, and swamps to the open sea. Their tracks are 3 toed and webbed."*

Devil's Rock - the very same the ancient scene of an 'Anishinaabe' Indian encounter with the Memegwesi, a semi-aquatic Littlefolk, who the Indians caught stealing fish from their nets?

## MEMEGWESI

The Memgwesiwak are a race of Little People of Native American legend that live in hollow rocks or underground caverns near large bodies of water. They are, in presentation, essentially, a type of semi-aquatic dwarf or faerie, similar in many respects to those of Europe, and yet occupying an environmentally diverse position, in what was then, a new land. Yet, within the mythology surrounding these 'little people', there is the possibility of a link between a primaeval race that may have once existed around the globe. Could the *Memegwesiwak* represent an aquatic form of the proto-pygmy, similar to the dwarves and Aelfs of Europe, or is their presence in North America an affectation of the mythical beings brought to this land during the age of colonialism by myriad explorers of diverse languages and customs?

**What's in a name?** The name *Memegwesi* comes from an Ojibwa word meaning: *"hairy-faced dwarf"* and is pronounced *may-may-gway-see.*

285

Its plural is, *Memegwesiwag*. Also known as *Maymaygwayshi*, *Mee'megwee'ssi*, *Mekumwasuck*, *Memegwecio*, *Memegwicio*, *Memekwesiw*, and *Nagumwasuck*. Although it is commonly espoused that their name comes from the Ojibwe word for hairy, *"memii"*, some researchers believe that their name is related to the word for butterfly, *"memengwaa."*

**Monstrous Measurements:** Child-sized. 3 – 4 ft tall. Monkey-like. Completely hairy, including the face. Bighead. Narrow face. Flat nose. Longbeard. Old-looking and ugly. Short arms. Bowed legs.

**Terrifying Tracks:** Tiny, baby-sized footprints.

**Beastly Behaviours:** Believed by the local Indians to be a dwarf-like creature that dwells on the riverbanks and beside lakes or in cliffs and large boulders. They are generally benign but will cause mischief or steal things or throw rocks at people's houses if they are not shown respect. They are shy and will hide if spotted by humans. They are excellent swimmers and characteristically raise their arms out of the water when surfacing. They can also utilise logs and sticks as makeshift watercraft. They are incredibly strong and can even uproot trees. Sometimes they will challenge people to tests of strength. Capable of fashioning stone arrow points, drums, baskets, and rudimentary coverings from chickadee skins. Carves rock art. Has a peculiar nasal voice that sounds like the drone of a dragonfly. Plays pranks on humans on stormy nights and smokes tobacco, which the local Indians would traditionally leave as an offering when traversing through its territory. In Ojibwe traditions, it is believed that only children and medicine men can see the Memegwesi.

**Deadly Diet:** Eats fish and wild rice.

**Hairy Habitat:** *Memegwesi* dwell in riverbanks, caves, or boulders in the Lake Superior area of central Ontario, northern Manitoba and Saskatchewan, Canada; and northern Minnesota; northern Wisconsin; northern Michigan and Maine; USA.

## Scary Sightings:

*Lake Timiskaming Legend:* There is a story of a local Indian tribe encountering and even capturing one of these beings on Lake Timiskaming. *'The Indians were passing the high ledge of rock a few miles below Haileybury, where the water was very deep and where they had set their nets. They found that somebody had been stealing fish. They proceeded to watch the nets and soon saw three Me*'*megwe*'*s*'*i come out astride of an old log for a canoe, using sticks for paddles. The Indians pursued them, the fairies meanwhile hiding their faces. Finally, the Indians caught one. Then one Indian said, "Look behind!" When the fairy turned quickly, they got a glimpse of how ugly he was. The Indians then took a knife from this fairy and the rest disappeared, riding their log through the rock wall to the inside, where they could be heard crying, as this was where they lived. The Indians then threw the knife at the rock and it went right through to the inside to its owner.'*

*Split Rock Channel & Memegwesi:* Another tale recounted by Diamond Jenness, in his book, *'The Ojibwa Indians of Parry Island, their social and religious life'* unfolds in an almost duplicate manner: *"At the north end of Parry sound, in what white men call Split Rock channel, there is a crag known to the Indians as Memegwesi's crag. ("Memegwesi is a friendly manido, or rather a band or family of manidos. They may play pranks on the Indians, but never harm them.") Some natives once set night lines there, but their trout were always stolen. At last, one of the men sat up all night to watch for the thief. At dawn, he saw a stone boat approaching manned by two Memegwesi, one a woman, the other bearded like a monkey. The watcher awakened his companions, and they pursued the stone boat, which turned and made for the crag. Just as the thieves reached it, the woman turned around and called to the Indians, 'Now you know who stole your trout. Whenever you want calmer weather, give us some tobacco, for this is our home.' The boat and its occupants then entered the crag and disappeared, but the Indians still offer tobacco to these Memegwesi whenever they pass their home."*

*Cabbage Town Monster:* On a warm summer's day in August of 1978, a local man named 'Ernest', from the neighbourhood of Cabbagetown, Toronto, was searching for a kitten that had gone missing from a litter that he and his wife had been raising. Whilst searching in the vicinity of their Parliament St. apartment, he came across a 'cave' at the bottom of a narrow passageway between his building and the one next door. Deciding that he'd better search the cave to make sure that the kitten hadn't wandered inside, he began to crawl inside, flashlight in hand, to see if he could find it. Until, when he was approximately 10 ft. inside the cave, he was confronted by something he described as *"a living nightmare that I'll never forget."* He said of the monster: *"it was long and thin, almost like a monkey, three feet long, large teeth, weighing maybe 30lbs with slate-grey fur. It was the eyes that truly stood out, orange and red and slanted.* In a strange turn of events, Ernest claimed that the creature spoke to him, saying, *"I'll never forget it. It said, 'Go away, go away,' in a hissing voice. Then it took off down a long tunnel off to the side. I got out of there as fast as I could. I was shaking with fear."* He stated, *"The last I saw the creature, it was heading off into the dark. The passage seemed to drop down very quickly and go a long way back."*

Following his encounter, Ernest spoke reluctantly to The Toronto Sun Newspaper, who found out about his experience and agreed to discuss his encounter only if his last name was not revealed. Ernest, accompanied by a reporter from the newspaper, reluctantly returned to the location of his strange sighting in March of 1979, where they discovered the corpse of a cat half-buried in the tunnel. Later, Toronto's Sewer Department thoroughly inspected the tunnel as it was feared that children might try to enter it and noted that it connected to the sewer system. Leading some researchers to speculate that it was an access point used by a subterranean dwelling creature to reach the surface and yet others to propose that the creature was one of the legendary river-dwelling dwarves, known to the Algonquin tribes as *Memegwesi*, that thrived in the city's rivers and streams before the city's expansion when many of them were built over.

**Beastly Evidence:**

*Spirit Holes:* The Ojibwa believed Little Wild Indians named Memegwesi inhabited splits and cracks in rocks and that the impossible man-made holes (drilled into solid rock) that often appear in structures like those in America's Stonehenge in North Salem, New Hampshire, were made by them; causing them to take the precaution of offering up a little tobacco in votive fashion, when passing their alleged homes, to ensure the little dwarfs' favour.

*Anencephalic Infants:* Modern folktales, alleging the discovery of the physical remains of tiny people are found throughout the United States, with the almost universal mystery disappearance of the remains, usually after being sent to the Smithsonian or some other such reputable institution for analysis, being featured prominently in these modern folktales. One such disappearance that may have contributed to these tales, but for which we have some evidence, came from a cave in the San Pedro Mountains in the 1930s. Leading some to believe that a race of cave-dwelling 'little people' had dwelt there in former times. The tiny corpse, which was sitting, cross-legged in an upright position, had a flat skull and tan skin, was approximately 7 inches tall and would have likely stood 1 foot tall when standing. The tiny mummy was largely dismissed as an anencephalic fetus by scientists, which was criticised by its proponents, who argued that the mummy had a full set of teeth. Unfortunately, the little mummy disappeared in the 1950s before further testing could be done.

*Pygmy Graveyard:* A graveyard unearthed in the 1830s in Coshocton County, Ohio, was believed to contain skeletons belonging to a pygmy race. The graves, which were approximately 3 feet long, were arranged with their heads facing west, giving rise to the theory that they were sun-worshippers. Interestingly in William J. Bahmer's *"Centennial History of Coshocton County"*, he writes that the missionary, David Zeisberger had suggested in 1778 the possible existence of little peoples in North America and believed that a certain burial ground, near Cochocton, Ohio, contained several remains of a pygmy race, about 3 ft. in height. Unsurprisingly, as with all of these legends, the locations and physical evidence of their discovery are missing. It should be noted that these disappearances largely occurred at a time when people in the old world were unearthing and cataloguing much of Egypt and Greece and the public was becoming keenly interested in the history of past peoples, thus making the alleged disappearance of these artefacts suspicious.

_Pictographs:_ Pictographs on the Semple River near Oxford House in northeast Manitoba that depict alleged stick figures of Memegwesiwag with lines running from their heads are said to commemorate the spot where the dwarfs cured a woman. The story runs as follows:

### The Legend of the Oxford House Rock Painting:

'A woman of the Oxford House Band was very sick. The woman's family asked an old man named Mistoos Muskego to come and cure her of her illness. The old man tried again and again to cure the woman, but nothing seemed to work. Finally, the old man said that there was only one hope left and that was to go and ask the men who lived in the rock if they could give him the powerful medicine needed to cure the woman. The old man left in his canoe and paddled up to where he knew the men who lived in the rock dwelt. (This spot is today a high granitic rock face rising sharply straight upwards from the Semple River even as it was in Misttos Muskegos' day). The old man was very powerful and used his power to enter into the rock unto the home of the men who lived in the rock. The old man talked for a long time with the men who lived in the rock and asked for the medicine that would cure the woman and in the end, he was given the medicine he requested. The old man then left the rock and paddled back to the home of the woman who was ill. The medicine of the men who live in the rock was given to the woman who was ill. This medicine cured the woman. The old man said that all should remember it was the men who lived in the rocks who were powerful and could give medicine to a powerful old man. The old man then made a paint and asked all people to come with him to the home *of the men who lived in the rocks. The old man and the people then paddled their canoes up to the solid rock where the old man left his canoe and stood on the rock ledge by the water. He told the assembled people how he had received the medicine. He then said that no one should forget the men who lived in the rock and that he would draw a painting of them. (He then drew a painting approximately two feet high, stick figured and with lines running from the head, giving a rabbit-eared look). The people now would remember [where] the men who lived in the rock lived and what they looked like and all returned home.'*

As told to C.J. Wheeler in the Cree First Nation of Bunibonibee (Oxford House). Adapted from de Wheeler, C. J. (1975). The Oxford House pictograph: The May May Quah Sao are alive and well at Oxford House. Dans J. Freedman et J. H. Barkow (eds.), Proceedings of the Second Congress, Canadian Ethnological Society (p. 701-714). Canadian Ethnology Service Paper 28(2), Mercury Series. Ottawa: National Museum of Man.

## Beastly Theories!

<u>Hidden Homes:</u> In its infancy, Toronto had numerous streams and waterways that were surrounded by thick forests. As the city expanded, these waterways were built over and became a subterranean network of underground streams, hidden beneath the sprawling metropolis and intersecting with its sewer systems. Did this expansion of the city spell the end of the *Memegwesi* that thrived in these rivers in ancient times? Or do they still exist in much-depleted numbers beneath the city, functionally extinct, emerging only after dark to feed upon the scraps left behind by our civilisation?

<u>Faerie Folklore:</u> The *Memegwesiwak* bare all the hallmarks of other little people legends and are very likely the product of Native American legends cohabitating with European faerie lore. The superstitious lore surrounding the behavioural do's and don'ts when interacting with *Memegwesi* also tend to support this notion. They are described as benign unless disrespected, and then they are

troublesome and mischievous, playing nasty pranks on people for fun and hiding things or stealing. They act as warnings against the wilderness for children, with those wandering away or breaking likely wilderness survival taboos or trespassing upon their territory (which in reality, were likely inhabited by predatory animals all too willing to prey upon a child) being taken away by the little people and never being seen again. They are territorial, unpredictable, possess magical qualities, and can be placated or even invoked to aid a person if the right offerings are made. Although it is clear that Native American tribes had their own beliefs in faerie-like beings before the arrival of the Europeans, one cannot help but reach the inescapable conclusion that the fairies and elves of Ireland, Scotland, England, Norway, France, etc. had already had an irreversible influence upon their character and form, by the time that these tales were written recorded.

_Proto-Pygmies:_ Is there any scientific credibility to the reports of little hairy men in North America and other diverse locations around the world? And, could there be any fact behind the little people fictions that pepper First Nations folklore? Maybe! In 2003, fossil remains of what has been affectionately dubbed, 'The Hobbit', were found in a cave on the island of Flores in the eastern Indonesian archipelago. This species (_Homo Floresiensis_) was believed to be a pygmy form of Homo erectus that stood only 3ft 6 in tall and that may have lived as recently as 12,000 years ago. This discovery would seemingly add some weight to the proliferation of Little People legends that are peculiar in their uniformity throughout many diverse cultures and nations.

Desna River at dawn. Ukraine.

## RUSALKA

Manifestations of the Rusalka are endemic throughout the Slavic folklore of Eastern Europe and Russia, where she has persisted since pagan times, as a benevolent water deity that arises from the water in the spring to give moisture to farmer's fields and crops. Later, in the 19th century, however, the personification of the Rusalka took on a darker tone and she was framed as the drowned soul of an abused woman or a murdered girl, who would lure young men into the water with her beautiful looks or voice; before wrapping her long hair around their legs and pulling them beneath the water, or tickling them to death, (presumably until they drowned) as she laughed. And it is this latter form, often being portrayed as *'hideous and hairy'*, that concerns us here.

**What's in a name?** The name *Rusalka* Plural, *Rusalki,* is derived from the Latin word *Rosālia,* which is used to denote the period of Pentecost, and likely entered into Slavic usage via the Byzantine Church of the medieval period, through its Greek rendition of ρουσάλια. She is also known as the *Vodyanitsa* ("the water maiden"). *Chertovka* ("she-devil"), *Khitka* ("adbuctor"), *Loskotukha* ("tickler" or "she who tickles"), *Shutovka* ("she-joker"), *Kupalka* ("bather"), and *Mavka* ("the dead")

**Monstrous Measurements.** There are two primary types reported: The first that is more closely related to the old pagan fertility deity or water nymph is something like a beautiful naked mermaid, with green or garlanded hair, though she is pictured as having legs rather than a fishtail. The second type is ugly and hairy, with large drooping breasts and long tangled hair that hangs around a grimacing monkey-like face. In the north of Russia, Rusalka is only portrayed as a hideous hairy woman with drooping breasts.

**Beastly Behaviours:** Lives in the forest during the summer and the water the rest of the year. Fond of tree-climbing, swinging on the branches, and diving from trees on the riverbank into the water. Excellent swimmer and diver. Fast runner. Can jump far. Has a shrill cry and a cackle-like laugh. Sometimes wears a covering of green leaves or old rags it obtains from humans. (Many Ukrainian and Byelorussian songs feature Rusalka begging human girls to give them clothes). Drowns people by tickling them to death. Has a mischievous nature. Likes to play pranks on fishermen by emptying their nets, replacing the fish with water plants and mud, or putting out their campfires by ringing the water out of their wet hair. They also play tricks on animals, like geese, whose wings they entangle, so that they cannot fly.

**Deadly Diet:** Rusalka are said to be fond of Hemp and Rye, in some regions and, like many other Wildmen, are alleged to raid farmer's fields at night, grazing on their crops.

**Hairy Habitat:** Rivers, streams, and forests in Eastern Europe and Russia.

**Scary Sightings:**

_1830s/40s:_ The Russian novelist Ivan Turgenev was said to have told his friends Guy de Maupassant and Gustave Flaubert a story of a harrowing encounter he had with a female Rusalka in his youth, in the 1830s or 1840s, in the dense forests where he used to hunt, around the Desna River, Ukraine.

_"On this particular foray into the forest, Turgenev had found a quiet river and overcome with a desire to swim in it, stripped, dived in, and was leisurely floating past the grasses and roots, when he felt a hand touch his shoulder. Somewhat startled, he turned to see a frightful creature with a vast, wrinkled smiling face, staring hungrily at him. It had two large breasts that floated in front of it and a mass of tangled, sun-bleached hair, which hung around its face and fell down its back. Turgenev, overcome with fear, began to swim frantically to the bank and was pursued by the monster, which all the while was continuously touching his neck, back, and legs and cackling with delight. Almost mad with terror, he reached the bank and ran at full speed through the woods, leaving his gun and clothes behind, while the dreadful woman kept pace with him, growling. Finally, worn out with fear and exertion, he was ready to drop to the ground when a boy, who had been watching his goats, came to his aid with a whip and flogged the fearsome beast, who ran away howling in pain. Turgenev last saw her disappearing among the leaves of the trees, almost like a female gorilla. Later, the shepherds told Turgenev that the creature was a madwoman, who had lived in the wood thirty years on the charity of the shepherds, spending most of her days swimming in the river."_

**Beastly Evidence:** There really is no evidence for the Rusalka as a living being other than Turgenev's anecdotal encounter. Indeed, apart from this tenuous link with the wildman, we do not have any evidence that it is representative of a flesh and blood animal at all. Except that, the assignation of Turgenev's encounter, as being that of a Rusalka, may be evidence of the use of culturally pervasive appellations to describe that for which the witness has no words. And the Rusalka as a Wildwoman could simply be the colloquial equivalent of calling a large unknown lizard a dragon, or a gorilla, a wildman of the woods. And, even though the Rusalka's existence, at some point in history, is implied through the continuation of the myths and legends that disseminate themselves through the symbolic naming of streams, rivers, and woods, throughout this vast region, and which continue to inspire the creation of modern tales, like the famous opera, 'Rusalka', written by the legendary composer, Antonin Dvořák in 1900, who based his Libretto upon its folklore; it does not occupy a position anymore tangible than the mermaids and nymphs of other nations.

*Alexander Pushkin's Rusalka. Dnieper bottom. Rusalka and her daughter. Original Art by I. Volkov, engraving. (Originally from NIVA magazine, page 87) By I. Volkov - pushkin.aha.ru by Golubchikov Aleksandr.*

### Beastly Theories!

*Fertility Wights*: In ancient times, the Rusalka were originally Slavic fertility wights or spirits that watered and nurtured crops. Some have even associated their myth with a belief in the benevolent Mokosh', the Old Slavic goddess of fertility and protectress of women. Later, in the nineteenth century, the character of the Rusalka changed and it became viewed as a malevolent trickster and an unclean spirit, borne out of the spirit of a female drowning victim or the murder of a young woman. Could the identification of the Rusalka with the wildman have grown out of this relatively recent time, wherein the beautiful water nymph became an ugly-faced, hairy and licentious Wildwoman?

*Waterbound Wildwoman!* Conversely, many tales of Wildmen testify about their love of water. Could the ancient Slavic folklore surrounding this water Nymph be based upon ancient encounters with this water-bound Wildwoman, reinterpreted over the ages into romantic folklore and prose? Certainly, Russian novelist Ivan Turgenev's harrowing encounter in the Desna River, Ukraine; indicates that the Wildwoman has a human-like ability to swim, even if not fully aquatic, which may account for many tales of the treacherous Rusalka luring young men, seduced by her voice, into deep water where they would be terrified by her ugly face and hairy breasts as she entangled their feet with her long hair or tickled them to death (by drowning). Interestingly, in various neighbouring eastern European nations, tales of the Rusalka testify to her occupation of the water and forest and field at different times of the year. Could these distinct accounts be observations of the migratory journeys and seasonal foraging in the lifecycle of the wildman?

Водные глубины. Омут Холст, масло (1907) Ву Дженеев Иван Алексеевич.

*Mermaid:* Although water-bound, the Rusalka is more closely related to a nymph-like being than a mermaid and is always depicted with legs, whether in water or on land. Furthermore, her common representation as to the unhappy female victim of a suicide, drowning or murder, is likely an early psychological coping mechanism for rural religious communities to come to terms with the misfortunes that life can inflict upon the living; or even a religious warning to the unfaithful upon the loss of an unbaptised child, or of a virgin who was drowned, of the dangers of foregoing the virtuous milestones of religious life.

*"DANGER!! Do not swim or play around here."* A kappa is depicted as a metaphor for drowning on a sign near a pond in Fukuoka.

## KAPPA

Japan is a country where superstition and tradition coexist peacefully alongside the modern world. In line with the precepts of their most ancient and culturally ingrained religion of Shintoism and the slightly newer (6th century AD) religion of Buddhism; Japanese people hold much of the natural world as sacred and often show reverence or respect (matsuri) by honouring or worshipping the multitudinous gods and spirits that are believed to inhabit the forests, mountains, rivers and streams of their islands. Within this complex and unending gradient of revered beings are the Yokai, a class of demons among whom the most prominent, or famous, is the Kappa, a malevolent, cucumber-loving Merbeing that inhabits rivers and lakes throughout Japan. But is this mythical merman just another player in the paranormal pantheon of Japanese folklore, or could there be a flesh and blood beast hidden behind the chimeric characteristics of the cryptid Kappa?

**What's in a name?** The name *Kappa* literally means "River Child" or "River Sprite." It is also known as *kawatarō* ("river-boy"), *Komahiki* ("horse-puller"), *Kawatora* ("river-tiger"), And *Suiko* ("water-tiger"). Other commonly used names are *Kawachi*, *Kyuusenbuu*, *Masunta*, *Mujima*, and *Ningyo*. In total, there are over 80 different names for the Kappa.

**Monstrous Measurements:** Half human and half turtle or frog. Ape-like face. Long hair. Both bipedal and quadrupedal. Height, 3 – 4 ft. Estimated weight, 20-50 pounds. Dish-like hollow in the top of the head (called a 'Sara') where water is kept. Turtle-like carapace on its back. Scaly or slimy limbs. Webbed hands and feet. Three anuses?

**Terrifying Tracks:** Webbed Feet. Teardrop-shaped. 22cm long and 12cm wide. Stride 50-60cm apart.

**Beastly Behaviours:** Active in summer. Changes colour like a chameleon, according to match surroundings. Has superhuman strength. Can swim like a fish and smells like fish. Primarily aquatic, but will occasionally venture onto land. Tries to drown children, solitary travellers, and animals and drink their blood and eat their livers in a vampire-like fashion, or remove a mythical organ from their anus called the shirikodama. Lecherous creature, reputed to rape female swimmers, as depicted in an 18th-century painting called: '*A kappa rapes an ama diver underwater*' from Utamakura (Poem of the Pillow). Likes to wrestle humans. Cries pearls instead of tears. Credited with having taught the art of bone setting and other medical practices to humans. Has a depression on its head full of liquid, which must be full whenever a kappa is away from the water. If damaged or spilt, it will die. (Possibly indicating an animal that breathes oxygen through water and must bring its own supply of oxygenated water from its watery abode in order to breathe when making short forays onto dry land.)

**Deadly Diet:** Favourite food is the cucumber (at festivals, offerings of cucumber are often made to the kappa). It is also fond of Japanese eggplant, noodles, and fermented soybeans. But has an alleged aversion to iron, sesame, and ginger. It is also reputed to kidnap children and animals to drink their blood and eat their livers.

**Hairy Habitat:** Kappa are said to be most prevalent in the rivers, lakes, ponds (occasionally the ocean), and mountains in Saga prefecture on the southern Japanese island of Kyushu; and the Saragaishi River, Honshu, Japan; but are also reported throughout Japan.

**Scary Sightings:**

<u>1978</u>: In November of 1978, two construction workers named Makoto Ito and Toshio Hashimoto were fishing from a seawall near the US Navy Base in the Japanese port city of Yokosuka when they saw what they described as a Kappa. Ito said of the creature they observed: *"It just popped up from beneath the surface and stood there. It was not a fish, an animal, or a man. It was about 3 meters (feet, perhaps?) in height and was covered in thick, scaly skin like a reptile. It had a face and two large yellow eyes that seemed to be focused on us."*

<u>1970s</u>: Two policemen claimed to have seen a creature hunched over at the side of a country road at dusk. The officers slowed down and approached the figure, thinking that it might have been a child, lost or in trouble. As they approached, the figure stood up to its full height and they could see that, instead of being a child, the figure was a strange creature that looked like a cross between a monkey and a frog, with outsized claws and large piercing eyes. The creature made a high-pitched 'chattering noise' before running on two legs across the road and disappearing into the undergrowth.

<u>1984</u>: On August 1st, 1984, at about 11 PM, a squid fisherman by named Ryu Shirozaki was walking home from a local pier after work and passing near the Kuta River of the town of Tsushima in the Nagasaki prefecture, came across what he thought to be a group of children playing at the water's edge. Thinking it strange to see children playing in the river so late, Shirozaki approached the beings and was shocked

to see several creatures with swarthy faces, spindly arms and legs, and skin that glistened in the moonlight. Unsure of what he was seeing, he called out to them as he approached, which caused the creatures to panic and quickly disappear into the water. The next morning, Shirozaki discovered a set of slimy, teardrop-shaped footprints on the nearby pavement and a strange jellylike substance that was in the process of coagulating in the hot sun. This apparent trackway stretched for around 20 meters. Each print measured about 22cm long and 12cm wide, and they were spaced roughly 50-60cm apart. Rumour quickly spread around the town that Kappa' had been seen, prompting the local police to conduct a forensic investigation, sadly leading to inconclusive results, apparently due to the paucity of the sample that was collected.

**Beastly Evidence:**

*A Handy Relic!* These mummified remains of a Kappa, which include a foot and an arm with hand attached, are believed to have been given to the Miyakonijo Shimazu family after a Kappa was shot on a riverbank in 1818. Currently on show at the Miyakonojo Shimazu Residence, in Miyazaki prefecture on the island of Kyuushuu in Japan. To date, they have not been subjected to scientific analysis.

*A Mummified Monster!* A kappa mummy is on display in Imari, Saga Prefecture, at the Matsuura Brewery, where it was discovered inside a black box during some renovations during the 1950s. There are several other purported specimens of Mummified Kappa remains dotted around Japan. It is significant to note that it was popular for artists to craft these mythical creatures using the body parts of real animals like monkeys, birds, and fish during the Edo period, from 1603 to 1867. And, although the remains we see today are 'relatively ancient', their age does not, in itself, validate their authenticity.

*Art and Literature:* Representations of the Kappa are numerous in Japanese art and literature and there is no shortage of woodcuts, paintings, and sculptures of this semi-mythical animal. Many of which often exhibit many simian characteristics in their artistic interpretation of this extraordinary creature. Whether this is simply a case of artists pulling features from nature to express something that defies description is unclear; although as one trails through the multitudinous personifications of Kappa portrayals, it becomes clear that more than one type of creature is responsible for the legends surrounding this cryptozoological chimaera.

*Japanese Netsuke (small sculpture) of a Kappa, donated to the Metropolitan Museum of Art in 1910 by Mrs Russell Sage.*

## Beastly Theories!

*A Menagerie of Merbeings*: Any casual observer of Kappa lore will observe that there not only appear to be several animals amalgamated into the most common manifestation of the *Kappa* but that there are, in fact, several types of Kappa in Japanese lore that vary in physical form and behaviour. This has led many to assume that this mythical monster could be represented by several known and yet-to-be-discovered animals. All of which may reside under the folkloric moniker '*Kappa*' within rural areas of Japan. One of these proposed identities and the primary theoretical subject of this chapter is that of an amphibious hominoid, answering to several descriptions and numerous names throughout history. A semi-aquatic wildman, or an aquatic swamp ape, covered in perpetual slime from its daily dives into the weeds and murk and living in or around abundant pools and rivers, where it can easily feed upon the available flora and fauna. Another possible identity is either an unknown species of bipedal *amphibious reptile* or a small surviving therapod dinosaur-like *Coelophysis*: Perhaps a large undiscovered species of *carnivorous turtle* or an *outsized Japanese giant salamander*, lying dormant on the river bottom for long periods and occasionally surfacing to make a quick protein snack of whatever may be walking by. This aggressive salamander can grow to almost 8 feet in length and if it were to grab a child, for example, in its powerful jaws, it would almost certainly succeed in drowning it. Some have even suggested that an extinct form of primitive amphibian called the *Temnospondyli* could account for the legend of the *Kappa*.

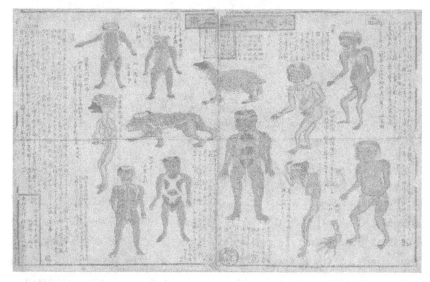

*Kappa drawings from mid-19th century Suiko juni-hin no zu* 水虎十二品之図 *(Illustrated Guide to 12 Types of Kappa) (1850).*

*Myth and Legend:* As with so many alleged cryptids around the world, the kappa is ingrained into the religion, superstition, and folklore of the Japanese culture, making the extraction of fact from fiction near impossible to effect. However, within this mythology, we can see the traces of cautionary tales, similar to the Kelpies legends of the ancient Scots or the Nakki of the ancient Fins, which are used to warn children about the dangers of water and certainly what we see in Japan, even in this modern era is something similar. Indeed, signs featuring Kappa drowning warnings are still frequently erected next to dangerous bodies of water. Could the kappa be nothing more than an imaginary bogeyman to ward away unwary children from the water's edge? This certainly seems more plausible than the possibility that a malevolent monkey turtle that eats cucumbers and livers and extracts imaginary organs from your anus exists undiscovered in the pools and rivers of rural Japan.

*Offering of cucumbers to Kappa at the Kappa-dera temple, in the Kappabashi area of Tokyo.*

_Sublime Superstition:_ In an area called Kappabuchi in the City of Tono, in Iwate Prefecture, Northeast Japan, an area once said to have been home to many Kappa; there is a 500-year-old Jokenji temple, where tourists flock to a clear stream that brooks through a well-tended grove, where _'Kappa Fisherman'_ or for want of a better term, _'kappa whisperers'_ are brought out, with handmade fishing poles, fully baited with cucumbers; to entice the shy and reclusive kappa to show himself to the onlookers. Behind the magnificent temple, which according to legend, was saved from a fire when the local Kappa community poured the water from their dish-shaped heads upon the flames that threatened to consume it, there lies a kappa shrine, which is said to give abundant milk to expectant mothers who pray there. Japan is filled to the brim with ponds, graves, and shrines housing the effigies and religious relics of the Kappa, and several festivals are even devoted to honouring its mermanian deity. It is, however, this often picturesque and endemic devotion, which causes the most confusion for the cryptozoologist. Leaving the physical reality of an undiscovered corporeal animal obfuscated in the beautiful tributes of the culture that has chosen to honour it.

Sunset over the River Nile – Sudan

## WOADD-EL-UMA

The River Nile is the longest river in Africa, flowing for approximately 4,100 miles, through the nations of Tanzania, Uganda, Rwanda, Burundi, the Democratic Republic of the Congo, Kenya, Ethiopia, Eritrea, South Sudan, Republic of Sudan, and Egypt. Further south, from its outflow on the Mediterranean Sea and below Egypt, lies Sudan and it is here that the river's character changes radically as it flows through the somewhat shallower and rockier Cataracts of the Nile between Aswan and Khartoum. And it is here, at the Third Cataract of the Nile at Tombos/Hannek, an archaeological site of the Eighteenth Dynasty of Egypt, that we find the strange legend of a hairy water-bound *Wildman*, known locally as the '*Woadd El Uma.*'

**What's in a name?** *Woadd-el-Uma* means "*Son of the Mother*" in Arabic. It is also known as '*Amanit*'.

**Monstrous Measurements:** Man-sized, bipedal. Covered in reddish-brown hair. Females have visible breasts.

**Terrifying Tracks:** Tracks are 10 inches in length, with four unusually long, narrow toes and a large, fully opposable toe. The stride is 3 ft. Feet are pointed at a 70-degree angle, oblique to the direction of travel. Appears to move in a series of sideways hops.

**Beastly Behaviours:** Believed to be semi-aquatic and to live in rivers or next to lakes. Sometimes seen on land before floods.

**Deadly Diet:** Vegetarian, prefers fruit.

**Hairy Habitat:** Nile River, Northern Sudan.

**Beastly Evidence:** On June 17th, 1832, while conducting geological studies in northern Africa, Joseph Russeger, an Austrian geologist, found unusual human-like tracks left overnight in the sand along the Nile River near the third cataract. The mysterious tracks emerge from the water, heading towards Russeger's camp, then onto some marshy terrain, before returning to the river.

**Beastly Theories:**

*Wildman of the water:* Reports from around the world indicate that these unidentified hominids (*Wildmen*) are strong swimmers. Could the Woadd-el-Uma be part of an undiscovered species of upright amphibious ape, using the shallow waters in the cataracts of the Nile to hunt after dark and avoid detection by man?

*Night Raiders:* Perhaps local tribesmen, in the business of raiding encampments after dark by boat and leaving only their footprints as evidence, could account for stories of the Woadd -El-Uma and Joseph Russeger's own strange discovery of footprints travelling to and from the water. Russeger was seemingly convinced that he had observed trace evidence of an aquatic humanoid, emerging from the river after dark, but is this interpretation simply part of a tradition of 19th-century sensationalism that was carried on by many European explorers of strange and unusual lands; over spinning unremarkable encounters into mysterious yarns for a home audience ever hungry for tall tales?

*Swimpanzees:* Chimpanzees are native to Sudan (although critically endangered!). Could a curious member of this species have been responsible for the tracks that came from the river and walked around Russeger's camp one June night in 1832? It was long believed that apes could not swim. However, in 2013, two biologists, Renato Bender from the University of the Witwatersrand, Johannesburg and Nicole Bender from the University of Bern, published their report in the American Journal of Physical Anthropology concerning a chimp named Cooper and an orangutan named Suriya they had studied. Both animals had been raised by humans and had not only learned the art of swimming but diving, as well. Is it possible in the shallower, boulder-filled waters surrounding the 3$^{rd}$ cataract of the Nile, in Northern Sudan, that a local chimpanzee population could have mastered the art of swimming?

*Could the inhospitable environment of Scape Ore Swamp provide a protected habitat for a prehistoric creature to thrive undetected?*

## THE LIZARD MAN OF SCAPE ORE SWAMP

Scape Ore Swamp in South Carolina covers an area of approximately 91 square miles and is made up of heavily forested floodplains and hills. This murky morass in Lee County, South Carolina, with its sleepy County Town of Bishopville, comprised of a diminutive population of 3,471 persons, was the centre of national attention in the late 1980s, with tales of its residents being terrorised by a large, bipedal lizard man. But, is this extraordinary creature more a tale of tourism than cryptozoology and similar to other notorious cryptozoological hotspots around the globe, does the mercantile appeal of t-shirts and tours keep the cyclical talk about the monster alive for the *'good of the community?'*

**What's in a name?** Lizard Man, The Lizard Man Of Lee County, the Lizard Man of Scape Ore Swamp, Jabberwok, Reptile man.

**Monstrous Measurements:** Humanoid form. Height, 7 ft. *"wet like."* Greenish, Greyish or brown colour. Scaly skin, like a lizard, covered in snakelike scales, sometimes confused with hair. Glowing red eyes. Three-fingered hands.

**Terrifying Tracks:** Three-toed, clawed prints. 14 inches long, 6 inches wide, and 1 inch deep. Stride, 40 inches.

**Beastly Behaviours:** Amphibious. Aggressive. Possibly dangerous to humans. Damages vehicles. Pungent Odour.

**Deadly Diet:** Alleged to have been responsible for several missing cats and an attempted attack on a teenage boy.

**Hairy Habitat:** Scape Ore Swamp, Bishopville, South Carolina, U.S.A.

**Scary Sightings:**

<u>1988</u>: At 2 AM, on June 29<sup>th,</sup> 1988, seventeen-year-old Christopher Davies was on his way home from working the late shift when he ran a flat tire along the road next to Elmore's Butter Bean Shed on Browntown Road in Lee County, South Carolina. Little did he know, as he exited his vehicle that night, that he would have an encounter that would change his life forever? Just as Davis had just finished changing his tire, he heard a thump from behind and turned to see something that terrified him. He said:

*"I had finished changing the tire and was putting the things in the trunk. The moonlight was out. I turned around and saw a red-eyed devil. He was about 30 yards from me, in the field. It had really long arms. When he would run, his arms would swing. I ran to the driver's side and got in. When I was sitting in the car, I saw him from the neck down. I pulled off and after about 2 yards, he jumped on the roof. I could see the creature's three-fingered hand through the windshield. I saw hands, rough-looking, black-fingernailed hands. After he jumped up on the car, he grunted. A deep grunt. He grunted one time. The creature fell off."*

Later coaxed by his father to tell his story to the police, Davis reported his tale to Lee County Sheriff Liston Truesdale a fortnight later. Describing the monster a seven-foot-tall, green creature, with three fingers on each hand, that jumped onto his car as he fled from the area and held on to the roof of the vehicle while staring menacingly at him through his windshield before being thrown from the vehicle when Davis slammed on the brakes and sped off.

*1987/88:* Sheriff Liston Truesdale also received several more reports following Davis's, with one witness claiming to have seen the creature in the fall of 1987 and another witness, a colonel, claiming to have observed a tall brownish creature a few weeks after Davis' sighting. Truesdale also took a statement from 31-year-old George Holloway Jr., who claimed to have encountered the creature in the fall of 1987. The witness, who had cycled out to a natural spring at 00:30 am to drink some of its water, had lit a cigarette and noticed what he had at first believed to be a dead tree, suddenly stood up, *"like a man"*, to a height of 7 – to 8 ft. Just as the creature got up a car passed by, briefly illuminating the creature's eyes before it turned and went back into the swamp.

*2005:* Sightings of the Lizard Man seemed to have disappeared from the area, that is until October 2005, when a local woman filed a police report stating that she had seen two 'Lizard Men' outside her home, near the Scape Ore Swamp.

**Beastly Evidence:**

*Polygraph Pass:* Sumter Police Captain Earl Berry administered eyewitness Chris Davis with a polygraph test at the Sumter City-County Law Enforcement Centre on August 8th, 1988, which he passed. This led polygraph experts to assert that the results meant that *"Davis believes that he saw, what he says he saw."* The official polygraph report was never released, with Sumter Police Captain Earl Berry saying it was not allowed. It is curious to note that the test undertaken by Davis was requested and paid for by *Southern Marketing Inc.*, a company that had been newly formed for the express purpose of arranging personal appearances for Davis. Who, as revealed in the laudable façade of their own statement, had made their request to *'satisfy their minds'* as to the veracity of the boy's story and because they had *'observed some young boys picking on him one weekend.'* Needless to say, such efforts, nudged by a company with strong commercial ties to the outcome of Davis passing his polygraph test, can only be viewed, at best, with an acerbic scepticism.

*Eyewitness Sketch:* An eyewitness sketch drawn by Chris Davis after his sighting shows a strange 3 fingered, bipedal humanoid.

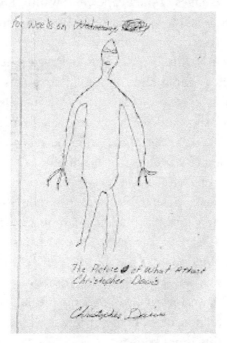

The sketch of the Scape Ore Lizard Man, made by Christopher Davis

*Car Trouble:* In 2008, a couple in Bishopville, South Carolina, reported to police that, as well as their vehicle being damaged similarly to the

Lizardman reports from twenty years earlier, their pet cats had gone missing and that their beds were scratched and shredded. Dixie Rawson said of the damage her car sustained: *"The whole front half of our van is chewed up. There are bite marks right through the front grill. Both sides of the van above the wheel wells were bitten and the metal is bent like a piece of paper."* Traces of blood were retrieved from the vehicle, tested, and subsequently believed to have come from a domestic dog or perhaps even a Coyote.

*Making Mischief:* It is interesting to note that before Christopher Davis had reported his sighting to Sheriff Truesdale, the Sheriff had investigated a report of a car damaged overnight while parked in the same area, on the edges of the Scape Ore Swamp. The car reportedly bore damage consistent with that made by an animal, with tooth marks, clawed scratches, hair, and muddy footprints left behind by the beast. Curiously, Sheriff Truesdale believed that this first report was the start of a whole rash of similar incidents that eventually culminated in Davis's strange encounter with the alleged 'lizard man'. Another strange aspect of Davis's report is that there are no photos of the damage that his car sustained and that his story regarding the extent of the damage his own car sustained often changed over the years. One would be remiss to overlook the classic *'cause and effect'* correlation at play within this tale, whether that be evidence supporting the activity of a marshland monster or a mischievous young man, making wild claims to cover up his misbehaviour, is anyone's guess. Undoubtedly, the untimely demise of Davis in 2009, in an apparently drug-related incident, points to a life lived outside the limits of the law. However, whether the illegality surrounding his tragic end is more indicative of his later life or the sad consequence of habitual criminality is not known.

*Tracks:* It has been claimed that during initial investigations into the damaged vehicles, police found and made casts of what looked like three-toed footprints that measured fourteen inches in length (currently housed at the South Carolina Cotton Museum in

Bishopville) and although these tracks would seem to offer some form of proof for the existence of the beast, sadly, they were proved to be demonstrably fake in a Destination Truth episode, aired in 2012, in which host Josh Gates, showed that the tracks, when overlaid, were identical to one another. A feature that would be impossible to replicate naturally if the trackway was that of a flesh and blood animal.

**Beastly Theories:**

*Black Bear Scare*: Black bears do inhabit this area and Chris Davis sighting, amongst others, might logically point in the direction of a (larger than usual) rogue ursine. Perhaps, if we attempt to reconstruct his sighting, substituting a bear for the *'creature'* to illuminate this theory, it might help us better understand what was seen that night. Let us assume that our large rogue bear, after a long and unsuccessful hunt, finally emerges from the swamp covered in mud and algae and, spotting the oblivious Davis changing his tire, and considering him fair game, charges the hapless boy. Davis, hearing the animal's approach, turns to face the beast and, unintentionally assuming a threat posture, causes the bear to rear up on its hind legs (to appear larger), its eyes reflecting red in his car's headlights. Davis then turns and gets into his car and drives off, reactivating the predatory instincts of the bear, which leaps on top of the terrified teenager's car, until finally being thrown off by the inertia of Davis slamming on the breaks. After which, he speeds off and does not see the creature again. Indeed, everything that Davis describes about the behaviour of his attacker can be explained away by the behaviour of a large rogue bear, and since the simplest explanation is usually the most plausible, the author believes that mistaken identity of a black bear is the most likely cause of this strange encounter.

*"They feast on The Flesh and Drink the blood of the living."* The Gill-Man, By Universal Pictures - Universal Pictures.

<u>*Aquatic Ape:*</u> Except for its assumed scaly texture, the lizard man also shares some descriptive features with other hairy humanoids in the USA. Could this apparent *Reptoid* be a type of North American *Freshwater Ape*, a variety of Bigfoot perhaps, or even one of the mysterious relict apes, or *'Napes,'* like the Florida *Skunk Ape* that has permanently adapted to a semi-aquatic lifestyle? Undoubtedly, as this chapter demonstrates, there is certainly evidence for a (semi) aquatic ape in this anecdotal primate pantheon that we have formulated. Would it be unthinkable for an animal as intelligent as an *ape* to become habituated (or even specialised) to life in the secluded watery wastelands of the southern states of the USA?

<u>*Therapod Dinosaur:*</u> There are many anecdotal reports, especially throughout the southern states of the USA, of what has affectionately been dubbed *'River Dinos'*. Could some of these sightings constitute a surviving Coelophysis, a small meat-eating dinosaur that lived in New Mexico in the late Triassic period? Regrettably, that seems unlikely, as this species did not resemble a humanoid and was far smaller than the *Lizard Man's* purported dimensions. However, perhaps a larger

species, such as *Therizinosaurus,* a therapod notable for its relatively small skull and elongated fingers with long claws, could be a better fit if seen under the right circumstances for the strange appearance of the *lizard man.*

| Therizinosaurus model at the Bristol Zoological Gardens, England.

*A Real Creature Feature*: The Lizardman or men appear to bear a very strong resemblance to the popular Gillman monster from the 1954 creature feature, *The Creature from the Black Lagoon!* Which raises the problem, as with all movie monsters, as to whether life apes film… or film apes life? Meaning: are the monsters we depict in our movies drawn directly from our shared superstitious subconscious and folkloric fables, or do the more imaginative among us draw upon these celluloid cryptids to describe what we encounter but cannot explain in our everyday lives?

*Dishonourable Discharge*: As with all cryptid reports, there is always a rash of hoaxes that follow them and the Lizard Man is no exception, as we see, for example, in the hoax perpetrated by Kenneth Orr, an airman stationed at Shaw Air Force Base. Orr claimed to have encountered the Lizardman and shot at it, On August 5th, 1988. As to why a person with such a 'responsible position' in society would want to risk his reputation with such a tale is not known, but this phenomenon is one that is encountered in cryptozoology time and again; that of the reliable witness with impeccable credentials risking it all for a bit of limelight and perhaps a small cash donation. It is also important to take into consideration the emotional draw that such publicised encounters can have on people suffering from *'attention-seeking behaviour'* and, of course, for the more commercially astute and entrepreneurially ready opportunists that always flock to such newsworthy tales. Of course, the best explanation for the continuation or 'survival' of most of these legends is that a rise in tourism normally follows and, once established, becomes needed as a continual boost to the local economy. Orr recanted this account two days later when he was arraigned for unlawfully carrying a pistol and the offence of filing a false police report. According to Orr, he had hoaxed the sighting to keep stories about the Lizard Man alive.

*On the Run:* Some have hypothesised that Davis's original story was an elaborate excuse given to his father for coming home late and to explain the damage caused to his car. It was, after all, his father who encouraged him to go to the police and file a report, which he then would have felt obliged to maintain once the police report became public. In a strange and maybe telling twist to this tale, some 20 years later, on Wednesday, June 17, 2009, Davis was shot dead in his home by two men armed with shotguns. Police later confirmed that his killing was due to a drug-related incident, saying that they had discovered 10 grams of marijuana and two scales in his kitchen. Could this fatal incident be connected to Davis's Lizard Man encounter? And is it more probable that the reason that Davis returned home that night in July 1988, scared out of his wits and with a damaged car, is that he was involved in selling drugs and after a life-threatening encounter with some competitors, was forced to spin an outlandish yarn to hide the fact from his family? A fact that, sadly, eventually cost him his life.

| *Honey Island Swamp: By Elisa Rolle.*

## HONEY ISLAND SWAMP MONSTER

Honey Island Swamp covers a vast expanse of 250 square miles, between the east and West Pearl Rivers, around 70,000 acres of which is a protected wildlife reserve. The swamp is largely impenetrable and overflowing with life, playing home to several large predators, such as cougar, red wolf, alligator, coyote, black bears, and perhaps, even something a little more unusual... a large, aquatic primate of an unidentified genus, known as the *Honey Island Swamp Monster*.

**What's in a name?** The Honey Island Swamp Monster is named after its alleged home, I Honey Island Swamp, Louisiana, USA.

**Monstrous Measurements:** Ape-like in appearance. Bipedal. Approximately 7ft. tall. Amber eyes. Human-like face. Covered with scraggly black hair from head to toe (sometimes described as grayish or reddish-brown). Broad shoulders. Long arms that hang down below the knees. Human-like hands.

**Terrifying Tracks:** Three webbed and clawed toes.

**Beastly Behaviours:** Good swimmer. Solitary, but occasionally seen in groups of 2 or 3. Emits calls that sound like moans, grunts, howls, and high-pitched shrieks. Emits a foul odour, like decaying flesh or rotten eggs. If seen, it will stand stock-still in an apparent attempt to mimic a tree stump but quickly flees when this subterfuge does not last! Dislikes eye contact. Will swim or climb trees to avoid detection.

**Deadly Diet:** There are no accounts of this animal eating, although it would be safe to assume, like most animals matching its description, that it may be omnivorous, feeding on the bountiful flora and fauna of the swamp.

**Hairy Habitat:** Secluded wetlands and swamps, like Honey Island Swamp, Louisiana.

**Scary Sightings:**

In 1963,_retired air traffic controller Harlan Ford claimed and his friend Ray Mills were deep in the woods trying to locate a camp they had noticed while flying over a remote area of the swamp outside Slidell, Louisiana. Thinking that they had found the site, the men stumbled through the undergrowth to a clearing where to their amazement, they found a large ape-like humanoid staring straight at them. Startled by their alarmed voices, the creature glared at them menacingly before running away on two legs into the dense woodland. Harland and Mills gave chase but were only able to find the creature's three-toed tracks. In a later interview for the 1970s television series, *In Search Of...* Ford said: *"I thought it might be a bear, and then it turned around."*

Another local man, Ted Williams, also claimed to have had two close encounters with the creature. In his interview for the classic cryptid television series, *In Search Of...* hosted by Leonard Nimoy, he said:

*"First time I ever saw it, it was standing plum still like a stump. I stopped and realized it wasn't a stump and it wasn't supposed to be there. When I stopped, it ran. It was dark gray, about seven foot high, it jumped a bayou. That was the first time I saw it..."*

*"...The next time I seen him was swimming the river (Pearl River), two of them, one was bigger than the other and faster than the other and they swam just like a human with them long overhead strokes. I tried to get one of them to look at me and the other one ran off and the other one wouldn't look at me. I could've shot it but I wouldn't on account it wouldn't look at me. It looked too much like a human to me, broad shoulders, arms hanging down below its knees, hands looked almost like a humans."*

Another man said that he saw the beast and ran towards it, only to find that it had inexplicably disappeared by the time he got there. The witness could not understand how it could have vanished and said that the animal *"couldn't have gotten very far in the time it took me to get to the spot where I first spotted it."*

**Beastly Evidence:**

*Tracks:* The three-toed, webbed and clawed footprint discovered by witness Harlan Ford and Ray Mills in Honey Island Swamp, Louisiana, bare more than a passing resemblance to those of a very large bull gator.

*Film:* After Harlan Ford died in 1980, his wife Yvonne found some 8 mm footage and a letter he wrote describing his encounters boxed up, along with plaster casts in the attic. This Super 8 footage (which Ford never made public) appears to show a large, hairy humanoid, walking from right to left, in the woods. If it is to be believed that Harlan Ford was indeed a hoaxer, one needs to ask why such footage was never exploited or offered to the usual media suspects.

**Beastly Theories:**

*Cajun Folklore:* Could the legends of the loup-garou/Rugarou be based on sightings of sasquatches, roughly translated by the local descendants of the French into a manifestation of European werewolf legends, melded with the Native American legends about wolf-walkers? Certainly, the huge, hirsute beasts that are described by witnesses are a match for some of the physiological characteristics of the Sasquatch.

*Monkey Business:* Local legends tell of a train crash that occurred in the early twentieth century, in which a travelling circus lost several chimpanzees. It is believed by some that the Honey Island Swamp Monster/s are the descendants of these former performative primates that have managed to adapt to their swampy surroundings. This explanation, of course, doesn't explain the bipedal gait observed in most sightings or account for the massive increase in size (7 ft) if the animals are chimps. However, the descendant of a single breeding pair occupying a unique environment and cut off from others of their species could explain the apparent Oligodactyly (loss of toe digits) and Syndactyly (webbed feet) observed in the alleged tracks of this beast.

*Tourist Trap:* There are currently several businesses that do good business on the back of the legend that came to prominence through Harlan Ford and Ray Mills encounter, and although many locals are still sceptical of the truth of their story, believing either that the story was concocted by Ford and Mills to keep people away from a new fertile hunting ground, or, that the two men fabricated the tracks using alligator castes to profit from the publicity; what is certain is that the part these men played in this mysterious story has certainly benefitted the local economy and those business owners who specialise in providing 'Swamp Monster' tours for curious visitors, who have undoubtedly benefitted from the attention that the creature has thrown their way.

_The Swimming Sasquatch:_ It is curious that the eyewitness, Ted Williams, described seeing the animals swimming during his encounter, as it was believed at that time that no ape species could swim and reports of sasquatch-like creatures engaging in such aquatic behaviour were uncommon. Indeed, one could argue that if Williams was hoping to convince other researchers that a sasquatch-like animal existed in the swamps of Louisiana, then this extraordinary detail would not have conferred much in the way of credibility upon his claim.

.

*Could rivers like these have played host to a species of semi-aquatic ape prior to China's industrialisation?*

## SHUIRENXIONG

This strange amphibious humanoid is just one of China's many mythological Merbeings, yet in contrast to its other *fish-man* entities and in keeping with the theme of this chapter, the *Shuirenxiong* is not a tailed Merbeing at all, but a humanoid entity, in the classical sense (bipedal, 2 arms, 2 legs...); and more akin to other suspected aquatic apes around the world. Like many anecdotal animals in the land of the dragon, it is steeped in mystery and indefatigably wrapped up in local folklore, which in Guangxi (which is home to china's largest percentage of minorities, including the Zhuang people, who make up 32% of the population) becomes a tangled contest of competing fables among the many archaic cultures that occupy the region, Yet, the historical sightings of these hairy watermen and their subsequent strange disappearance in the 1970s, point to the possibility of a flesh and blood animal, that once inhabited this region, that has now been driven from its habitat by the juggernaut of industrialisation that has overtaken this once agrarian land.

**What's in a name?** Shuirenxiong - literally means *"Water manbear."*

**Monstrous Measurements:** Bipedal. Hairy. Humanoid shape. Looks like a cross between a man and a bear. Has a rounded head, with long head hair, around 1.3 ft in length. Arms are long and its hands five-fingered, each finger ending in long nails 1 to 2 inches in length. The body is covered in short fur, which is yellowish on its body and black on its back.

**Beastly Behaviours:** Amphibious. Powerful swimmer. Found near water. Bipedal but can also move about on all fours. Has long fingers nails that it uses to play with its hair. Wary of humans and will dive into the water and quickly swim away if spotted.

**Deadly Diet:** Fish and crustaceans.

**Hairy Habitat:** Frequents Rivers around Heng County, southern Guangxi Zhuang Autonomous Region.

**Scary Sightings:**

*1940s:* A farmer named Huang Fangji encountered what he believed to be a small demon while travelling to Xinxing Village. The frightened farmer tried to beat the creature to death with his hoe, but the small hairy humanoid beat a hasty retreat and jumped into the water, swimming swiftly away until Huang lost sight of it.

*1940s/50s:* A local villager named Huang Shiyin was alerted by a strange splashing noise one day while fishing along the river. Looking in the direction of the disturbance, he noticed an odd-looking 'man' sitting on the riverbank and shouted for him identity himself. Upon seeing Huang, the 'strange man' immediately dove into the water and swam away, leaving Huang convinced that he had encountered the legendary Shuirenxiong.

*1950:* A perplexed old cowherd watched in wonder at the spectacle of two black Shuirenxiong wrestling each other alongside the Yu River. The battle went on for some time and the cowherd was able to observe the animals closely until both fell into the water, submerging together.

*1960s:* Gan Daxian and his father, two local residents of Heng County, claimed to have observed Shuirenxiong frequently in the early 1960s before the Xijin Hydropower Station was built in the country and said that the creatures could often be seen swimming in the rivers and basking on the riverbanks.

**Beastly Evidence:**

*Uneventful Expedition:* In June 1984, the *China Yeren Scientific Exploration and Study Society* sent one of its members, Professor Fang Zhongyou, on an expedition to the area. Sadly the expedition failed to find any evidence of these enigmatic aquatic animals. However, if the testimony from local villager Daxian and his father concerning the decline of sightings in coincidence with the construction of the Xijin Hydropower station are to be believed, then it is hardly surprising that Professor Zhongyou did not find evidence of species habituation more than 20 years after sightings had ceased to be reported.

**Beastly Theories:**

*Aquatic Apes: Oreopithecus Bambolii* was an aquatic Miocene ape that presumably subsisted on water plants and perhaps fishes and crustaceans as well. The species had an estimated weight of 66 to 77 lbs. and walked upright on two legs, just like a human. Could an extant yet rare species of *Orepithecus* still exist in some of the world's more pristine ecosystems?

Fossil of Oreopithecus Bambolii, an extinct ape: By Ghedoghedo - Own work, CC BY-SA 3.0, https://commons.wikimedia.org/w/index.php?curid=15086054

*Otterly Ridiculous:* It has been suggested that the Eurasian otter, which does inhabit this region, could be mistaken for a large aquatic primate. However, any local person would be familiar with these animals and unlikely to make such an extraordinary misidentification.

*Industrial Extinction:* The industrialisation of the developing world has had a negative impact on many fragile species, especially those already clinging on to existence in niche habitats and delicate ecological zones; and others whose specialisation has tied them to specific habitats and dietary requirements. Since there have been no sightings of the Shuirenxiong since the construction of the Xijin Hydropower Station in the 1960s, could it too have joined the long list of now-extinct species that the environmental havoc our march towards progress has wreaked upon the fauna of the natural world?

# BIGFOOT ON THE BRAIN!

There are those who could be forgiven for thinking that our current international obsession with Bigfoot started on May 29th, 2011; with the airing of the first Finding Bigfoot, episode on the Travel Channel. This delicious foray into *'bigfooting'*, sometimes awkwardly translated into television, was possibly one of the most universally appealing and ground-breaking shows about cryptozoology ever to grace the silver screen! Hosted by 4 contrary, yet congenial characters and neatly straddling pseudoscience and anecdotal authentication; the show made 'bigfooting' accessible to the masses with its simplistic methods of calling in the 'squatch' with tree knocks and howls and its ever tedious treks through the woods; preferably after dark and adorned with a modified ghostbusters getup, inclusive of night-vision-selfie-cam; to deliver those unflattering, under-chin close-ups of the cast, to a virgin audience, ever hungry for hairy men

However, to the longest-serving and long-suffering Sasquatch enthusiasts among us, the origination point, or at least the public nativity of this phenomenon can be traced back to two men (Roger Patterson and Bob Gimlin) who claimed to have filmed a strange encounter with a large, bipedal, female, hairy 'hominid', in Bluff Creek, California, in 1967! Although, their famous film with its hairy star, who has since become affectionately known as 'Patty', came some time after Ivan T, Sanderson's, 1962 book - Abominable Snowmen: Legend Come to Life; and certainly long after Shipton's famous photograph of the alleged tracks of a Yeti, captured during his 1951 Everest expedition; the fact remains that the PG film was and remains, the celluloid inauguration upon which the bigfoot legend begat international acclaim.

**What's in a name?** The name *Bigfoot*, was coined by newspaper columnist – Andrew Genzoli, in the Humboldt Times, after a series of large manlike tracks that were found near Bluff Creek in 1958, and like many of our mysterious and elusive candidates for cryptozoology, this name has become a catch-all identifier for a number of other *'Hairy Humanoids'* that may not be as closely related to *'Bigfoot'* as their hairy, upright forms suggest. In fact, as well as its other universally recognised nickname – *Sasquatch*; there are myriad other names for this cryptid in North America, both in the European population, where we find accounts going back hundreds of years and the First Nations population; wherein, legends of Cannibal Giants like *Bukwus*, *Dsonoqua* and *Omah*, et al. are ingrained into their traditions, art and archaeology!

**Monstrous Measurements:** The North American Bigfoot or Man-Ape, is a physically imposing species, standing somewhere between 7 – 9 ft. tall and weighing between 650 – 1000 pounds. It has a pointed head with a sloping forehead and a heavy brow-ridge. A flat face with a wide mouth. Deep-set eyes and a flat nose. Its body is bulky with wide shoulders, a huge chest, and long arms that hang below its waist. It is covered in hair, not fur, which varies in colour from dark brown to black, light brown to grey, with some reports even mentioning the occasional white Bigfoot encounter. Although it is not entirely clear whether these reports might be a fanciful interpretation, based upon the cultural misnomer that the Himalayan Yeti is white (which in general, it is not!)

**Beastly Behaviours:** Bigfoot are primarily nocturnal, even though many sightings do occur during the day, and appear to be solitary animals; although, family groups are also infrequently seen. They are naturally inquisitive animals and are often attracted to human activity and will sometimes even interact with people. These interactions often, characteristically, consist of a territorial, ushering out of the human intruder from the Bigfoot locale, through varying levels of harassment, such as rock or stick throwing, howls, growls, whistles, whoops, wood knocks, a strong overwhelming stench (which appears to be a form of a skunk-like deterrent) and if all else fails, face to face intimidation. Though, for the most part, despite their superior size and strength, Bigfoot tend to keep their distance from humans and will opt to move away, if seen or approached;

**Terrifying Tracks:** As its name implies, Bigfoot has BIG feet! Which in appearance are superficially similar to those of human feet; albeit on a much larger scale (averaging between 14 – 18 inches in length), with all of its toes being of a similar size and shape (the inner or big toe being slightly larger) and sitting in a straight line. It has a flat foot, that is broader and wider than humans and that appears to display unusual mid-foot flexibility; commonly known among Bigfoot researchers as the 'midtarsal pressure ridge'; a fascinating physiological feature which is observed in tracks, as an indentation seen towards the heel imprint; and which is believed to be the result of force transferred to the ground when the mid-tarsus 'flexes' as the heel lifts, causing the weight to be focussed under the forefoot. A most helpful adaptation, which may aid in supporting this large bipedal hominoid in the precipitous, rough topography of its environment

**Deadly Diet:** Bigfoot is believed to be omnivorous and has been observed eating roots, berries, grasses, corn, apples, clams, fish, larvae, rodents, deer, and other similar fayre. They are not (fortunately) believed to prey upon humans as a food source and although Native American folklore is replete with tales of Cannibal Giants kidnapping their womenfolk and predating upon their people (a behavioural characteristic attributed to ancient Hairy Humanoid reports around the world); these folk tales do not seem to be supported by modern-day Bigfoot encounters in North America.

**Hairy Habitat:** Traditionally, the North American Bigfoot is believed only to inhabit the montane forests of western North America, being found in the states of Northern California, Oregon, Washington, Idaho, and Alaska, in the USA and the provinces of British Columbia and South-Western Alberta, in Canada. However, there are Bigfoot-like reports throughout North America that are clearly outside of their traditionally known distribution zone! It should not surprise the reader to discover that Bigfoot reports outside of this traditional zone have risen exponentially with the advent of popular Bigfoot television shows. Even so, when one looks closely at these unexpected locales, a continuous stream of historical reports is reassuringly present in abundance, indicating that this species may occupy a wider distribution area than previously thought.

Note: several 'Bigfoot-like' sightings, like the Skunk Ape, for example, are allegedly representative of a distinct relict ape species, (coined: 'Napes' by Loren Coleman in the 1960s) which are reported in North America and other diverse locales around the world.

**Beastly Evidence:** In the field of cryptozoology and especially in *Hairy Humanoid* research, there are many vital indices that we can collect to assess the potential existence of unknown animal species, such as:

*Tracks:* It could be reasoned that tracks or footprints are the only true indisputable evidence that science possesses of these enigmatic *Hairy Humanoids*; and yet, in scientific circles at least; these frozen footsteps of the wildman are only considered soft evidence. Nevertheless, these plastered podiatric pedalisms can act as confirmation of habituation and even allow researchers to guestimate the step, stride, straddle, and angle of gait, of an animal, as well as aid in distinguishing between specimens, via the dermal ridges that these creatures possess, (similarly to humans) which are unique to each individual.

_Hair:_ Many hair samples that defy identification as known species, have been attributed to various Hairy Humanoids over the years. This is because hair is seen as easier evidence to obtain, due to its natural resistance to decay and its lack of appeal to scavengers. Many researchers are put off of collecting hair samples, however, due to the perceived cost of lab analysis. An experience that can be easily avoided by employing the use of a jeweller's optivisor to examine any prospective samples. Bigfoot researcher, Professor Jeff Meldrum advises that researchers look for hairs that have parallel-sided shafts, with blunt, worn tips, anywhere up to several inches long.

_Scat:_ This too can provide useful insight into the dietary habits of Hairy Humanoids, However, it should be noted that no one knows what their scat should look like. It is presumed that many of these animals are omnivores and that their scat may be similar in content and appearance to a bear or human, albeit on a larger scale. Unfortunately, without resorting to DNA analysis, it is visually impossible to determine that you are looking at _Hairy Humanoid_ scat. It is therefore imperative that other, clear signs (tracks, hairs, preferably even a sighting) be present, before resorting to the fiscally prohibitive route of DNA testing.

_Film and Photography:_ On October 20th, 1967, in an encounter that would ultimately change the course of their lives and _Hairy Humanoid_ research forever, Roger Patterson and Bob Gimlin captured 952 frames of 16-millimeter film, showing a large, hair-covered, bipedal hominoid with pendulous breasts, walking away from them at Bluff Creek, California. The film is held up as one of the most incontrovertible pieces of Bigfoot evidence in existence and often lauded within the 'community' as indisputable proof for the existence of a large undiscovered hominoid in North America; has since gone on to become the benchmark for all Bigfoot evidence. It is noteworthy that film evidence, especially in our current era of easily accessible, off the shelf CGI, that film alone does not automatically constitute a form of hard evidence and that anyone wishing to present their own celluloid encounter with a Hairy Humanoid to the general public should expect their findings to be dissected in a most undignified manner.

*Audio:* Alan Berry, captured one or more Bigfoot on tape at an altitude of 8,500ft. in the Sierra Nevada on October 21st, 1972. His high-quality audio recording - colloquially known as The Sierra Sounds, features strange speech-like sounds like: *"Gob –uh-gob-uh-gob, ugh, muy tail"* which, that when subjected to analysis were determined to have been made by an animal larger than an adult human male. Fascinatingly, the audio analysts also concluded that more than one 'speaker' was present and involved in the conversation.

Eric Reinhardt too, claimed to have heard similar sounds during a confrontation he had with a juvenile and large male Sasquatch while camping with his girlfriend in November 2018, in Monroe County, Montana. After being chased into his tent by a big male Sasquatch, after pursuing a smaller juvenile, whom Eric had mistaken for a car thief, he said: *"The big male started making strange noises at the juvenile. It was a very parenting tone. He spoke in a series of clicks and pops with his tongue. It wasn't just nonsense because the juvenile was responding with sounds too, which sounded more like a squealing noise. There were a couple of back and forth communications like this between them and then the juvenile headed into the woods with the adult right behind him."*

*Sticks and Stones & Nesting Homes:* There are scores of *Hairy Humanoid* groups online that consist of nothing more than photographs of sticks and stones. Indeed, this has become something of a feeder pill within the peripheral community which perpetuates an unhealthy cycle of confirmation bias. Whereas stick signs, nests, and rock stacking could certainly be a sign of 'activity', one should be cautious of attributing activity or habituation to these 'signs', without other indicators being present. In my recent documentary Sticks & Stones: UK Bigfoot, with British Bigfoot filmmaker – Christopher Turner, we examined the perils and pitfalls of attributing such 'signs' to bigfoot and logically hypothesised, that if Bigfoot-like creatures were the cause of a tree break or rock formation, that several other 'confirmatory signs' should be observable within the same area, such as:

- *Tracks/footprints:* an animal capable of placing two large tree limbs into an X formation, as a rudimentary territorial marker, would have to leave some evidence of its exertions. So, one would expect to find tracks in and around these large structures.
- *Hair:* Animals that habituate an area, often leave evidence of themselves behind like hair, for example. Again, a creature dragging and lifting large tree limbs would expect to snag a few hairs along the way. (A close examination of the structures for hairs, is mandatory!)
- *Scat/Bones:* Such large and energetic animals would require a high-calorie intake, and if habituating an area long enough to place various markers and structures about the place would need to stop to eat and after some time, defecate. Ergo, logically speaking, scat and animal remains should be present within the vicinity/area of said stick structures.

*Eyewitness reports*: As one might expect, North America and in especial, the USA has the largest number of eyewitness accounts in the world. This anomaly, it could be argued, is not due to a higher incidence of encounters, but rather, due to the presence of a large, media-engaged population that has imbibed the tenets of this pop culture phenomenon and disseminated its creed around the globe. This media hysteria is not all bad of course and has had some positive benefits; such as the creation of an environment in which many awe-inspiring investigators from multi-disciplinary fields, have felt emboldened to undertake this yoke; creating detailed databases of evidence and reports, from which lay researchers or citizen scientists, such as myself, can extrapolate vital data about the *Hairy Humanoid* mystery. It has also produced an indispensable timeline of sightings, some going as far back as the 1800s, with which to compare key details, like physiology, behaviour, habitat, and diet, etc. Eyewitness accounts are a form of direct testimonial evidence and if examined under proper testing conditions can be highly reliable. Nevertheless, the potential for memory distortions, environmental conditions, the effect of stress or trauma, and even blatant confirmation bias – or 'Bigfoot on the Brain', as it is often referred to in the 'community', means that this form of evidence requires evidential support in the form of tracks, hair, scat, etc.

*eDNA:* The development of eDNA (DNA that is collected from soil, seawater, snow, or air.) may seem like the magic bullet when it comes to finally solving the mystery of hairy humanoid habituation in various locales around the globe; however, this method is exhaustive of both time and resources; and a genuine smoking gun in the form of sightings, tracks, scat, etc. should be present, before employing it in the field.

*Come Prepared:* Finally, a simple lightweight evidence kit; comprising of - paper envelopes, a paper bag, tweezers, latex gloves (for collecting samples), a jewellers optivisor (for examining hair) and a can of minimally expanding insulating foam, a soft-bristled brush, 2 pieces of cardboard, and a paperweight (for casting speedy and lightweight tracks) - is more than sufficient to collect any impromptu evidence you may come across in the field. Remember, if it's easy to carry, you're more likely to bring it along!

## Beastly Theories:

*Surviving Gigantopithecus*: A surviving, 'evolved' Gigantopithecus Blacki; a huge Pleistocene ape, known only from jaw fragments found in southern China and Vietnam. As much as this fossil ape would seem to be to most Bigfoot believers, the golden ticket to the main event: i.e. - a paleontological promissory of an evolutionary forefather to our modern-day bigfoot phenomena, there are some understandable difficulties with this theory; the most obvious of which is the subjective speculation upon which the physiological dimensions of this animal has been reconstructed. In fact, were it still in existence today, it might be more gorilla-like in appearance and very likely, although not categorically, quadrupedal.

Bigfoot is a creature that is subject to an ever-increasing burden of poly-philosophies that have been arbitrarily placed upon it by communities as ideologically far apart as anthropologists and alien abductees! And yet, somehow; there is a loose symmetry that pervades throughout these contending creeds and a shared love for our hairy humanoid friends that at its very base, allows for some form of communication between these estranged encampments!

However, most current researchers realise that the continuing absence of a specimen (alive or dead) is detrimental to the concept of Bigfoot as being a bonafide undiscovered animal and perceive that with its growing pop culture popularity, that they are in a race against time to prove its existence and to prevent it from permanently becoming a creature of modern folklore and fable.

Let the hunt begin!

*Excerpt from Beasts of the World (Vol.1) Hairy Humanoids, written by Andy McGrath*

# ACKNOWLEDGMENTS

I would like to thank:

Doug Hajicek, Alex Hajicek, Dr Karl Shuker, Richard Freeman, Don 'Jeff' Meldrum, David C. Xu, Professor Zhou Zhang, Gary Opit, Tony Healy, Paul Cropper, Dean Harrison, Dmitri Bayanov (RIP), Marie Jeanne Koffmann (RIP), Michael Newton (RIP), Jon Downes, Karac St Laurent, Aleksandar Petakov, Eli Watson, Scott Carpenter, Seth Breedlove, Christopher Turner, Captain Darren Howe, Peter Byrne, George Eberhart, John Green (RIP), Bob Gimlin, Russell Accord, Boris Porshnev (RIP), Jordi Magraner (RIP), Igor Bourtsev, Linda Godfrey, Cliff Barackman, James 'Bobo' Fay, Todd Disotell, J. Richard Greenwell (RIP), Grover Krantz (RIP), Paul Sinclair, Jason Parsons, Ivan T. Sanderson (RIP), Grover S. Krantz (RIP), Bernard Heuvelmans (RIP), Dr Peter Hocking. Pops McGrath and Yossi and Ruti Ron.

To my Wife and beautiful Daughters, I do everything for you.

All my love,

Aba Xxx

*Beasts of the World (vol.1): Hairy Humanoids* is the first in a seven-part series - which seeks to investigate the history, evidence, and common theories surrounding parallel classes of cryptid creatures that have been reported in diverse locations around the world.

The 2<sup>nd</sup> instalment in this new series – *Beasts of the World (vol.2)*, is due for release in the summer of 2022.

*Beasts of the World (vol.1): Hairy Humanoids* and its associated media and merchandise is the intellectual and commercial property of Andrew M.L. McGrath. *(Copyright 2021)*

For all publishing enquiries, please contact: https://hangar1publishing.com/pages/contact

For personal appearances and bookings, please email: andyronmcgrath@gmail.com.

# BIBLIOGRAPHY

## MAN APES

**Ucumar, 9-14:** *Location*: Argentina, Peru, Bolivia, Ecuador, Venezuela and Colombia, South America. *Sources*: https://cryptidz.fandom.com/wiki/Ucumar, https://www.radioenciclopedia.cu/cultural-news/legends/south-america-lives-the-legend-of-the-ucumar-20191118/, https://cryptid-quest.tumblr.com/post/187449080039/cryptid-of-the-day-ucumar-description-described, Pablo Latapi Ortega, *"Ucumar, the Argentinian Yeti,"* Contactos Extraterrestres, April 16, 1980. Simon Chapman, The Monster of the Madidi: Searching for the Giant Ape of the Bolivian Jungle (London: Autumn, 2001)

**Jez-Tyrmak, 15-18:** *Location*: Central Asia and Tibetan Plateau. *Sources*: George M. Eberhart, Mysterious Creatures, a Guide to Cryptozoology, Volume 1 & 2. CFZ Publications, 2010 pp. 176, 283, 482. Timelife Books - *The Himalayas*, pp. https://www.kg.undp.org/content/kyrgyzstan/en/home/ourperspective/ourperspectivearticles/2016/i-know-of-no-other-such-country.html. http://forteanzoology.blogspot.com/2011/01/dale-drinnon-clarifications-on-dzu-teh.html, https://www.sacred-texts.com/lcr/abs/abs26.htm.

**The Big Grey Man of Ben MacDhui (Am Fear Liath Mòr) 19-26:**
*Location*: Ben MacDhui Mountains, Scottish Highlands, UK. *Sources*:
Richard Frere, 'The Big Grey Man of Ben MacDhui',
https://www.spookyisles.com/big-grey-man-ben-macdhui/
https://www.scotsman.com/arts-and-culture/big-grey-man-ben-
macdui-2507058 http://www.biggreyman.co.uk/legend.html, https://
paranorms.com/am-fear-liath-mor/, https://www.
undiscoveredscotland.co.uk/usscotfax/outdoors/greyman.html,
https://www.undiscoveredscotland.co.uk/usscotfax/outdoors/
greyman.html, https://hauntedauckland.com/site/big-grey-man-ben-
macdhui-britains-bigfoot/.

**Jogung, 27-33:** *Location*: Australia. *Sources*: George M. Eberhart,
Mysterious Creatures, a Guide to Cryptozoology, Volume 1. CFZ
Publications, 2010, pp. 283. Rex Gilroy, *"Giants from the Dreamtime"*-
The Yowie in Myth and Reality. 2001, http://karlshuker.blogspot.com/
search?q=quinkin, https://en.wikipedia.org/wiki/Paranthropus,
https://en.wikipedia.org/wiki/Australopithecine, https://www.
yowiehunters.com.au/what-is-a-yowie, https://catalogue.nla.gov.au/
Record/6421816, http://www.australianyowieresearchcentre.com/
yowie-names/.

**Orang Dalam, 34-38:** *Location*: Malaysia, East Asia. *Sources*: George M.
Eberhart, Mysterious Creatures, a Guide to Cryptozoology, Volume 2.
CFZ Publications, 2010, p435, https://malaysianwildlife.org/malayan-
sun-bear-helarctos-malayanus/, https://malaysianwildlife.org/lar-
gibbon-hylobates-lar/, https://www.worldwildlife.org/ecoregions/
im0144#:~:text=The%20Peninsular%20Malaysian%20Montane%
20Rain,spectacular%20and%20endemic%20crested%20argus, https://
en.wikipedia.org/wiki/Peninsular_Malaysian_rain_forests,

**Ngoloko, 39-43:** *Location*: Kenya, Mt Kilimanjaro. *Sources*: George M.
Eberhart, Mysterious Creatures, a Guide to Cryptozoology, Volume 2.
CFZ Publications, 2010, p414, J.A.G Elliot, *"The Ngoloko: A Mystery of
the African Bush,"* Blackwood's Magazine 202 (1917): pp. 609 – 617.
Loren Coleman and Patrick Huyghe, the Field Guide to Bigfoot and

Other Mystery Primates. pp. 102, 103, https://www.yourlocalguardian. co.uk/news/1297969.startling-secrets-of-ostrich-people/, https://en. wikipedia.org/wiki/Ectrodactyly, https://rarediseases.org/rare-diseases/ectrodactyly-ectodermal-dysplasia-cleft-lippalate/#:~:text= Ectrodactyly%2C%20which%20is%20also%20known,be% 20affected%20in%20some%20individuals, https://www.tripadvisor. com/blog/4-incredible-regions-to-observe-kenyas-wildlife/.

WILDMEN

**Almasti 47-66:** *Location*: Caucuses Mountains & Mongolia/China. *Sources*: Dmitri Bayanov, *In the Footsteps of the Russian Snowman*, pp. 9, 21, 36,37,46,49, 51, Abdul Hassan Ali Masudi, *Meadows of Gold and Mines of Gems*, translated from Arabic by Aloys Sprenger. London. 1841, V, I, p.440, 'Story told by Koumykov Feitsa, 67 years, Kabardian of Kurkujin', Story told by Pchoukov Mohamed', Story told by Khakonov Danial, 65 years, pensioner, Kabardian, from Karmakovo', 'Story told by Kochokoev Erjib, 70 years, Kabardian, an inhabitant of Stary Cherek'. 'Story told by Didanov Dina, 40 years, Kabardian, an electrician at Baksan', 'Story told by Khadji Mourat, 23 years, Azerbaijani, chauffeur at Belokany', 'Story told by Omarov Ramazane, 37 years, Lakh, director of the veterinarian and zoological station of the district of Tliarata, in the Republic of Dagestan'. 'Story told by Akhaminov Khouzer Bekanlouk, 55 years, Kabardian, farmer at Planovskoye': All stories sourced, quoted, paraphrased, abridged, and reinterpreted from: Marie Jeanne Koffmann's, *'The Almasty – Yeti of the Caucasus,'* reprinted by The Relict Hominoid Inquiry 4:79-105 (2015), https://onlinelibrary.wiley.com/doi/pdf/10.1002/ggn2.10051, https://www.channel4.com/press/news/was-russian-bigfoot-actually-african-slave,

**Yeren, 67-86:** *Location*: China. *Sources*: George M. Eberhart, Mysterious Creatures, a Guide to Cryptozoology, Volume 2. CFZ Publications, 2010, pp. 628 – 632, David C. Xu, Mystery Creatures of China, the Complete Zoological Guide, Coachwhip Publications, 2018. pp. 73-84. Loren Coleman and Patrick Huyghe, The Field Guide to Bigfoot and Other Mystery Primates, Anomalist Books, 2006. pp.130, 131. https://www.isu.edu/media/libraries/rhi/research-papers/Zhou_Tracking-the-Chinese-Wildman.pdf, https://www.isu.edu/media/libraries/rhi/brief-communications/Footprint-Evidence-of-Chinese-Yeren.pdf, https://en.wikipedia.org/wiki/Yeren, https://en.wikipedia.org/wiki/Chinese_Academy_of_Sciences, http://www.bjreview.com/print/txt/2007-12/17/content_90934.htm, https://www.scmp.com/news/china/society/article/2160570/dreamers-crackpots-or-realists-diehards-trail-chinas-bigfoot, https://www.odditycentral.com/news/this-man-has-spent-the-last-22-years-looking-for-bigfoots-chinese-cousin.html, https://whc.unesco.org/en/list/1509/,

**Basajaun, 87-95:** *Location*: Basque Country, Aragon, Pyrenees of Spain and France. *Sources*: George M. Eberhart, Mysterious Creatures, a Guide to Cryptozoology, Volume I. CFZ Publications, 2010, p66, Webster W. *Basque Legends*. London: Griffith and Farren, 1877, *Antiquity*, 56:31-41, Olivier Décobert, "The case for Neanderthal survival: fact, fiction, or faction?" Myra Shackley (1982), Magraner J. *Les hominidés reliques d'Asie Centrale*. Valence: *Troglodytes*, (1992), Vinson, Julien (1883). I. Les trois Vérités, X. Basa-Jaun aveuglé. Le Folklore du Pays Basque. Paris: Maisonneuve et Larose. pp. 10–11, 43–45, https://www.isu.edu/media/libraries/rhi/brief-communications/ANCIENT-REPRESENTATIONS-OF-THE-WILDMAN-IN-FRANCE.pdf, , https://www.ancient-origins.net/myths-legends-europe/basajaun-0014222, https://www.sacred-texts.com/neu/basque/bl/bl20.htm, http://karlshuker.blogspot.com/search?q=basajaun, https://www.bbc.co.uk/news/uk-england-suffolk-35050026.

**Bar-Manu, 96-106:** *Location*: Chitral and Karakoram Ranges, North-West Frontier Province, Pakistan. *Sources*: Jordi Magraner: *Oral Statements Concerning Living Unknown Hominids: Analysis, Criticism, And Implications For Language Origins*, http://www.wildlifeofpakistan.com/blogs/index.php?blog=2&p=134&more=1&c=1&tb=1&pb=1Jordi Magraner´s Oral Statements Concerning Living Unknown Hominids, https://en-academic.com/dic.nsf/enwiki/1129708, http://www.bigfootencounters.com/biology/jordi.htm, Ahmad Siddiqui, Dr

Raheal (16 February 2014). *"In search of an elusive creature".* www. thenews.com.pk, Graziosi P. *Anthropological research in Chitral - Italian expeditions to the Karakorum (K2) and Hindu Kush, in scientific reports V, Prehistory-anthropology, vol. I,* p. 57-236, Leyde, 1964. *L'Homme Erik, Aspects sociaux et religieux de l'ancien royaume de Chitral au Nord Pakistan, Memoire de DEA en Histoire Religieuse, Université Jean Moulin Lyon III,* 1991, https://www.isu.edu/media/libraries/rhi/research-papers/MAGRANER-formatted.pdf,, https://blogs.scientificamerican. com/tetrapod-zoology/the-strange-case-of-the-minnesota-iceman/.

**Mari-Coxi 107-114:** *Location*: Serro dos Parecis, Mato Grosso State, Brazil. *Sources*: Percy Fawcett & Brian Fawcett, Exploration Fawcett, Weidenfeld & Nicolson (28 July 2016), https://www.britannica.com/place/Mato-Grosso, http://karlshuker.blogspot.com/search?q=percy+fawcett, https://cryptidz.fandom.com/wiki/Maricoxi, https://www.astmh.org/education-resources/tropical-medicine-q-a/major-tropical-diseases, https://www.britannica.com/list/9-mind-altering-plants.

**Yowie, 115-128:** *Location*: Primarily found in Queensland to Victoria, Coastal Mountains. *Sources*: Tony Healy and Paul Cropper, The Yowie: In Search of Australia's Bigfoot. Anomalist Books (2006) pp. Out of the Shadows; 1994 – Paul Cropper and Tony Healy, Bigfoots and Bunyips; 1996 – Malcolm Smith, Eberhart 2, p639, https://www.thesun.co.uk/news/8402922/bigfoot-yowie-apeman-living-australia/, https://en.wikipedia.org/wiki/Yowie, https://www.abc.net.au/local/stories/2014/12/09/4145054.htm, https://www.facebook.com/pg/yowiehunters.com.au/photos/?tab=photos_albums, https://www.dailymail.co.uk/news/article-7519813/The-remote-Queensland-town-sightings-Yowie-else.html, https://www.youtube.com/user/YowieSightings/videos, https://www.yowiehunters.com.au/queensland, https://www.yowiehunters.com.au/yowiesigns, https://www.dailymail.co.uk/news/article-7312415/Yowie-hunters-claim-10-foot-beast-stalked-bushland-ran-cave.html, https://www.news.com.au/lifestyle/real-life/news-life/yowie-researcher-dean-harrison-reveals-proof-creature-exists/news-story/548e364c7d9bf54f12b8c1e8608e52f6, https://www.yowiehunters.com.

au/yowie-art-sculptures, https://www.news.com.au/lifestyle/real-life/
news-life/yowie-researcher-dean-harrison-reveals-proof-creature-
exists/news-story/548e364c7d9bf54f12b8c1e8608e52f6.

## RELICTS

**Yeti, 131-145:** *Location*: Himalayan Mountains of Nepal, Kashmir, India
and Bhutan; Southern Tibetan Plateau, southern Xinxiang Uyghur
Autonomous Region, northwest Yunnan province, China. *Sources*:
Eberhart 2, p632. *Abominable Snowman – Legend Come to Life* - by Ivan
T. Sanderson (1961) pp. 6-11 & 459. Hillary, Sir Edward P. *Nothing
Venture, Nothing Win*. New York: Coward, McCann and Geoghegan.
1975. Tom Slick, *"The Yeti Expedition,"* Explorers Journal 36 (December
1958): 5-8, Reinhold Messner, *My Quest for the Yeti* (New York: St
Martin's, 2000); Peter Byrne, *The search for Big Foot: Monster, myth or
man?, In Search Of The Abominable Snowman: Bad-Boy Child Of The
Tibetan Monkey God*, by William F Romain, *A Checklist of Hypotheses
for the Yeti*, Oliver D. Smith. https://www.atlasobscura.com/places/the-
yeti-scalp-of-khumjung-khumjung-nepal, https://www.neatorama.
com/2020/01/15/Taxonomania-An-Incomplete-Catalog-of-Invented-
Species/, https://www.alpfmedical.info/freshwater-monster/yeti.html,
https://www.atlasobscura.com/articles/saga-of-the-yeti-hand?fbclid=
IwAR0KWxOub1d8phaOufSR18SgtDXlBxosHovMOy-
4N2kLvhakyoTyiBdLsXI.

**El Sisemite', 146-152:** *Location*: Guatemala: Central & South America.
*Sources*: Green 1978, p.133. Sanderson 1961, pp.159 & 161-162. Michael
Howard. 1974, *Kekchi Religious Beliefs and Lore regarding the Jungle*,
National Studies. Vol.3: pp. 34-49, G. G. B. *"Guatemala Myths."* The
Museum Journal VI, no. 3 (September 1915): 103-115, *Forbidden
Archaeology: The Hidden History of the Human Race*, Michael A. Cremo
and Richard L. Thompson (Bhaktivedanta Book Publishing, 1996),
http://www.bigfootencounters.com/creatures/sisimite.htm, http://
www.bigfootencounters.com/biology/duende.htm, https://itsmth.
fandom.com/wiki/Sisemite, https://www.penn.museum/sites/
journal/416/, http://forteanzoology.blogspot.com/2010/07/dale-

drinnon-sisimite-tzitzimitl.html, https://itsmth.fandom.com/wiki/ Sisemite, https://www.penn.museum/sites/journal/416/, https:// puzzleboxhorror.com/encyclopedia-of-supernatural-horror/sisemite-central-america/, https://bigfooteruption.com/worldwide/north-america/central-america/guatamala/sisemite/, https://tamastslikt. wordpress.com/2012/04/13/maya-folklore/.

**Skunk Ape, 153-168:** *Location*: North America: Florida everglades. *Sources*: Kyle Mizokami, *Bigfoot-like Figures in North American Folklore and Tradition*, Loren Coleman and Patrick Huyghe, *The Field Guide to Bigfoot and Other Mystery Primates*, Anomalist Books, 2006. http:// www.bigfootencounters.com/creatures/skunkape.htm, https://en. wikipedia.org/wiki/Skunk_ape, https://www.westpalmbeach.com/the-skunk-ape/, https://youtu.be/gMOrXd-pI04,

## LITTLEFOOT

**Teh-Lma/The Little Yeti, 171-176:** *Location*: Choyang River Valley, Nepal, & Nepal/Bhutan/Tibet/Sikkim state, India. *Sources*: Peter Byrne, "frogs lure Abominable Snowman," New York Journal-American, June 15th, 1958, George M. Eberhart, Mysterious Creatures, a Guide to Cryptozoology, Volume 2. CFZ Publications, 2010, pp.564, *The Himalayas: The World's Wild Places*, TIMELIFE BOOKS. https:// aimeecrocker.com/exploits/the-abominable-snowman/ https://en. wikipedia.org/wiki/Sloth_bear#Distribution_and_habitat, http:// publications.americanalpineclub.org/articles/12195932400/Himalaya-Nepal-Slick-Johnson-Nepal-Snowman-Expedition,

**Nimbinjee, 177-186:** Location: New South Wales, Queensland. Sources: George M. Eberhart, Mysterious Creatures, a Guide to Cryptozoology, Volume 2. CFZ Publications, 2010, pp.283, 285, The *Yowie: In Search of Australia's Bigfoot*. Tony Healy and Paul Cropper, Anomalist Books, Gary Opit docs and photos used with kind permission (Pinkney, 2003). Patricia Riggs, associate editor of The Macleay Argus.

**Orang Pendek, 187-194:** *Location*: The Kerinci Regency of central Sumatra and Kerinci Seblat National Park. *Sources*: George M. Eberhart, Mysterious Creatures, a Guide to Cryptozoology, Volume 2. CFZ Publications, 2010, pp 146, https://cliffbarackman.com/research/orang-pendek-project/orang-pendek-project-data-index/orang-pendek-project-1232013/, https://www.theguardian.com/science/2011/oct/07/evidence-elusive-orang-pendek, https://en.wikipedia.org/wiki/Orang_Pendek, https://www.vice.com/en/article/j5585p/meet-the-man-searching-the-jungles-of-indonesia-for-a-mythical-pint-sized-bigfoot, https://cliffbarackman.com/research/orang-pendek-project/about-the-orang-pendek/. https://cliffbarackman.com/research/sound-recordings/possible-orang-pendek/, https://en.wikipedia.org/wiki/Sumatran_lar_gibbon.

**Nittaewo, 195-201:** *Location*: Sri Lanka. *Sources*: Hill, W. C. Osman (1945), *Nittaewo, an Unsolved Problem of Ceylon*. Colombo: Loris. pp. 4, 251–62, George M. Eberhart, Mysterious Creatures, a Guide to Cryptozoology, Volume 2. CFZ Publications, 2010, pp. 417-418, A.T. Rambukwella, *"The Nittaewo of Mahalenama,"* Loris 10 (December 1966); 367-370. Heuvelmans, Bernard (1955) *On the Track of Unknown Animals*, Routledge, Nevill, Hugh *"The Nittaewo of Ceylon,"* The Taprobanian 1 #3 (February 1886), Rambukwella Captain A.T., *the Nittaewo - The Legendary Pygmies of Ceylon*. Journal of the Royal Asiatic Society of Ceylon.1963, https://en.wikipedia.org/wiki/Nittaewo, http://serendib.btoptions.lk/article.php?issue=70&id=1716#page,

**Agogwe, 202-207:** *Location*: Zimbabwe. *Sources*: Burgoyne, Cuthbert *"Little Furry Men,"* Discovery: The Popular Journal of Knowledge, Vol. 19 (1938), Sanderson, Ivan T. (1961) *Abominable Snowmen: Legend Come to Life*, Chilton, Eberhart, George M. (2002) *Mysterious Creatures: A Guide to Cryptozoology*, pp. 39. Heuvelmans, Bernard (1955) *On the Track of Unknown Animals*, Routledge, Hichens, William *"African Mystery Beasts,"* Discovery: The Popular Journal of Knowledge, Vol. 18, No. 216 (December 1937), Coudray, Philippe (2009) *Guide des Animaux Cachés, Editions du Mont, Heini Hediger, ("Auf der Spur eines neuen*

*Menschenaffen,"*) Das Tier 1 (October 1960): 49; Charles Cordier, *"Deux anthropoïdes inconnus marchant debout, au Congo ex-Belge,"* Genus 29 (1963): 2-10; Charles Cordier, *"Animaux inconnus au Congo,"* Zoo 38 (April 1973): 185-191; https://lonewolfonline.net/agogwe/, https://www.phantomsandmonsters.com/2014/06/agogwe-little-men-of-forest.html, http://www.unknownexplorers.com/agogwe.php,

MONKEY MONSTERS

**Salvaje, 211-219:** *Location*: Puerto Ayacucho, Venezuela. *Sources*: Loren Coleman & Patrick Huyghe, *The Field Guide to Bigfoot and Other Mystery Primates,* Anomalist Books, (2006); pp. 78, 79. Marc E.W. Miller and Khryztian Miller, *"Further Investigation into Loy's Ape in Venezuela,"* Cryptozoology 10 (19910: 66-71.) Alexander Von Humboldt, *Personal narrative of a Journey to the Equinoctial Regions of the New Continent, during the Years 1799-1804* (1825) (New York: Penguin, 1995), pp. 207-208. Rolf Blomberg, *"Rio Amazonas",* Almqvist&Wiksell, 1966.

**Nandi Bear, 220-227:** *Location*: Uganda, the highlands of Kenya. *Sources*: Loren Coleman and Patrick Huyghe, *The Field Guide to Bigfoot and Other Mystery Primates,* Anomalist Books, 2006. pp.104 and *Eberhart, George M. (2002) Mysterious Creatures: A Guide to Cryptozoology* Heuvelmans, Bernard (1955) *On the Track of Unknown Animals,* Routledge, Shuker, Karl P. N. (1995) *In Search of Prehistoric Survivors: Do Giant 'Extinct' Creatures Still Exist?,* Blandford, Shuker, Karl *"A Fossil Nandi Bear?,"* Fortean Times 380 (June 2019), Pocock, Reginald I. (1930). *The Story of the Nandi Bear,* Natural History Magazine 2: 162–169, http://www.philippe-coudray.com/PDF/A%20GUIDEBOOK%20TO%20HIDDEN%20ANIMALS%20WEB.pdf,

**Isnachi, 228-232:** *Location*: Southern Ecuador & Peru. *Sources*: Loren Coleman and Patrick Huyghe, *The Field Guide to Bigfoot and Other Mystery Primates,* Anomalist Books, 2006. pp 76, George M. Eberhart, *Mysterious Creatures, a Guide to Cryptozoology, Volume 2.* CFZ Publications, 2010, pp 276, Peter J Hocking *"Large Peruvian mammals Unknown to Zoology"* Cryptozoology 11 (1992) 38 – 50. Peter J Hocking *"Further investigation into Unknown Peruvian mammals"* Cryptozoology

12 (1996) 50 -57. Chapman, Simon (2001) *the Monster of the Madidi: Searching For the Giant Ape of the Bolivian Jungle*, Aurum, Blake, C. C. 1862, *"Past life in South America."* The Geologist 5:323-330. Cartelle, C., and W. C. Hartwig. 1996. *"A new extinct primate among the Pleistocene megafauna of Bahia, Brazil."* Proceedings of the National Academy of Sciences 93:6405-6409. Hartwig, W. C., and C. Cartelle. 1996. *"A complete skeleton of the giant South American primate Protopithecus."*, Nature 381:307-311. https://raftingmonkey.com/2017/02/12/monkey-megafauna/,

**Devil Monkey, 233-239:** *Location*: Large-tailed Primate of North America. *Sources*: Chad Arment *"Virginia Devil Monkey Reports"*, North American Biofortean review 2, no.1 (2000): 34-37, https://pinebarrensinstitute.com/user-submitted-encounters/2018/9/4/user-submitted-cryptid-sighting, http://frontiersofzoology.blogspot.com/2012/03/devil-monkeys-demolished.html, http://www.unknownexplorers.com/devilmonkeys.php.

**Kra-Dhan/Bekk-Bok, 240-244:** *Location*: Nepal & Vietnam. *Sources*: Loren Coleman and Patrick Huyghe, *The Field Guide to Bigfoot and Other Mystery Primates*, Anomalist Books, 2006. pp 136, George M. Eberhart, *Mysterious Creatures, a Guide to Cryptozoology*, Volume 1. CFZ Publications, 2010, pp. 307, Ivan T. Sanderson: *"Abominable Snowmen: Legend come to Life"* (Philadelphia: Chilton, 1961). pp. 244-245; *"Abominable Jungle-men,"* Pursuit, no. 10 (April 1970): 36-37. Sports Afield, (May 1957): *"I Met the Abominable Snowman"* (A True Story), by George Moore M.D.

DOGMEN

**The Beast of Bray Road, 247-254:** *Location*: Bray Road, Elkhorn, Wisconsin. *Sources*: Godfrey, Linda S. (2003). *The Beast of Bray Road: Tailing Wisconsin's Werewolf*. Black Earth, Wisconsin: Prairie Oak Press, https://thoughtcatalog.com/christine-stockton/2018/08/beast-of-bray-road/, https://www.wisconsinfrights.com/elkhorn-werewolf-photo/, https://www.theguardian.com/us-news/2021/aug/14/wisconsin-wolves-hunters-300-kill-limit, https://www.

nationalgeographic.com/animals/article/wisconsin-wolf-hunt-killed-one-third-state-population, https://walworthcountycommunitynews.com/1991/12/29/tracking-down-the-beast-of-bray-road/, https://www.werewolves.com/more-than-a-single-word/.

**Old Stinker - The Werewolf of Hull, 255-262:** *Location*: Hull, Yorkshire, England. *Sources*: Andy McGrath, *Beasts of Britain*, Hangar One Publishing, (2021), https://theconversation.com/why-we-should-welcome-the-return-of-old-stinker-the-english-werewolf-67797, https://www.dailymail.co.uk/news/article-3591219/Hull-residents-spot-fanged-beast-human-like-features-nicknamed-Old-Stinker.html, https://www.yorkshirepost.co.uk/arts-and-culture/truth-behind-those-sightings-hulls-beast-barmston-drain-werewolf-1789077,

**The Adlet, 263-266:** *Location*: Greenland, Alaska (USA) and Canada. *Sources*: Boas, Franz (1888). "The Central Eskimo". Annual Reports. Bureau of American Ethnology. 6: 470–666. Boas, Franz (1982). "The Folklore of the Eskimo". Race, language, and culture. U of Chicago P. Rink, Signe (1898). "The Girl and the Dogs: An Eskimo Folk-Tale with Comments". American Anthropologist. 11 (6): pp. 181–87, Sonne, Birgitte (1990). The Acculturative Role of Sea Woman: Early contact relations between Inuit and Whites as revealed in the Origin Myth of Sea Woman. Commission for Scientific Investigations in Greenland, Green, Thomas A. (2008). The Greenwood Library of World Folktales: North and South America. Greenwood Press, https://www.adn.com/features/article/alaska-folklore-five-mythical-creatures-last-frontier/2012/06/13/, http://fantasy-faction.com/2021/mythological-creatures-of-alaska-fantasy-close-to-home, https://www.mythical-creatures-and-beasts.com/adlet.html.

**Skinwalker, 267-277:** *Location*: Arizona, New Mexico. *Sources*: Keene, Dr Adrienne, *"Magic in North America Part 1: 'Ugh!' at Native Appropriations"*, 8 March 2016. Kluckhohn, C. (1944). *Navaho Witchcraft*. Boston: Beacon Press, Eller, J. & Blackwater, N. (1999). *The Navajo Skinwalker, Witchcraft, and Related Phenomena* (1st Edition Ed.). Chinle, AZ: Infinity Horn Publishing. Brunvand, J. H. (2012). *Native*

*American Contemporary Legends.* In J. H. Brunvand, *Encyclopaedia of Urban Legends* (2nd Edition ed.). Santa Barbara, California, United States of America, https://www.legendsofamerica.com/navajo-skinwalkers/, https://allthatsinteresting.com/skinwalker, https://ksltv.com/447719/mystery-of-utahs-skinwalker-ranch-very-much-alive/, https://thoughtcatalog.com/jacob-geers/2016/10/14-facts-about-skinwalkers-that-will-100-scare-the-shit-out-of-you/, https://www.legendsofamerica.com/navajo-skinwalkers/, https://www.hitc.com/en-gb/2021/10/28/what-is-a-skinwalker-tiktok/, https://rivercityghosts.com/the-terror-of-the-skinwalker-the-native-american-boogeyman/.

**Hyena Man, 278-282:** *Location:* Arabian Peninsula, the Levant, North Africa, And the Horn of Africa. *Sources: "The Magicality of the Hyena: Beliefs and Practices in West and South Asia"* (PDF). Asian Folklore Studies, Volume 57, 1998: 331–344. June 2008. Archived from the original (PDF) on 2008-06-25. https://en.wikipedia.org/wiki/Werehyena, https://inthedarkair.wordpress.com/2015/10/26/malicious-myths-the-were-hyena/, https://villains.fandom.com/wiki/Werehyena.

## AMPHIBIOUS ANTHROPOIDS

**Memegwesi, 285-292:** *Location:* Lake Superior area of central Ontario, northern Manitoba and Saskatchewan, Canada; northern Minnesota; northern Wisconsin; northern Michigan, Maine, USA. *Sources:* George M. Eberhart, *Mysterious Creatures, a Guide to Cryptozoology,* Volume 1. CFZ Publications, 2010, pp. 351, Johann G. Kohl, Kitchi-Gami: *Wanderings Round Lake Superior* (London: Chapman and Hall, 1860), pp. 358-366, Regina Flannery-Herzfeld, *"A Study of the Distribution and Development of the Memegwicio Concept in Algonquian Folklore,"* master's thesis, Department of Anthropology, Catholic University of America, 1931, John E. Roth, *American Elves* (Jefferson, N.C.: McFarland, 1997), pp. 9-10, 38-40, 114, 137- Selwen Dewdney and Kenneth E. Kidd, *Indian Rock Paintings of the Great Lakes* (Toronto, Canada: University of Toronto Press, 1967), pp. 12-24. Sr. Bernard Coleman, *"The Religion of the Ojibwa of Northern Minnesota,"* Primitive Man 10 (1937): 33-57, Jennes, Diamond, *The Ojibwa Indians of Parry*

*Island, their social and religious life*, Ottawa: National Museum of Canada, J. O. Patenaude, printer. 1935. vi, pp. 115. As told to C.J. Wheeler in the Cree First Nation of Bunibonibee (Oxford House). Adapted from de Wheeler, C. J. (1975). *The Oxford House pictograph: The May May Quah Sao are alive and well at Oxford House.* with J. Freedman and J. H. Barkow (eds.), *Proceedings of the Second Congress, Canadian Ethnological Society* (p. 701-714). Canadian Ethnology Service Paper 28(2), Mercury Series. Ottawa: National Museum of Man. http://temagami.nativeweb.org/tale-folklore-20.html, http://www.native-languages.org/memegwesi.htm, https://www.planet-today.com/2018/01/strange-encounters-with-bizarre-tunnel-dwelling-monsters.html, https://www.planet-today.com/2018/01/strange-encounters-with-bizarre-tunnel-dwelling-monsters.html, https://squeakyspooky.livejournal.com/22649.html, http://www.native-languages.org/memegwesi.htm, https://www.facebook.com/Mishkiki.Org/posts/the-little-peoplean-anishinaabe-legendthe-memegwesi-little-people-can-do-magnifi/726197461511728/, http://stonestructures.org/html/underworld.html, https://imagesdanslapierre.mcq.org/wp-content/uploads/2018/09/Activity3_Ann_1_STUDENT_EN_FORM.pdf,. https://ojibwe.lib.umn.edu/main-entry/memegwesi-na.

**Rusalka, 293-298:** *Location:* Danube, Dnieper and Volga River. E. Europe and Russia. *Sources:* George M. Eberhart, *Mysterious Creatures, a Guide to Cryptozoology, Volume 2.* CFZ Publications, 2010, pp. 488, *In the Footsteps of the Russian Snowman*, Dmitri Bayanov, (CFZ PRESS) pp. 138 - 139. Guy De Maupassant, *The Complete Short Stories*, Cassell, London. 1970, Vol.3, pp. 192 – 195. Dmitri Bayanov, *Historical Evidence For The Existence Of Relict Hominoids*, International Centre Of Hominology, Moscow 121614, Russia, Pp. 38-39. The Struggle for Troglodytes, Boris Porshnev. pp. 51-52. https://en.wikipedia.org/wiki/Mavka,http://www.encyclopediaofukraine.com/display.asp?linkpath=pages%5CM%5CA%5CMavkaIT.htm, https://imgur.com/gallery/9yRVeHi.

**Kappa, 299-306:** *Location:* Saga prefecture on the southern island of Kyushu, Japan. *Sources:* Catrien Ross, *Supernatural and Mysterious*

*Japan* (Tokyo: yen books, 1996), pp. 31, 99. *The Field Guide to Bigfoot and Other Mystery Primates by Loren Coleman and Patrick Huyghe*. pp. 138. Donald Alexander Mackenzie, *Myths of China and Japan* (London: Gresham, 1923), pp. 350-351. https://www.dailymail.co.uk/sciencetech/article-2644036/Are-bones-water-demon-Remains-mythological-Kappa-Japan.html, https://www.ancient-origins.net/news-mysterious-phenomena/are-mummified-remains-unidentified-creature-proof-mythological-kappa, http://pinktentacle.com/2008/05/seven-mysterious-creatures-of-japan, http://mysteriousuniverse.org/20, https://paranormal-world.fandom.com/wiki/Kappa_Encounters.

**Woadd -El-Uma, 307-309:** *Location*: Third Cataract of the Nile River, Sudan. *Sources*: George M. Eberhart, *Mysterious Creatures, a Guide to Cryptozoology, Volume 2.* CFZ Publications, 2010, pp. 617. http://www.sci-news.com/biology/science-chimpanzees-orangutans-swim-dive-01319.html, http://www.sci-news.com/biology/science-chimpanzees-orangutans-swim-dive-01319.html#:~:text=Chimpanzees%2C%20Orangutans%20Can%20Swim%20and%20Dive%2C%20Biologists%20Prove, https://a-z-animals.com/animals/location/africa/sudan/,

**The Lizard Man of Scape Ore Swamp, 310-319:** *Location*: Scape Ore Swamp, Bishopville, South Carolina, U.S.A. *Sources*: Loren Coleman and Patrick Huyghe, *The Field Guide to Bigfoot and Other Mystery Primates*, Anomalist Books, 2006. Pp. 62, Blackburn, Lyle (2013). *Lizard Man: The True Story of the Bishopville Monster*. Anomalist Books, Linda S. Godfrey (28 August 2014). *American Monsters: A History of Monster Lore, Legends, and Sightings in America*. Penguin Publishing Group. p. 278. Radford, Ben. *"Episode 16 - The Lizard Man of Scape Ore"*. Squaring the Strange, Fortean Times 333 (Nov 2015) *"Attack of the Lizard Man!"*, Houston Chronicle (1988-08-13) *"To keep a monstrous legend alive/Man admits lying about Lizard Man"*, Houston Chronicle, mark Opsasnick and Mark Chorvinsky, *"Lizard Man,"* Strange Magazine, no. 3 (1988): pp. 34, 36. *"Youth Who Saw 'Lizard Man' Gets an Agent"*. San Francisco Chronicle. 1988-08-02. https://pubs.usgs.gov/circ/circ1173/circ1173a/chapter12.htm, https://www.strangecarolinas.com/2018/06/lizard-

man-museum-bishopville-sc.html, http://www.bigfootencounters.
com/articles/remember.htm, https://cryptidarchives.fandom.com/
wiki/Lizard_Man_of_Scape_Ore_Swamp, https://www.
strangecarolinas.com/2018/06/lizard-man-museum-bishopville-
sc.html, https://en.wikipedia.org/wiki/Bishopville,_South_Carolina,
http://www.theparanormalguide.com/blog/the-lizard-man-of-lee-
county.

**The Honey Island Swamp Monster, 320-324:** *Location*: Honey Island
Swamp, Louisiana, USA. *Sources*: https://offscreen.com/view/
homespun_horror, Loren Coleman, *"Three Toes are better Than Five,"*
Fortean Times, no. 98 (June 1997):44; Dana Holyfield, *Encounters with
the Honey Island Swamp Monster* (Pearl River, La: Honey Island
Swamp Books, 1999).

**Shuirenxiong – The Water Man Bear, 325-329:** David C. XU,
Mysteries Creatures of China, the Complete Cryptozoological Guide.
Pp. 113,114. (Coachwhip) 2018, Yu Wang, Shanhai Xunzong: Shijie
Guaishou Zhi Mi (Tracking Mountains and Seas: World Monsters
Mysteries.

# PHOTOS & ILLUSTRATIONS

## MAN APES

**Ucumar:**

*"In 1957, the Brazilian newspaper 'Ultima Hora de Rio de Janeiro' reported that the villagers of Tolar Grande were terrorised by eerie calls emanating from the mountains!"* Source: By kevin.j from Córdoba, Argentina - Flickr, CC BY-SA https://commons.wikimedia.org/w/index.php?curid=5935568.

*"The Ucumar is said to be fond of the cabbage-like insides of the Payo plant (Aechmea distichantha)"* Source: By Gklekailo - Kalugaringon nga buhat, CC BY-SA 3.0, https://commons.wikimedia.org/w/index.php?curid=14791499

*"Could the endangered and rarely seen account for some sightings of the Ucumar?"* Source: By Steve Wilson: from Chester, UK - Rare Spectacled or Andean Bear, CC BY 2.0, https://commons.wikimedia.org/w/index.php?curid=83135367

*"Gigantopithecus lower jaw (cast) from the Cenozoic of eastern Asia. Public display, Cleveland Museum of Natural History, Cleveland, Ohio, USA"*

**Jez-Tyrmak:**

*"Could a type of giant Man-Ape, or "Big Yeti," exist here on Tibetan Plateau? "*

**The Big Grey Man of Ben MacDhui (Am Fear Liath Mòr):**

*"A trifling 1.9% of Scotland landmass is covered by urban sprawl, if a giant, 'Man Ape' could survive undetected anywhere in Britain, then surely it would be here!"*

*"Professor Norman Collie."*

*"A Brocken Spectre occurs when the sun casts an enormous shadow in front of an observer".*

**Jogung:**

*"In 1960, two prospectors observed a group of huge gorillas ranging in height from 7 – 10ft. tall, as they destroyed their hut, at Lake Ballard, Western Australia."*

*"Quinkin' Rock Art, some of the worlds most extensive and ancient rock painting galleries surround the tiny town of Laura, Queensland."*

Public Domain, https://commons.wikimedia.org/w/index.php?curid=10662386

**Orang Dalam:**

*"Are the stories of Malaysia's 'Man Ape' simply the folktales of yesteryear repackaged for a modern audience, or could this ape-like giant have a basis in biology?"* By Kai Gan, CC BY 3.0, https://commons.wikimedia.org/w/index.php?curid=57569865

*"Could the indigenous Senoi people of Peninsular Malaysia, who are also sometimes referred to as Orang Dalam ("man of the interior"), have inspired the legends of this mysterious 'Man-Ape?"* Source: *By Internet Archive Book Images - https://www.flickr.com/photos/internetarchive-bookimages/14583642829/Source book page: https://archive.org/stream/womenofallnationo1joyc/womenofallna-tiono1joyc#page/n225/mode/1up,* No restrictions, *https://commons.wikimedia.org/w/index.php?curid=43414342*

**Ngoloko:**

*"An Aerial photograph of the Tana River which is in the Rift Valley, Kenya"* Source: By SGT R.A. Ward, U.S. Marine Corps - http://www.dodmedia.osd.mil; VIRIN: DM-SD-01-06042, Public Domain, https://commons.wikimedia.org/w/index.php?curid=14786431

*"An advert for P.T. Barnum's "Feejee Mermaid" around 1842. "* Source: By P. T. Barnum or an employee - Newspaper advert, Public Domain, https://commons.wikimedia.org/w/index.php?curid=6798674

*"Could isolated tribes like the Vadoma (or Ostrich people) have been viewed through the eyes of 19th century Europeans as a form of ancient man?"* Source: By Thfk - Own work, CC BY-SA 4.0, https://commons.wikimedia.org/w/index.php?curid=38644505

## WILDMEN

**Almasti:**

*"Caucasian mountains. Kabardino-Balkaria. Russia. "*Source: By kikiwis, CC BY 3.0, https://commons.wikimedia.org/w/index.php?curid=56135016

*"Uncontacted indigenous tribe in the Brazilian state of Acre".* By Governo do Acre c/o Gleilson Miranda - https://www.flickr.com/photos/fotos-doacre/3793140069/in/set-72157621833492035, CC BY 2.0, https://commons.wikimedia.org/w/index.php?curid=24286114

*"Model of Homo Neanderthalensis elder man in The Natural History Museum, Vienna".* Source: By Jakub Hałun - Own work, CC BY-SA 4.0, https://commons.wikimedia.org/w/index.php?curid=113008114

**Yeren:**

*"Virgin forest in Shennongjia Forestry District, Hubei, China".* Source: By Evilbish - Own work, CC BY-SA 3.0, https://commons.wikimedia.org/w/index.php?curid=32980667

*"Inscription in cliff face next to the entrance of the "Yeren Cave" in Western Hubei Province, China. The inscription reads "Ye Ren Dong" ("Wild Man Cave")."* Source: By Rolf Müller - Own work, CC BY-SA 3.0, https://commons.wikimedia.org/w/index.php?curid=751903

*"Frontispiece depicting Adam Schall von Bell and Matteo Ricci, China Illustrata by Athanasius*

*Kircher "Source*: The frontispiece of Athanasius Kircher&#039;s China Illustrata. This scan is from http://www.deutsches-museum.de/bib/entdeckt/alt_buch/buch0900.htm, Public Domain, https://commons.wikimedia.org/w/index.php?curid=5631986

*"The Great Wall of China".* Source: By Severin.stalder, CC BY-SA 3.0, https://commons.wikimedia.org/w/index.php?curid=26549385

**Basajaun:**

*"Irati Forest, Navarre, Spain"*, By JavierOlivares - Own work, CC BY-SA 4.0, https://commons.wikimedia.org/w/index.php?curid=79416055

*"A depiction of a Wildman alongside a person, commonly assumed to be its "Shower" or "Handler"*, adorns a portal in an 11th-century church in Semur-en-Auxois.

*"The god Pan (pictured here with Daphnis) an ancient embodiment of the Wildman?"* Source: Public Domain, https://commons.wikimedia.org/w/index.php?curid=2292318

**Bar-Manu:**

*"Tirich Mir is the highest mountain of the Hindu Kush range located in Chitral District of Pakistan"* Source: By Shah Tahsin Anwar - Own work, CC BY-SA 4.0, https://commons.wikimedia.org/w/index.php?curid=59412081

*"Almost all of Magraner's Barmanu eyewitnesses identified the Minnesota Iceman as a match for the animal they encountered. Could the sensational image of this Barnumesque hoax have reached even here, influencing the minds of these isolated shepherds? "* Source: Darren Naish - Tetrapod Zoology: "The Strange Case of the Minnesota Iceman," Jan. 2, 2017 (Scientific American Blog Network), Public Domain, https://commons.wikimedia.org/w/index.php?curid=67834028

**Mari-Coxi:**

*"Could a tribe of Wildmen live hidden within the impenetrable forests of the Amazon?"* By Martin St-Amant (S23678) - Own work, CC BY-SA 3.0, https://commons.wikimedia.org/w/index.php?curid=6356904

*"Colonel Percy Harrison Fawcett. Colonel Percy Harrison Fawcett in 1911"*. Source: User Daniel Candido on pt. Wikipedia, Public Domain, https://commons.wikimedia.org/w/index.php?curid=1297422

*"Pachon Navarro: The Double Nosed Andean Tiger Hound"* Source: By 99bea - Own work, CC BY-SA 4.0, https://commons.wikimedia.org/w/index.php?curid=45080320

**Yowie:**

*"Jamison Valley in the Blue Mountains, New South Wales, Australia"* Source: Diliff - Own work, CC BY-SA 3.0, https://commons.wikimedia.org/w/index.php?curid=5403298

*"Although Indigenous stories of the Hairy Man are common, there appear to be relatively few examples of rock art that show Yowie-type creatures. Groote Eylandt Archipelago, home to the Anindilyakwa people."* Source: The Anindilyakwa Land Council Newsletter No 16 (November 2015)

*"Reconstructed Homo Naledi skull"* By Martinvl - Own work, CC BY-SA 4.0, https://commons.wikimedia.org/w/index.php?curid=44792709

RELICTS

**Yeti:**

"Photograph of an alleged yeti footprint found by Michael Ward, taken at Menlung glacier on the Everest expedition by Eric Shipton in 1951". Public Domain

*"A 'female' Yeti scalp that was discovered by Sir Edmund Hilary in 1960 and extensively examined by specialists at the field museum in Chicago turned out to be a fake made from the skin of a Serow (Himalayan –goat-antelope)"* Photo: Nunò Nogueira, 2006. (Creative Commons.)

*"The Pangboche Hand. 'In 1960, Sir Edmund Hilary examined the mummified hand of a 'yeti' at Pangboche monastery and declared it a mix of human and animal. However, it was later revealed by Peter Byrne that he had removed a phalanx and finger bone from the hand in 1959 and replaced them with human phalanges."* Photo: Sir Edmund Hillary - Epitaph to the Elusive Abominable Snowman. LIFE Magazine. 13 January 1961.

**El Sisemite':**

*"Montane Forests of Guatemala",* By Salix Oculus - Own work, CC BY-SA 4.0, https://commons.wikimedia.org/w/index.php?curid=63309259

**Skunk Ape:**

*"Could the vast wilderness of the Florida Everglades hide the existence of an unknown species of Ape?* " By Chauncey Davis from Cape Coral, FL, USA - Everglades and Turner River Uploaded by Closedmouth, CC BY 2.0, https://commons.wikimedia.org/w/index.php?curid=19057696

*"One of two photos of the creature that has since become known as the Myakka Skunk Ape. Even at first glance, it certainly becomes clear why our witness identified an 'orangutan' as the closest match to this curious beast. Yet, in its size, colouration, elongated fangs and especially its glowing eyes, if genuine, it can only be representative of an, as yet unknown, ape species.* "Anonymous:

<u>LITTLEFOOT</u>

**Teh-Lma/The Little Yeti:**

*"Could small rivers and streams provide valuable protein sources like fish, lizards, insects and frogs, to feed a population of diminutive yeti-like creatures known locally as 'Teh-lma?"* Source: By Sam Litvin - Himalaya, CC BY 2.0, https://commons.wikimedia.org/w/index.php?curid=79496541

*"Could an unknown regional variety of Hoolock Gibbon have adapted to the environmental sparsity of the Himalayas?"* Source: By Dr Raju Kasambe - Own work, CC BY-SA 4.0, https://commons.wikimedia.org/w/index.php?curid=37410544

**Nimbinjee:**

*"The Nimbin Valley and Nimbin Rocks in the Northern Rivers of NSW":* By Kpravin2 - Own work, CC BY-SA 4.0, https://commons.wikimedia.org/w/index.php?curid=79197523

**Orang Pendek:**

**Nittaewo:**

**Agogwe:**

## MONKEY MONSTERS

**Salvaje:**

*"Puerto Ayacucho, Venezuela"* By Daniela 1997 books - Own work, CC BY-SA 3.0, https://commons.wikimedia.org/w/index.php?curid=32364789

*"De Loys' Ape"* By Francois de Loys - Montadon, George (1929). " Découverte d&#039; UN singe d&#039; apparence anthropoïde en Amérique du Sud&quot. Journal de la Société des Américanistes 21 (1): 183-195. DOI:10.3406/jsa.1929.3665., Public Domain, https://commons.wikimedia.org/w/index.php?curid=71142086

*"The Yanomami are the largest relatively isolated tribe in South America. They live in the rainforests and mountains of northern Brazil and southern Venezuela"*, By Sam Valadi - Yanomami Mom & Baby, CC BY 2.0, https://commons.wikimedia.org/w/index.php?curid=87444816

Nandi Bear:

*"Kenyan Tealands"* – By Bjørn Christian Tørrissen - Own work by uploader, http://bjornfree.com/galleries.html, CC BY-SA 3.0, https://commons.wikimedia.org/w/index.php?curid=22879800

*"Sketch of the track found by F. Schindler found near the Magadi Railway"* (Fair use)

*"Giant short-faced hyena (Pachycrocuta brevirostris) could this species be responsible for some sightings of the Nandi Bear?"* Cast of the holotype skull at the Musée Crozatier: By Musée Crozatier - Own work, CC BY-SA 4.0, https://commons.wikimedia.org/w/index.php?curid=93221225

**Isnachi:**

*"A historical restoration of Protopithecus brasiliensis an extinct genus of large New World monkey that lived during the Pleistocene"*. *"Yanachaga–Chemillén National Park, Peru"*. Photo by E. Lehr. Creative Commons Attribution 3.0

## DOGMEN

*A police sketch of the creature, an animal rescue worker described as being like,*

*"A big dog with a human face." Seems to have a suspiciously Bigfoot-like appearance* (Sketch by Andy Rawlins.)

*"Publicity photo of Chaney in full make-up,* by Horror Monsters File: Horror Monsters No1PgiCrop.png, Public Domain, https://commons. wikimedia.org/w/index.php?curid=85963519

**The Adlet:**

*"Could this be the view that the ancient Inuit beheld as Norse settlers reached their lands from across the sea?"* By Hannes Grobe, AWI - Own work, CC BY-SA 2.5, https://commons.wikimedia.org/w/index.php? curid=2978422

*"Wolf killed by Inuit hunter, March 29, 1914, near Schei Island, Greenland",* by Edward Alphonso Goldman - The Wolves of North America, Vol. I, Public Domain, https://commons.wikimedia.org/w/index.php? curid=32665929

**Skinwalker:**

*"An American Indian medicine man. Oil painting. The picture is housed in the Wellcome Collection and is on display"* (Public Domain)

*"Skinwalker Ranch superintendent Thomas Winterton".* (KSL-TV)" (Fair Use)

*"A Navajo Medicine Man",* by Edward S. Curtis. USA, 1900. The picture is housed in the Wellcome Collection and is on display. (Public Domain).

**Hyena Man:**

Rural Village in Ethiopian Highlands –Wikicommons

*"A hyena as depicted in a medieval bestiary. "* By Aberdeen Bestiary - http://en.wikipedia.org/wiki/File:Hyena_bestiary.jpg, Public Domain, https://commons.wikimedia.org/w/index.php?curid=17552530

*"Hyena Men of Harar, Ethiopia"*, by Karoline.Piegdon - Own work, CC BY-SA 4.0, https://commons.wikimedia.org/w/index.php?curid=64093627

## AMPHIBIOUS ANTHROPOIDS

**Memegwesi:**

*"Devil's Rock - the very same the ancient scene of an 'Anishinaabe' Indian encounter with the Memegwesi, a semi-aquatic Littlefolk, who the Indians caught stealing fish from their nets?"* By Jean-Paul Lefaivre, CC BY-SA 3.0 https://commons.wikimedia.org/w/index.php?curid=46645494

**Rusalka:**

*"Desna River at dawn"*. Ukraine, By George Chernilevsky - Own work, Public Domain, https://commons.wikimedia.org/w/index.php?curid=82439234

*"Alexander Pushkin's Rusalka. Dnieper bottom. Rusalka and her daughter."* Original Art by I. Volkov, engraving. (Originally from NIVA magazine, page 87) By I. Volkov - pushkin.aha.ru by Golubchikov Aleksandr, Public Domain, https://commons.wikimedia.org/w/index.php?curid=6590216

*"Водные глубины. Омут Холст, масло (1907)"* Бy Дженеев Иван Алексеевич - http://www.art-catalog.ru/picture.php?id_picture=21934, Public Domain, https://commons.wikimedia.org/w/index.php?curid=68440544

**Kappa:**

*"DANGER!! Do not swim or play around here."* A kappa is depicted as a metaphor of drowning on a sign near a pond in Fukuoka"*, by Sehremis - Own work, CC BY-SA 4.0, https://commons.wikimedia.org/w/index.php?curid=74407491

*"Japanese Netsuke (small sculpture) of a Kappa, donated to the Metropolitan Museum of Art in 1910 by Mrs Russell Sage"*, This file was

donated to Wikimedia Commons as part of a project by the Metropolitan Museum of Art. See the Image and Data Resources Open Access Policy, CC0, https://commons.wikimedia.org/w/index.php?curid=58789126

*"Kappa drawings from mid-19th century Suiko juni-hin no zu"* 水虎十二品之図 (Illustrated Guide to 12 Types of Kappa) (1850): By Juntaku - Internet, Public Domain, https://commons.wikimedia.org/w/index.php?curid=19920237

*"Offering of cucumbers to Kappa at the Kappa-dera temple, in the Kappabashi area of Tokyo"*. By Jeanjung212 - Own work, CC BY-SA 4.0, https://commons.wikimedia.org/w/index.php?curid=64109430

**Woadd -El-Uma:**

*"Sunset over the River Nile – Sudan"*, by David Haberlah at the English-language Wikipedia, CC BY-SA 3.0, https://commons.wikimedia.org/w/index.php?curid=13322538

**The Lizard Man of Scape Ore Swamp:**

*"Could the inhospitable environment of Scape Ore Swamp provide a protected habitat for a prehistoric creature to thrive undetected?"* By Ned Trovillion, U.S. Fish and Wildlife Service - http://www.public-domain-image.com/public-domain-images-pictures-free-stock-photos/nature-landscapes-public-domain-images-pictures/wetlands-and-swamps-public-domain-images-pictures/swamp-water-landscape.jpg, Public Domain, https://commons.wikimedia.org/w/index.php?curid=24943796

*"The sketch of the Scape Ore Lizard Man, made by Christopher Davis"*. (Fair Use)

*"They feast on The Flesh and Drink the blood of the living."* The Gill Man, by Universal Pictures - Universal Pictures, Public Domain, https://commons.wikimedia.org/w/index.php?curid=88865134

# AFTERWORD

Go to HangarıPublishing.com to learn more about the Author and stay up to date with their newest releases.

CPSIA information can be obtained
at www.ICGtesting.com
Printed in the USA
BVHW031512020922
646141BV00014B/727